Gotamī, those principles
of which you know:

‘These principles lead to dispassion,
not passion;
to being unfettered,
not fettered;
to getting rid of,
not heaping up;
to few wishes,
not many wishes;
to contentment,
not discontentment;
to seclusion,
not socializing;
to arousal of energy,
not laziness;
to being easy to support,
not hard to support.’

You may definitely hold:

‘This is Dhamma,
This is Vinaya,
This is the Teaching of the Buddha.’

—The Buddha,
Aṅguttara Nikāya 8.53,
Pali Vinaya 2.258–9.

Also by Bhikkhu Sujato through Santipada

A History of Mindfulness
How tranquillity worsted insight in the Pali canon

Beginnings
There comes a time when the world ends...

Sects & Sectarianism
The origins of Buddhist schools

A Swift Pair of Messengers
Calm and insight in the Buddha's words

Dreams of Bhaddā
Sex. Murder. Betrayal. Enlightenment. The story of a Buddhist nun.

White Bones Red Rot Black Snakes
A Buddhist mythology of the feminine

SANTIPADA is a non-profit Buddhist publisher. These and many other works are available in a variety of paper and digital formats.

http://santipada.org

Bhikkhuni Vinaya Studies

Research & reflections on monastic discipline for Buddhist nuns

BHIKKHU SUJATO

SANTIPADA

SANTIPADA

Buddhism as if life matters

Published in 2012 by Santipada.
Printed and distributed by Lulu.com.

ISBN 978-1-921842-15-3

Typeset in Gentium using LuaTeX.

Cover drawing by Darryl Gradwell.

Contents

'Disputes about livelihood or the pāṭimokkha *would be trivial, Ānanda.*
But should a dispute arise in the Sangha about the path or the way,
such a dispute would be for the harm and unhappiness of many,
for the loss, harm, and suffering of gods and humans.'

—The Buddha,
Sāmagāma Sutta
(Majjhima Nikāya 104.5)

INTRODUCTION

In the past few decades a quiet change has been taking root in the traditional forms of Buddhist monasticism. Women, for a long time excluded or marginalized, have been moving towards the center. Whether in international conferences, bookstores, or retreat centers female monastic teachers are present, and are among the most popular and effective presenters of Buddhism in the international forum. This prominence is unprecedented, for in the annals of Buddhist history, female teachers are rare to the point of vanishing. And yet, while the female presence has become the norm in the public face of Buddhism, women still lack acceptance within the central monastic institutions, especially in the Theravādin and Tibetan traditions. It can hardly be a coincidence that those regions where women have the least acceptance and opportunity are also those that deny women the full ordination into the state of a bhikkhuni.

2 In the earliest form of Buddhism, as laid down by the Buddha himself, women who wished to commit themselves fully to their spiritual practice were granted the opportunity to practice as bhikkhunis, fully ordained nuns. As bhikkhunis, they had their own organized women's communities which were supported by the Buddhist faithful so that the women could strive to realize the highest Awakening. A small but extraordinary literature of these awakened nuns still survives today.[1] Seeing such examples of realized practitioners awakens an inspiration and a faith that this is possible.

3 Supporting the balanced and stable growth of the bhikkhuni order requires efforts on many levels: building monasteries, encouraging women

[1] Principally the Therīgāthā of the Pali Canon.

with a renunciate inclination, taking part in Sangha dialogue, and education. Such work has been ongoing through the Buddhist world in the last few decades.

4 One area where some special work is necessary is in textual study. The bhikkhuni movement is by its very nature cross-sectarian, as the modern Theravādin nuns seek their bhikkhuni ordination lineage from the East Asian bhikkhunis, who themselves originally received the ordination lineage from Sri Lanka. This means that questions of comparative textual study, especially in the area of Vinaya, become imperative. My own researches into Buddhist meditation texts had already shown me the importance of comparative study, so it was natural for me to bring this perspective to bear in the case of Bhikkhuni Vinaya.

5 Over the years I have accumulated a number of essays in response to specific questions discussed among the international community of monastics and scholars who have been engaging in these matters. In certain cases I found that it was possible to clear up perceived difficulties without too much trouble. In other cases, the more I looked, the more problematic the texts became. So this work is concerned with problem-solving: looking at difficult or controversial areas, highlighting the most accurate textual data, and looking at different possibilities for interpretation. It is not meant to be a guide to monastic conduct, and does not attempt to be complete or systematic. Along the way I offer a little advice for those seeking practical guidance. Usually, despite the forbidding textual complexities, the ethical issues are really quite simple.

6 One important point. Decisions on how to interpret and practice monastic discipline for Buddhist nuns must be made by the nuns themselves. Monks have no right under Vinaya to enforce any interpretation or practice on the nuns. Our role must be to support and encourage, to educate when needed, to offer advice when it is wanted, and to remain silent when it is not.

0.1 The Nature of Vinaya

7 What kind of thing is the Vinaya? Etymologically the word stems from the prefix *vi-* (= English dis-, de-), here having a separative implication; and

the stem *naya*, lead. This yields the meaning 'leading away'. In this sense it is frequently used in a simple ethical context: *rāgavinayo, dosavinayo, mohavinayo*; the 'leading away of greed, hatred, and delusion'.

8 More specifically, however, *vinaya* is used in the sense of ethics, where it carries the suggestion of that which 'leads away' from bad behavior. This may be applied in the context of lay ethics, such as the famous *gihivinaya* of the Sīgāla Sutta;[2] but normally it is a shorthand term used for Buddhist monastic discipline. Generally, all matters pertaining to monastic deportment and behavior may be considered as *vinaya*.

9 *Vinaya* is also the specific texts that deal directly with monastic conduct. Within this more narrow meaning there are a range of texts to consider. The Buddhist texts contain many discourses that speak in everyday terms of matters of monastic life, from inspiring verses such as the famous Rhinoceros Sutta,[3] to prose passages such as the three sections on ethics found in the preliminary to the Gradual Training, especially in the Sīlakkhandha of the Dīgha Nikāya.[4] Several Suttas address more technical matters of monastic jurisprudence, such as the discussion of the seven ways of settling disputes found in the Sāmagāma Sutta.[5]

10 Usually, however, *vinaya* refers to the Vinaya Piṭaka, that is, that section of the Buddhist canon that deals extensively and in detail with monastic conduct.[6] In good postmodern spirit we must not forget our plurals; there are many Vinayas, each stemming from a different community of Buddhist monastics in ancient India. While we are always tempted to trace these

---

[2] Dīgha Nikāya 31. This is the Pali version of this sutta. For corresponding texts in Chinese, Sanskrit, Tibetan, etc., for this and other suttas, see www.suttacentral.net.

[3] Sutta Nipāta 1.3.

[4] Dīgha Nikāya 1–13. This passage, which in various forms is found in each Nikāya, as well as the Vinaya and Abhidhamma Piṭakas, is indispensable to an understanding of Buddhist monasticism. It depicts an approach to ethics that is not legalistic, like the Vinaya Piṭaka, but based on the aspiration to live the best possible life for the sake of spiritual growth.

[5] MN 104.

[6] The Pali Vinaya Piṭaka has been translated in its entirety into English by I.B. HORNER as *The Book of the Discipline*. No other Vinaya has been fully translated into English. Nevertheless, the Bhikkhuni Suttavibhaṅga of the Dharmaguptaka has been translated by HEIRMANN; that of the Mahāsaṅghika by HIRAKAWA; and the Lokuttaravāda into French by NOLOT. Apart from these, only fragments of translation into European languages have been done, a major hindrance in our understanding of comparative Vinaya.

back to an assumed 'original Vinaya', we should not forget that the texts themselves suggest that there has always been a degree of flexibility and variation among the communities.

11 The various meanings discussed above are often conflated, in ways that may or may not be felicitous. On the positive side, we remember that the ultimate purpose of practicing monastic disciple is ultimately for eliminating greed, hatred, and delusion; that is, we keep *vinaya* so we can achieve the *vinaya* of defilements.

12 Less usefully, it is common to fudge over the difference between *vinaya* as the name of a body of texts, and *vinaya* as the conduct of Buddhist monks and nuns. This causes the highly misleading assumption that if something is mentioned in the Vinaya Piṭaka that it must be what the monks and nuns actually do; or the opposite, that what monastics do must be in the Vinaya Piṭaka. Both of these are very far from the reality of monastic life. It would be better to think of the texts of the Vinaya Piṭaka as a framework which provides the shared context within which monks and nuns negotiate their behavior in accordance with their own social contexts, interpretive approaches, and ethical values. Some monastic traditions take a literal approach to Vinaya and regard simply following the rules as the main thing, while others think of Vinaya as a contextual guideline which must be adapted in time and place.

13 These different perspectives are never entirely separate: no matter how literally one wishes to apply Vinaya, some things must be altered to suit circumstances of time and place; and conversely, no matter how ready one is to adapt the principles, some facts about human existence just don't change.

14 This difference in interpretive approaches is often confused with a completely separate issue, that is, whether one *cares* about Vinaya at all. Within contemporary monastic circles, there are many monks and nuns who are just not very sincere about what they are doing. They ordain, not from a genuine spiritual vocation, but to get an education, a livelihood, or because of social expectations. In other cases, they may have a spiritual vocation, yet Vinaya plays little role in this. For such monastics the Vinaya is just a set of tales from the far-off past, with no relevance to their lives. In such

cases I think it is quite proper to question whether there is any benefit in being ordained.

15 But among those who care about Vinaya a variety of interpretive approaches exists, and these approaches quite manifestly work for those who practice them. We are used to hearing from the Suttas, for example, that practice of ethics is the foundation for *samādhi*. Those who are committed to a literal interpretation of Vinaya believe, and may indeed experience for themselves, that punctilious attention to details of behavior supports their meditation. On the other hand, it is undeniable that many recognized meditation masters, from all traditions, do not in fact maintain such a rigorous approach to Vinaya; yet their *samādhi* may well be better than many of the strict Vinaya monks.

16 This is not to say that strict Vinaya has no purpose. If we look at the ten reasons the Buddha gave for laying down the Vinaya, many of them are not just for individual purification, but are concerned with communal stability.

17 > 'Therefore, monks, I shall lay down a training rule for the bhikkhus for ten reasons: the well-being of the Sangha; the comfort of the Sangha; the restraint of bad-minded persons; the comfortable living of virtuous monks; the restraining of defilements pertaining to this life; the warding off of defilements pertaining to the next life; the inspiration of those without faith; the increase of those with faith; the long-lasting of the True Dhamma; and the support of the Vinaya.'[7]

18 Vinaya helps to build a community in a way that individual meditation abilities cannot. There is no doubt that the Vinaya has been a major force in maintaining the extraordinary longevity of the Buddhist Sangha, which can stake a claim to be the oldest continuous human organization.[8] While some would prefer to write off monasticism as a medieval archaicism, in the face of the Sangha's ability to reinvent itself it would be premature to dismiss the monastic Sangha just yet.

19 In a world riven by greed, the Vinaya shows a way of contentment. In a world of suspicion, the Vinaya teaches us to build communities based on trust. In a world obsessed with vengeance and violence, the Vinaya tells

---

[7] Pali Vinaya 3.21. Similar lists are found in each Vinaya.

[8] The Jaina Sangha may be older.

us that discipline is best fostered through gentleness and forgiveness. In a world dominated by the imposition of power upon the powerless, the Vinaya bases itself on consensus and equality for all. The Vinaya appeals to our noblest ethical principles, and offers a clear and explicit framework for applying these in living communities.

20 This book is a defense of the Vinaya. Its purpose is to inspire faith in the Vinaya through understanding of its subtleties. But it does not go about that defense in the usual way, by an insistence on every detail and an apologetic for the monastic institutions that are supposedly built on the Vinaya's foundations. On the contrary, it focuses on a discussion of what may be the most contentious Vinaya issue of all: the role of women. It is here that Vinaya is at its weakest, and if it survives this critique, it can survive anything. But if the Vinaya cannot face up to a close and critical scrutiny of its treatment of women, we must ask ourselves: despite the many wonders found in the Vinaya, does it have any chance of surviving at all? If the Vinaya is founded upon the exclusion of half of humanity, does it even deserve to survive?

21 The place of bhikkhunis, as fully ordained mendicants within the institutional structure of the Sangha, is a litmus test for the Sangha of our time. The notion of a bhikkhuni is deeply problematic for modern Buddhists, for it challenges the assumptions behind sectarianism. Conservative Theravādins are happy to have 'Mahāyāna bhikkhunis', as long as they are not 'Theravādins'. But the Buddha had never heard of 'Theravāda' or 'Mahāyāna'. Vinaya says nothing about ordination lineages, nothing about Mūlasarvāstivāda, nothing about Dharmaguptaka, nothing about Theravāda, nothing about Tibet, nothing about China, and nothing about Sri Lanka or Thailand.

22 This question cuts to the heart of our relation with our ancient Buddhist heritage. Why do we expect Buddhist monastics to keep the Vinaya rules? Because they were laid down by the Buddha, of course. It is this which gives them their universality within the Buddhist world. But those same texts which resonate with the fundamental authority of the Buddha himself say nothing of Mahāyāna or Theravāda. The distinction between Theravāda and Mahāyāna does not stem from the Vinaya, but is a hangover from ancient rivalries, as recorded in the polemical histories of the schools. So

the conservative position reveals its irreducible incoherence: the rules are essential because they come from the Buddha, but the bhikkhunis must be excluded because of sectarian rivalry, which had nothing to do with the Buddha.

23 One of the most important lessons I have learned as a monk is that Vinaya is *reasonable*. This is far from obvious, as many of the things that are said to be Vinaya are excessive, hurtful, or irrational. In my experience, almost always such things are not, in fact, found in the Vinaya texts themselves; or if they are found, they have a context and a purpose that helps us understand why they are there. For much of this book, I shall be attempting to demonstrate that some of the assumptions and commonly held assertions about bhikkhunis are untrue, or at least, that there may be other ways of looking at things. I want to rescue the Vinaya from the fundamentalists. When Vinaya is presented in a way that is overly rigid and dogmatic, open-minded and good-hearted people turn away from it.

24 Without pretending to be an objective witness—for such a thing is impossible—I try to shelve as many assumptions as possible, and read implications out of the texts. I am not interested in making definitive statements as to what is the right and the wrong way to practice Vinaya. In certain cases I make recommendations based on my research and opinions. However, given that I have deliberately sought out the most difficult and controversial areas, it is hardly likely that a widespread agreement is possible. I am more interested in bringing accurate information and a critical sensibility to the debate, so that at least we can be sure how certain, or uncertain, the grounds for our opinions may be.

25 In discussing Vinaya widely for many years among living monastic communities, I have come to realize that no two people will ever agree about everything. And yet life goes on. There is a degree of acceptance of diversity, which is always elastic, and varies from person to person, time to time, place to place, and context to context. Our commonality does not stem from an agreement as to every detail of the Vinaya, but from our choice to use the Vinaya as a common text that provides an environment for dialogue. The text itself is the commonality. This makes it all the more imperative, as monastics from different traditions come ever closer and share more deeply and more frequently, that we learn to deal with the

common basis, the canonical Vinayas themselves, rather than the late commentarial treatises that have come to serve as the guide for monastic conduct in every tradition. And it makes the task of seeking out and evaluating the real similarities and differences a task of urgency.

0.2 Vinaya in Context

26 The Vinaya is a set of conventions that are intended to guide or govern behavior. It evolved based on precedent in the manner of common law. In the early period of the Buddha's ministry there was no Vinaya as we know it. The Buddha taught by example, and by extolling the ideal life for the monastics. The level of spiritual development of the Sangha was high, and there was no need for a set of regulations. The Buddha even refused Sāriputta's request to establish a Vinaya, saying that he would do so at the right time.[9] This would only come when defilements started to emerge within the Sangha. After incidents where monks began to seriously misbehave, the Buddha began to lay down rules. Gradually these came to be systematized, with detailed procedures, classifications, and penalties.

27 The penalties are typically gentle. In most cases, simply a confession; in certain contexts an item improperly obtained must be relinquished; more serious offenses required a period of probation and suspension of status within the community. The most serious cases deserved expulsion. There was no question of corporal punishment or imprisonment. The gentleness of the Buddha is even more striking when we consider that, in his day, it was considered normal for the authorities to inflict harsh punishments that are abhorred by all civilized people today, such as flogging, torture, imprisonment without trial, and capital punishment. In addition, the Vinaya is based on confession: generally, a monastic must admit to their guilt before they can be punished.

28 Such a system, based on mutual consent and sincerity, is wide open to abuse by the unscrupulous. It has always been difficult to properly discipline bad monks, but the Buddha apparently felt that, as a spiritual movement, it was better to err on the side of trust and gentleness than

[9] Pali Vinaya 3.9.

to insist on harsher disciplinary measures. The ongoing success of the Buddhist monastic orders is a testament to this policy.

29 Since there is little or no ability within the Vinaya to enforce punishment on an unwilling monk, Vinaya has by and large failed to address the needs of those with no integrity. Insincere monks can simply join the Sangha, and as long as they get away with it, can continue with bad behavior. Only the coercive power exercised through secular law can have any real impact on such monastics. It is important to acknowledge this, for we must avoid wasting our time by trying to use Vinaya to deal with such problems. It doesn't work, and never will.

30 Those who are already spiritually advanced, on the other hand, have no personal need for the Vinaya. Like the Sangha in the early days of the Buddha, or like the fabled Pacceka Buddhas of antiquity, they operate from a mature, internalized sense of ethics. This does not mean that spiritually advanced individuals need not keep Vinaya; on the contrary, they should keep Vinaya, not for themselves, but for the sake of the community at large. As spiritual leaders, their respect for Vinaya will inspire those still struggling, and maintain the coherence and faith of the community.

31 While Vinaya is of limited use, then, for those who are either very bad or very good, it is highly effective at helping the great number of us who fall in-between. For these, Vinaya provides a clear sense of right and wrong, a set of guidelines that can be applied very widely across many circumstances, and which furnishes the security that comes from knowing one's conduct is, when judged according to a revered set of sacred principles, blameless. The Vinaya, as a set of conventions, speaks primarily for those who are sincerely interested in the spiritual path, but who are in need of communal support to maintain their discipline.

32 Holding the textual ideal close to hand as we grapple with the real life complications, the conventions should constantly point beyond themselves. We do not keep the rules for the sake of the rules. The Vinaya, having been set up to redress the falling away from the spiritual heights of the early Sangha, serves to re-orient us back towards those heights. The conventions are pointing beyond convention.

33 In much of the Buddhist world, the number of monks is falling dramatically, the Sangha feels less and less relevant, and inspiring leadership is

hard to find. Attempts to reform Buddhism in traditional lands have failed, not because they don't enforce the rules strictly enough, but because they do not address the actual problem. Too often, monks simply have no spiritual vocation, but ordain out of cultural expectations, and the idea of practicing Dhamma is entirely irrelevant. The scriptures are studied, if at all, simply as a set of legends with no relation to actual living. Until this changes, attempts at reform will continue to fail.

34 There is, however, a different face to Buddhist monasticism, one which is not based on fulfillment of a cultural ideal, but on a thirst to find the true Dhamma. This new monasticism lives in an uneasy relationship with the traditional Sangha institutions. It is not about giving a mass of students a standardized grounding in conventional Buddhism. It is about re-discovering the essence of Buddhist monastic life in a way that speaks to us.

0.3 Bhikkhunis in History

35 The traditional story, found in the canonical scriptures of all existing schools, says that the bhikkhuni Sangha originated when Mahāpajāpatī Gotamī, the Buddha's aunt and foster-mother, approached him to ask for ordination. The Buddha repeatedly refused, but after being beseeched by Ānanda, he agreed. However, he laid down eight 'rules of respect' (*garudhamma*) for Mahāpajāpatī as her ordination, which insist that the nuns must always pay respects to the monks.

36 I don't believe that story, and have discussed why at length in my *White Bones Red Rot Black Snakes*. But in any case, the bhikkhuni Sangha was established, and a code of conduct (Vinaya) was drawn up to regulate their conduct, paralleling the Vinaya for the bhikkhus. The bhikkhuni Sangha apparently throve in the Buddha's time, with thousands of women ordaining. They set up monasteries, wandered the country, taught, organized themselves and, most importantly, achieved Awakening. The songs of Awakening of the early bhikkhunis are recorded in the ancient verse collection, the Therīgāthā.

37 After the Buddha passed away, we don't hear all that much about the bhikkhunis, and there are no later literary works to compare with the

Therīgāthā. But large numbers of bhikkhunis are said to have attended ceremonies in the time of Aśoka. Aśoka himself always mentions bhikkhunis alongside bhikkhus in his edicts, strictly adhering to politically correct usage. But the most famous contribution of bhikkhunis is in the story of how the Bodhi Tree was taken to Sri Lanka by Saṅghamittā, Aśoka's daughter. She subsequently established a bhikkhuni Sangha in Sri Lanka, which flourished for over 1000 years. The same source—the Sinhalese Vinaya commentary, preserved in Pali and Chinese versions—says that the bhikkhuni Sangha was established in 'Suvaṇṇabhūmi' (Lower Burma or Thailand) under the leadership of the monks Soṇa and Uttara in the same period. Thus bhikkhunis have been intrinsic to Buddhism of South and South-east Asia since the beginning.

38 The texts say little about the bhikkhunis in later times. However, bhikkhunis are mentioned about as often as monks in ancient Indian inscriptions. They appear in positions of influence, as donors of large monuments, as teachers, as learned students of the scriptures.[10]

39 But the most momentous turn of events in bhikkhuni history came in 433 CE, when a shipowner called Nandi left Sri Lanka bound for China. He took with him some bhikkhunis, led by Ayyā Sārā.[11] When in China, they conferred ordination on Chinese nuns, thus establishing the bhikkhuni lineage there. The rites were evidently carried out using the Dharmaguptaka Vinaya. Presumably the Vinaya masters of the time decided that the Dharmaguptaka Vinaya was essentially similar to that of the Sinhalese Theravādins of the Mahāvihāra, an opinion that is shared today by scholars who have done comparative work on the matter. The bhikkhunis flourished in China, and subsequently spread to Korea, Japan, and Vietnam. Buddhism was well established in Vietnam long before the period of Chi-

[10] SCHOPEN, *Bones, Stones, and Buddhist Monks*, p. 249.

[11] Chinese accounts at T50, № 2059, p. 342, b11–c7; T50, № 2063, p. 939, c6–p. 940, a3; and T50, № 2063, p. 941, a8–b2. English translation: 'The First Chinese Bhikkhunis' (http://santifm.org/santipada/2010/the-first-chinese-bhikkhunis/). Sārā's name is often reconstructed as Devasārā or Tessarā. She is not mentioned in Sri Lankan sources, so any reconstruction is tentative. But the first element in her name as found in Chinese is the character 鐵, which is never used as a phonetic element, but only in its meaning of 'iron'. The Pali for 'iron' is *ayas*, and the honorific for bhikkhunis is *ayyā*. It seems likely, then, that she was referred to as Ayyā Sārā (Venerable Sārā), and the Chinese translator misheard the name as Ayassārā (Iron Sārā).

nese domination, and it seems likely that they had their own bhikkhuni Sangha, perhaps of the Mūlasarvāstivāda lineage, before adopting the Chinese system still in use today. The bhikkhuni Sangha was never established in Tibet and related areas.

40 It seems that the bhikkhuni Sangha flourished in southern Asia for around 1500 years. In the 11th century CE, Sri Lanka underwent a period of turmoil, at the end of which the bhikkhunis were no longer. It is impossible to determine the exact circumstances that led to their disappearance. It is possible that small numbers continued in later years, but there is no evidence that I know of.

41 In those regions known today as Burma and Thailand, it is difficult to trace the history of the order established under Soṇa and Uttara. There are occasional scraps of evidence—an inscription here, a painting in a temple there. In colonial times, a few travel records mention seeing women in the ocher robes. Conventional wisdom has it that there were no bhikkhunis in these lands until the modern period, but it is premature to conclude this. Taking all the little hints together, it seems possible that the bhikkhunis did maintain a quiet presence. One of the latest and clearest mentions of bhikkhunis in Burma is discussed by Maung Paw:

> 42 In January 21 1788, the kings made another proclamation stating that:
>
> 43 Any male or female who are of age 19 and who are:
>
> - free of any incurable disease;
> - free from any criminal offenses or fugitive from law;
> - free from financial indebtedness—not bankrupt person.
>
> 44 Those free of the above could be permitted to be ordained as Bhikkhu for male and Bhikkhuni for female. There is another proclamation forbidding any king's slave from taking ordination as Bhikkhu or Bhikkhuni. Whoever so monk ordained the king's slave will be harshly punishable by law. (March 30, 1810).
>
> 45 In the same month, the king made another proclamation stating that all legally ordained Bhikkhu or Bhikkhuni be monitored by the king's men to check on the legal status of their Sangha life and their orderly observation of the rules of the Monks.[12]

---

[12] Maung PAW, pp. 36–37. PAW cites his source as Dr. Than TUN, *The Chronicle of King's Proclamation* (excerpt from 'Ideas and Views'), August 2001.

46 If our source does not mislead us, until recent years the bhikkhunis were present in Burma, and possibly in Thailand as well. Buddhism in those lands was diverse and often did not have a strong central control. Local customs flourished, and many regions owed little allegiance to the putative government. It was not until the challenges of the colonial era that cohesive nation states in the modern sense were formed. And as these states were formed under Western influence, Western models lay behind the new forms that Buddhism was shaped into.

47 In Thailand, for example, the modern reform movement was shaped by the towering figures of King Mongkut and his son Vajirañāṇavarorasa.[13] As a Prince, Mongkut ordained as a bhikkhu in 1824 and went to practice meditation. However, he was disappointed that the monks did not understand what they were doing and could only repeat what had been passed down by the tradition. He criticized this attitude, calling it *āciṇṇakappikavāda.* This term harks back to the Second Council, where one of the contested issues was whether it was allowable to follow what had become customary. Mongkut became convinced that contemporary Thai Buddhism had become a mass of superstition and was in need of reform. Mongkut had an incisive, analytical mind, and he embarked on a detailed study of the Buddhist texts, always pointing back to the rational teachings of original Buddhism as found in the Pali Canon. During his time in the Sangha he was zealous in his study of Western knowledge. He developed a friendship with a certain Bishop Pallegoix, who lived nearby in Bangkok, and they exchanged lessons in Pali and Latin. He had many discussions on religion with Western missionaries, who he impressed with his skeptical and questioning attitude. Later, as king, he corresponded with Pope Pius IX, emphasizing the spirit of religious tolerance found in Thailand. Mongkut began to re-envisage Thai Buddhism along the Western lines of the Vatican hierarchy.

48 Following on from the reforms instituted by Mongkut, Thailand eventually adopted a Sangha Act in 1902, under the guidance of Vajirañāṇavarorasa, then head of the Dhammayuttika Nikāya. Thailand thus became the first Buddhist country to attempt to control the Sangha using a modern, Western-style legal instrument. A Council of Elders was established as the

[13] For the Burmese experience see GUTTER.

ruling body of the Sangha; their decisions were absolute and could not be appealed or disputed. The Sangha Act was modeled on the structure of secular Thai society, and successively remodeled to reflect the changes as Thailand went from being a monarchy to a democracy (1941), then in 1962, a military dictatorship. Subsequent democratic reform has failed, however, to result in a democratic reform of the Sangha Act.[14]

49 The current Sangha Act defines the Sangha as male-only, and sets up a Vatican-style system of titles, positions, and bureaucratic administration, all with the avowed intent to protect the Vinaya and serve the Sangha.[15] It may be more than simple coincidence that both the Vatican and the Thai Sangha have a problem accepting ordained women within their ranks. In insisting that bhikkhunis can have no place within the Thai Buddhism, the Sangha is placing more emphasis on the modern legal structures derived from Western models, rather than the Buddhist scriptures on which their tradition, and the modern reform of that tradition, is supposed to be based. And while bhikkhuni ordination is sometimes decried as a Western, feminist interpolation in the Asian tradition, the reality is that the four-fold community, including the bhikkhuni Sangha, is the authentic heritage, while the insistence on a male-only Sangha is a modern, Western-derived innovation. History, it seems, is not without a sense of irony.

0.4 The Vinaya Texts

50 In the spirit of great Buddhist reformers like Mongkut, we return to the earliest texts and seek a renewal of faith from the wellsprings. Today, we have access to a much broader array of texts than was available in Thailand in the 19th century, and can benefit from the huge amounts of work that have been done in archeology, recovery of manuscripts, digitizing of texts, linguistic research, and much more.[16] But before we dig deeper, we need

[14] A succinct summary of this process is found in PUNTARIGVIVAT.

[15] Available online at www.songpak16.com/prb_all.htm.

[16] One long-standing error that still bedevils discussion of bhikkhunis in Thailand is the claim by VAJIRAÑĀṆAVARORASA in his *Vinayamukha* (3.268) that the bhikkhuni order had already died out by the time of the Buddha's parinibbana. This argument is effectively refuted by the footnotes in the English translation, apparently inserted by the translator, but remains widely repeated in Thailand. It was based merely on the fact

to clarify what the Vinaya texts actually are, and to define some of the terms we will meet throughout our study.

51 The canonical Vinayas are divided into two main sections, the Suttavibhaṅga and the Khandhakas.[17] The Suttavibhaṅga contains the famous lists of *pāṭimokkha* rules (*sikkhāpada*)—227 for bhikkhus and 311 for bhikkhunis in the Pali recension[18]—together with a mass of explanatory and background material.

52 The bare lists of rules are called the *pāṭimokkhas*, and these are recited in the fortnightly *uposatha* ceremony by the bhikkhu and bhikkhuni communities. This ceremony is the key to the collective identity of the Sangha, and is regarded as an essential act in maintaining the harmony of the community. It is still maintained in many monastic communities to this day. Thus the *pāṭimokkhas*, as well as being legal texts, also perform a ritual function.

53 But the *pāṭimokkhas* do not appear as independent texts within the canonical Vinayas. They only occur embedded in the explanatory matrix of the *vibhaṅga*. This text as a whole is called the Suttavibhaṅga, the 'analysis' (*vibhaṅga*) of the 'basic text' (*sutta*). Confusingly, *sutta* here means the *pāṭimokkha* itself, not the 'Suttas' in the normal sense of 'Discourses'. In the Tipiṭaka as a whole, the Collection of Discourses (Suttapiṭaka) is sepa-

---

that bhikkhunis were not mentioned in the deathbed scene of the Mahāparinibbāna Sutta. This is already a weak argument, and contrary to many other Pali sources, some of which Vajirañāṇavarorasa discusses and dismisses. The evidence for the survival of the bhikkhunis in India from archaeology and northern texts, which Vajirañāṇavarorasa did not have access to, places the matter beyond doubt.

[17] This picture is primarily derived from the Pali Vinaya. It is complicated by the inclusion into the Pali canon of the later compilation the Parivāra, the existence of several quasi-canonical texts in translations, such as the Vinaya-mātikās, and the extended, complex structure of the Mūlasarvāstivāda Vinaya.

[18] The number of rules varies somewhat in the different Vinayas. But when examined closely, the differences are almost entirely in the most minor category of rules, the *sekhiyas*, which are concerned primarily with matters of etiquette. Several passages in the Suttas refer to the 'approximately 150 training rules', which seems to refer to the *pāṭimokkha* rules leaving out the *sekhiyas* and the seven *adhikaraṇasamathas*. (The *adhikaraṇasamathas* are not counted in one of the earliest enumerations of the *pāṭimokkha* rules, at Parivāra pp. 146–8.) It thus seems that in the Buddha's day, only the '150' or so rules would have been recited at the fortnightly *uposatha*. Of course, many of the *sekhiyas* would still have been followed, as ordinary good manners, but they had not yet been formalized as part of the recitation.

rate from the Collection of Discipline (Vinayapiṭaka). Originally, however, *sutta* meant 'thread', and the Vinaya describes the *pāṭimokkha* as like a thread that holds the holy life together.[19]

54 Since the *pāṭimokkhas* do not occur independently within the canon, they are sometimes regarded as 'paracanonical'.[20] But this is misleading. If 'canon' means 'a collection of sacred books accepted as genuine' and 'para' means 'beside' or 'beyond',[21] the implication is that the *pāṭimokkha* lurks as an outsider hoping to be accepted in the inner circle. But its authority has never been questioned, and it directly underlies the very substance of the Suttavibhaṅga, and indirectly, much of the Khandhakas. A better term might be 'protocanonical': it was already unquestionably authoritative at the time when the full canon was compiled, and forms the foundation upon which the 'canonical' Vinaya was built as a commentary. In our discussion we will be constantly reminded of the distinctions between these clearly demarcated strata of the texts.

55 The rules of the *pāṭimokkhas* are divided into eight classes, of different levels of seriousness and in certain cases with different procedures for transgressors.[22] They address everything from murder to table manners. There are many different versions of the *pāṭimokkhas* in existence, and they all preserve a remarkably similar set of rules. It is noteworthy, though, that the bhikkhu *pāṭimokkha*, when compared across all versions, is significantly more consistent than the bhikkhuni *pāṭimokkhas*. The *vibhaṅgas* introduce three more classes of rules.[23]

---

[19] Pali Vinaya 3.9.

[20] E.g. PREBISH in his *A Survey of Vinaya Literature*. The word 'paracanonical' meaning 'semi-canonical' seems to be mainly used in speaking of the Pali Canon.

[21] Oxford English Reference Dictionary.

[22] The bhikkhu *pāṭimokkha* in Pali consists of 4 *pārājikas* (expulsion), 13 *saṅghādisesas* (suspension), 2 *aniyatas* (undetermined; this category applies to the bhikkhus only), 30 *nissaggiya pācittiyas* (entailing forfeiture of some kind of material object with confession), 92 *pācittiyas* (entailing confession), 4 *pāṭidesanīyas* (acknowledgement), 75 *sekhiyas* (rules of deportment), and 7 *adhikaraṇasamatha* (means of settling issues).

[23] *Thullaccaya* ('grave offence'; usually these fall on an incomplete commission of a *pārājika* or *saṅghādisesa*); *dukkaṭa* ('wrong-doing'; a minor offence); *dubhāsita* ('wrong speech'; minor verbal transgressions). Unlike the *pāṭimokkha* categories, these are not necessarily common to all traditions. The Mahāsaṅghika group, for example, does not have a category called *dukkaṭa*, and instead uses *vinayatikkrama* in a similar sense. Hence these categories were likely to have been formalized in the sectarian period. In the

56 The *vibhaṅgas* follow a set pattern. They start with the events leading up to the laying down of the rule, which is told as an origin story (*nidāna*). The matter is reported to the Buddha, who lays down the rule (*paññatti*). Then there may follow secondary cases leading to modifications of the rule (*anupaññatti*). After the final rule formulation, there is a word by word analysis of the rule (*padabhajanīya*), judgments in various further cases (*vinītavatthu*), and a list of exemptions from the rule (*anāpatti*). While this formal pattern is followed in all the existing Vinayas, the details of the analyses differ greatly.

57 Complementing the rules-with-explanations of the Suttavibhaṅga are the twenty-two chapters of the Khandhakas. While the Suttavibhaṅga is essentially proscriptive—it says what not to do—the Khandhakas are more prescriptive—they focus on what should be done. They lay down such things as ordination procedures, means for carrying out the *uposatha* and other ritual activities, duties in building and maintaining monasteries, observances regarding footwear, medicines, and all manner of other details. Just as the Suttavibhaṅga is constructed on top of the *pāṭimokkha*, it would seem that the Khandhakas are constructed on top of the various *saṅghakammas*. Like the *pāṭimokkha* rules, the *kammas* are common to all traditions, and would seem to predate the explanatory material in which they are embedded. However, the structure of the Khandhakas is not as clear and stereotyped as the Suttavibhaṅga, so it is not as easy to tease out the earlier and later strata. There's much overlap between these two texts, showing that they evolved together as an interdependent whole.

58 Appended to the twenty main Khandhakas are two chapters on the First and Second Councils, dealing with how the Sangha organized itself following the Buddha's passing away.

0.5 Schools

59 As Buddhism grew and spread about ancient India, it gradually evolved into various schools. The first schism, between the Mahāsaṅghika and Sthavira, probably occurred in the post-Aśokan period, and was driven by

account of the First Council in the Pali Vinaya we find *dukkaṭa* used in a general sense of 'wrong-doing'; the term has not yet been formalized as a class of offence.

a dispute on the nature of the arahant. Subsequent schisms occurred due to other doctrinal issues, such as the nature of impermanence (Sarvāstivāda) and the understanding of not-self (Puggalavāda). In many cases, however, the schisms simply occurred due to the expansion of Buddhism during the Aśokan period, and the subsequent individual development of relatively isolated communities. All of these schools achieved an independent status within 400–500 years after the Buddha's passing away.[24]

60 These schools all pre-date the emergence of Mahāyāna, and contrary to the statements of both modern academics and Theravādins, there is no good reason to seek a special link between the Mahāyāna and the Mahāsaṅghika, still less between the Mahāyāna and the defeated Vajjiputtakas of the Second Council. In fact, the Mahāyāna evolved gradually and in complex ways, both borrowing from and rejecting the teachings and practices of many of the early schools. In ancient India, monastics who followed the Mahāyāna teachings would have lived among the communities of one or other of the early schools. There has never been a distinctively Mahāyāna Vinaya as such. Mahāyānists would take ordination in one of the early schools. Their practice was modified by various sets of 'Bodhisattva precepts', but these were not meant to replace the early Vinaya, but to modify or extend it, especially in areas where it was felt that the letter of the law had obscured the higher spiritual values of compassion and wisdom. In some respects, though, the so-called 'Bodhisattva precepts' reveal a sectarian defensiveness that belies their supposedly higher spiritual values.

61 Mahāyāna monastics today still acknowledge their adherence to the Vinaya codes of early schools. Sangha in the East Asian traditions of China, Taiwan, Korea, Vietnam, and related traditions follow the 'Four Part Vinaya' of the Dharmaguptaka school. This is preserved in a Chinese translation by Buddhayaśas and Chu Fo-nien between 410–412 CE.[25] An excellent English translation of the Bhikkhunivibhaṅga with extensive notes and explanations is available.[26] Central Asian Sangha in the Tibetan, Bhutanese, and Mongolian traditions practice the Mūlasarvāstivāda Vinaya. This exists

---

[24] These questions are discussed in detail in my *Sects & Sectarianism*.

[25] T22, № 1428, pp. 714–778.

[26] Ann HEIRMANN, *Rules for Nuns*.

in a complete Tibetan translation of the ninth century by a team of translators, as well as a partial Chinese translation by Yi Jing in the early 700s. While these texts are very similar, there are certain differences, and there is some question as to the exact sectarian affiliation. Considerable quantities of the Mūlasarvāstivāda Vinaya have been recovered in Sanskrit also, as have several *pāṭimokkhas* and other Vinaya materials. Little of this material is available in English translation.

62 The number of early (pre-Mahāyāna) schools is conventionally reckoned as '18' in number, but there were both many more and many less than that. Many more, because if all the individual names and local variants were to be compiled, we would have over thirty schools. Many less, because these schools fell into a much smaller number of about four groups of schools; and of the individual schools, a few names crop up again and again. It seems likely that many of the names mentioned only occasionally were little more than local branches, perhaps just one monastery, who may not have possessed an independent textual tradition.

63 In discussions of Vinaya, the same group of names is repeatedly mentioned as the chief Vinaya schools, and due to the perseverance of the ancient redactors and translators, we are lucky enough to possess actual Vinaya texts from most of these major Vinaya schools. The exception is the Puggalavāda group of schools; despite the fact that they were one of the largest wings of Indian Buddhism, we only possess a single late Vinaya summary in Chinese translation.[27]

64 Of the existing Vinayas, the Mahāvihāravāsin is the only one of which we have a complete edition in an Indic language (Pali). This forms the basis for the modern Theravāda school. My basic education has been in this school, and it remains the tradition with which I am most familiar. Although I try to use the texts of other schools as best I can, the Pali texts are still the most accessible and clearest to me. I usually use the Pali form for Indic words, not because it is the 'original' or 'correct' form, but because it is the one I am most familiar with.

65 However, it is prudent to avoid using the name Theravāda in reference to early Buddhism, as it invites a series of misunderstandings. The modern Theravāda school is commonly believed to be identical with the Elders

[27] T24, № 1461. Summarized by CHAU, pp. 117–122.

who formed in opposition to the Mahāsaṅghikas at the first schism. But this is by no means the case; rather, the modern Theravādins are one of the schools who descended from those ancient Elders. To avoid confusion I refer to that original group of Elders by the Sanskrit form Sthaviras. The ancient Sthaviras underwent several subsequent splits, and one of the dozen or so resulting schools formed in Sri Lanka, based at the monastery known as the Mahāvihāra. This community called themselves, among other titles, the Mahāvihāravāsins, 'Dwellers at the Great Monastery'. This title, though clumsy, has the great virtue of being specific and unambiguous: we can go to the ruins of the Mahāvihāra, stand there, and know that we are speaking of the community at this place. Since before the Common Era, the Sri Lankan Sangha had divided into three main monastic traditions, one of which was the Mahāvihāra; the others were the Abhayagiri and the Jetavana. These were unified under the Mahāvihāra in the reign of Parakramabāhu I around 1165 CE. It was around that time that the Sinhalese school also started to gain prominence in Burma and Thailand, gradually supplanting the various forms of Buddhism that had thrived up until then, although never completely overtaking the earlier forms. Since the Mahāvihāravāsins used Pali as their ecclesiastic language, it is also common to refer to their texts as the 'Pali'. In this work, I refer to this school as either the Mahāvihāravāsins or the Pali school when speaking in historical context, and reserve Theravāda for the modern school.

66 Most of the other extant Vinayas were translated into Chinese around the fifth century CE.[28] Apart from the Chinese and Pali texts, the most important for our concerns is the Hybrid Sanskrit version of the bhikkhuni Vinaya of the 'Ārya Mahāsāṅghika Lokuttaravādin' school, who we will refer to more economically as the Lokuttaravādins. This is based on manuscripts, probably written in the 11th–12th centuries in the final phase of Indian Buddhism, and taken to Tibet, from where they were retrieved by Rāhula Sāṅkṛtyāyana and brought back to India in 1935–38.

67 There is no clear *a priori* reason to assume that any of these texts is more authentic than any other. In fact, all of them have undergone a long period

---

[28] A history of the introduction, translation, and adoption of the Indian Vinayas into China may be found in YIFA, pp. 3–8.

of redaction, and include much late material, along with a common core which is probably inherited from the earliest times.

68 The main Vinaya schools and their principle relations may be summed up as follows. At the left is the basic division into the root schools of Mahāsaṅghika and Sthavira. Then follows the division of the Sthaviras into three great groups of schools. Finally we have the schools for who we possess actual Vinaya texts. I mention the language of the original texts (with the hypothesized language in brackets for those texts which exist only in translation), and the language of the translated texts.

Table 1: Main Extant Vinaya Texts

First schism	Main groups of schools	Main Vinaya schools	Language (original)	Language (translation)
Mahā-s	Mahā-s	Mahāsaṅghika	(Hybrid Sanskrit)	Chinese
		Lokuttaravāda	Hybrid Sanskrit	
Sthavira	Vibhajjavāda	Mahāvihāravāsin	Pali	
		Dharmaguptaka	(Gandhārī)	Chinese
		Mahīśāsaka	(Sanskrit)	Chinese
	Sarvāstivāda	Sarvāstivāda	(Sanskrit)	Chinese
		Mūlasarvāstivāda	Sanskrit (partial)	Tibetan, Chinese
	Puggalavāda		?	

Chapter 1

A QUESTION OF INTERPRETATION

BHIKKHUNI VINAYA IS A COMPLEX, MISUNDERSTOOD, YET CRUCIAL field of study. We cannot assume that our understanding of the monks' Vinaya will be an adequate guide. So before going on to discuss bhikkhuni Vinaya as such, I would like to address some interpretive problems.

1.1 What can we expect from Vinaya?

2 No text is perfect, and no text ever contains the seeds of its own interpretation. A text can never speak for itself. Left to itself, a text sits on the library shelf and gathers dust. It will only speak when a human being, full of wishes, neuroses, limitations, and expectations, picks it up, and because of some desire or interest, opens it and starts to read. They do not know the text, or they would not bother to pick it up. The very fact of engagement with a text implies a gap, a lack, which the reader hopes the text will go some way to fill.

3 But the author of that text knows nothing of this. They have no idea who will read their text, why, and to what ends. Shakespeare tells us that the devil may quote scripture to his purpose; and the Buddhist texts make it very clear that Māra speaks words of compassion.

4 Every text is both deficient and excessive. Deficient, because it cannot explain all its terms, and must leave much unsaid. The author can never fully express all they have in mind. This problem is addressed in fiction by Jorge Luis Borges, with his infinite libraries, or his *aleph*, through which all points in the universe can be seen simultaneously. The *aleph*, by a dire twist of fate, comes into the hands of a poet who sets out to express everything, and by doing so steals the meaning from the world. The problem becomes all the more acute the further we are in time and place from our subject. Our texts are full of haunting and ambiguity. The inquiring mind, the lost soul seeking truth, cannot help but insert itself in these gaps, fill out the non-existent with the reassurance of the existent.

5 And texts are excessive, because they carry implications. Sounds, echoes, suggestions; all these and more convey meaning in a text, and this meaning can never be fathomed, least of all by the author. Each time we read a text, it says more to us than the author intended. It creates new connections in our minds, inspires fresh ways of thinking. The message we carry away with us will never be exactly that which the author had in mind, and frequently it will be something strange and unpredictable.

6 As a teacher, I am constantly reminded of these limitations. Even when dealing with the here and now, speaking closely with a small group of intelligent people, who I know well and who are sincerely trying to understand what I am saying, I have to keep reminding myself that each person in the room will go away with something different. Invariably, what is taken from a teaching is quite different from my intention; I have omitted something that would have clarified my meaning, or I have said something that carried an unintended connotation. This is not a problem with the teaching or with the students, it is the nature of communication and meaning. It is, in fact, this which gives communication its richness. Each seeing differently, we remain a community who can learn from each other.

7 In addition to these general problems, which must affect any attempt to interpret texts, there is a further pair of extremes that become particularly acute in addressing ancient religious scripture. Such texts are in the peculiar situation of having originated in a very remote time, place, and context; and yet being held to have an immediate and literal application to the present time, place, and context. And in trying to mediate

this gap, we often fall into the temptations of either overinterpreting or underinterpreting the text.

8 In overinterpreting the text, we give it a significance greater than it can reasonably bear. A chance remark becomes a timeless gem of wisdom; an offhand observation becomes a law for all eternity. Texts say so much, and only so much. We cannot expect them to yield all the answers that we want. Ancient scriptures are notoriously subject to this weakness. We want to be able to relinquish responsibility, to turn to an unimpeachable authority for answers so that we may lay down our burdens. Academics are no less susceptible to this temptation than devotees. Witness the attempts to pin down the date of the Buddha, with gallons of ink expended to narrow down the date by a few years here or there, when we may be out by centuries.

9 The opposite sin is to underinterpret the text. The scriptures are archaic, irrelevant, meaningless. 'It's impossible for monastics to live without money today'; so say those who have never tried. It is a simple matter to dismiss something we know little about, and finding errors in an ancient text requires no great intellect. But if we are to engage our tradition in a meaningful way, to establish the bhikkhuni Sangha as a continuation and reform of the Buddhist tradition, then we must take the texts seriously. We can criticize them, but such criticism must grant the texts the respect of careful and sympathetic study. It is not easy work, and there are few willing to do it, but there is no alternative.

10 We can take heart from the encouragement of the Buddha himself. It is a staple of modernist Buddhism to claim that the Buddha encouraged the spirit of inquiry, and that we should not take even our sacred scriptures merely on faith. It is less well known that the Suttas themselves provide concrete instructions and examples in how to interpret texts. A series of texts in the Aṅguttara Nikāya go so far as to say that one slanders the Buddha if one presents a scripture that was not spoken by the Buddha as if it were spoken by the Buddha (or vice versa); or if one presents a scripture requiring explanation as if it were one that did not require explanation (or vice versa).[1] A simplistic insistence on literalism is not merely untenable, but actually slanders the Buddha. He was too subtle, too aware of context, to be imprisoned in literalism. Our duty, if we are to take these injunctions

1 AN 2.23–2.26; see EĀ 18.9 (T2, № 125, p. 592, c29).

seriously, is to undertake the task of weening out the authentic from the inauthentic parts of our scriptures, and determining what they might mean in a given context. And that is no easy matter.

1.2 The Scope of Vinaya

11 How universally should we apply the rules? Practically, monastics vary widely in this. Some argue that times have changed so much that only the four *pārājikā* should apply; some suggest that it would be an improvement if the monks would keep even the five lay precepts. Rigorist monks declare that all the rules should be kept and should apply to all; yet it is not easy to find a monk who really keeps every single rule in a literal sense. This question opens into a vast field of ongoing dialogue and change in monastic practice.[2]

12 Perhaps we should leave aside, for now, the never-ending question of how best to apply the Vinaya in modern contexts, and consider a more limited question: how broadly were the rules meant to apply? In other words, what was the Buddha (or the redactors) *thinking* about when the rule was laid down? The Pali commentaries have faith that the Buddha laid down each rule as an expression of his omniscience,[3] and hence all rules are, in theory at least, universal and eternal in their application, at least as long as the current Buddha's dispensation lasts. This is used as the basis for Vinaya arguments down to the present day.[4] However the texts themselves present a humbler picture.[5] The Buddha addresses the actual situation before him. When unforseen situations come up, as they frequently do, he readily adjusts the rule. In particular he is more than willing to make allowances for areas that he had not geographically

---

[2] An example of this is discussed in 'Vinaya in Theravāda Temples in the United States', Paul David NUMRICH, Journal of Buddhist Ethics, V^OL 1, 1994.

[3] See the commentary to the Brahmajala Sutta; in Bhikkhu BODHI's translation, *The Discourse on the All-embracing Net of Views*, Buddhist Publication Society, 2007, pp. 122–5.

[4] An example of this is JETAVANA Sayadaw's argument for the establishing of the bhikkhuni order (Milindapañha Aṭṭhakathā, Hasāvatī Piṭaka Press, Rangoon, Burmese year 1311 (=1949), pp. 228–238), translated by Bhikkhu BODHI as 'Can an Extinct Bhikkhunī Sangha Be Revived?' in his *The Revival of Bhikkhunī Ordination in the Theravāda Tradition*. www.buddhanet.net/budsas/ebud/ebdha347.htm

[5] See ANĀLAYO, 'The Buddha and Omniscience'.

considered when laying down the rule, as for example the case of Soṇa, who asked for an allowance in regard to wearing shoes in the remote and rough country of Avanti.[6] Later redactors of the Vinaya took this as a precedent in making further allowances as Buddhism expanded beyond its initial frontiers; for example, the Haimavata Vinaya Mātikā depicts the Buddha allowing monks in the cold Himalayan regions to wear extra warm clothes.[7] Practically speaking, of course, virtually all monks and nuns take advantage of this principle in one way or another, and Buddhism has adjusted to the culture and climate in every country it has gone into, which is one of the major factors in its survival and spread until the present day.

13 If we cannot be certain that each rule was definitively and explicitly intended to apply universally, then let us ask a different question: what can we reasonably consider to be the scope of the rule within the thought-world of the early texts? This question is readily answerable, for that thought-world is clearly circumscribed, temporally, geographically, and culturally.

14 Temporally, the scope is given in the origin story for the bhikkhuni ordination itself: Buddhism was expected to last for 500 years, perhaps a millennium. While the prediction of the demise of Buddhism after this time is only found in this single dubious passage, this general time frame is implicit throughout the early texts. Clearly, the founders of early Buddhism were afraid that their religious message would die away within a few generations, and did not imagine that it would last more than a few hundred years at best.

15 Geographically, the early texts were limited to the Gangetic region of northern India, reaching as far south-west as the distant Avanti (now in the Western region of Madhya Pradesh), and in one or two passages to what is now Maharashtra (Assakā). To the north-west, the scope of awareness extended to Gandhāra, with one or two references to the 'Greeks' (*yona*; but they may have been known only by rumor). On the Eastern side lay Aṅgā, but this did not extend even as far as the mouth of the Ganges. There is no mention of, say Sri Lanka, or even of southern India.[8]

---

6 Pali Vinaya 1.194*ff*.

7 T24 № 1463 p. 846, c12–13: 爾時諸比丘雪山中夏安居。身體剝壞來到佛所佛聞已如此國土。聽著富羅複衣

8 See http://www.ancient-buddhist-texts.net/Maps/MP-index.htm.

16 Culturally, the texts have little to say about any cultures that differ from their own. There is one interesting reference to the fact that the Greeks have only two classes—masters and slaves[9]—but even in the legendary Jātakas, which ostensibly tell of events in far-distant ages of the earth, the culture remains remarkably like that of India in the 5th century BCE. Sadly, there is no hint that the Buddha knew of modern science, of Western civilization, of the global culture that has emerged after colonialism. And there is no text that affirms that in formulating a rule for nuns wandering along a lonely jungle path of Magadha in 500 BCE, the Buddha wanted that same rule to apply to a nun boarding an Airbus A380 in Changi Airport in 2009.

17 So this matter of the scope of the Vinaya texts remains subject to inference and interpretation. We can't expect the Vinaya to hand us all the answers. Different people will choose different things to preserve or adapt; but we should always be guided by the fundamentals of our ethics. In some northern lands, for example, the monastic year has been adjusted to shift the time of the rains retreat, which was laid down to accord with the Indian monsoon. It is hard to find fault with this. Other changes are less benign. For example, in cold climates, most monastics decide to wear jackets, even though this is against the Vinaya. In the Buddha's day, it seems, sleeved garments were a rarity, the special clothes of a prince or a warrior. So most monastics agree that in our different culture and climate, this rule need not be followed. But some monks stay in cold climates and refuse to wear warm jackets, wanting to follow the letter of the rule. So they live in highly heated buildings, at significant financial and environmental cost, instead of putting on a jumper. This choice values ancient Indian dress codes over the future of the planet. In such cases keeping to the letter of the Vinaya is, I believe, unethical.

1.3 The Layers of Text

18 We have remarked on the fact that the existing Vinaya texts include a set of rules called the *pāṭimokkha*, embedded within an explanatory matrix called the *vibhaṅga*. From the beginnings of modern Buddhist studies it

9 MN 93.6 Assalāyana.

has been recognized that these parts of the text form distinctive historical layers or strata. The *pāṭimokkha* is the earlier text, and the *vibhaṅga* was formed later. Moreover, the *pāṭimokkha* existed in its own right, as it still does, as an oral text, quite independent of the *vibhaṅga*. This is demonstrated by the presence of an array of textual markers—rhythm, grammatical case, vocabulary, length—that bind the *pāṭimokkha* rules into one coherent textual entity, despite the fact that it does not appear as such in the existing Vinayas.

19 For example, most of the *pāṭimokkha* rules use the particle *pana*, which serves to grease the flow from one rule to the next. Such markers are mnemonic devices to aid memorization and recital of the *pāṭimokkha* as an oral text, which is still recited each fortnight. But *pana* and the other markers only work when the *pāṭimokkha* rules are listed one after the other. Embedded within a complex matrix of explanatory and background material, as they are in the canonical Vinayas, these literary features become meaningless. This is one of the reasons we know that the *pāṭimokkha* existed as an independent text before the *vibhaṅgas*.

20 This invites us to question the relationship between the rule and its explanation. We shall see that, while the rules have much in common, the *vibhaṅgas* often differ completely. Take the first and most important of all monastic rules, the first *pārājika*, prohibiting sexual intercourse. This rule is preserved in near identical form in all Vinayas, but the background story is very different in each.[10] The Pali tells the long story of Sudinna's seduction by his former wife, largely borrowed from the well known account of Raṭṭhapāla, recorded in several Suttas. But while the Raṭṭhapāla Sutta versions are typically similar, only the Mahīśāsaka Vinaya preserves a similar background story to *pārājika* 1. The other Sthavira schools mention Sudinna but tell different stories, while the Mahāsaṅghika Vinaya doesn't mention Sudinna at all. The most plausible explanation of this state of affairs is that the rules stem from an early period, before the split of the Sangha into different schools, while the explanations largely arose later. The process of analyzing, explaining, and adjusting the rules must have been ongoing for many centuries after the Buddha's death.

[10] See ANĀLAYO, *Comparative Study*.

21 The question then becomes: what do we follow, the rules or the *vibhaṅga*? From the viewpoint of the Suttas, this would seem to be obvious. The standard exhortation on ethics for the monastics tells us to follow the rules: 'Dwell possessed of ethics, possessed of the *pāṭimokkha*, restrained with the restraint of the *pāṭimokkha*, perfect in conduct and resort, and seeing danger in the slightest fault, train by undertaking the training rules (*sikkhāpada*).'[11] In this standard exhortation, still recited regularly by the bhikkhus, there is no mention of a *vibhaṅga*, and no suggestion that one is bound to follow a particular interpretation of a rule.

22 There is little or no evidence that the *vibhaṅga* in anything like its current form existed in the Buddha's lifetime, and accordingly little justification for saying that the rulings of the *vibhaṅga* were intended by the Buddha to be authoritative. We do, it is true, find passages that are suggestive of the development of *vibhaṅga* material. For example, a stock passage says that a monastic teacher should know both *pāṭimokkhas* in full, well analyzed, well ordered, and well classified in both 'thread' (*sutta*) and 'supplement' (*anuvyañjana*).[12] This could well be understood, as the commentary does, as implying that one understands both the *pāṭimokkha* and the Suttavibhaṅga. But of course, the text itself falls short of establishing this. It merely shows that there was material 'supplementary' to the actual rules; the very choice of the word *anuvyañjana* emphasizes that this material was secondary to the rules themselves. No doubt such passages refer to a growing body of material which helped to explain, elaborate, and elucidate the brief rules of the *pāṭimokkha*, and no doubt such a process resulted in the Suttavibhaṅgas we have today. Whether any of that early supplementary material still exists is a matter for inquiry.[13] But it would certainly be unjustified to leap from such vague references to infer that a full-blown Suttavibhaṅga was in existence in the Buddha's day. Moreover, the purpose of this passage, it should be noted, is not to establish an authority by which monastics should practice. That has already been defined as the 'training rules' of the *pāṭimokkha*, or *sutta*. The purpose, rather, is to

---

[11] E.g. MN 6.2.

[12] E.g. Pali Vinaya 1.68: *ubhayāni kho panassa pāṭimokkhāni vitthārena svāgatāni honti suvibhattāni suppavattīni suvinicchitāni suttaso anubyañjanaso.*

[13] A small attempt was made by FRAUWALLNER, *Earliest Vinaya*, pp. 130*ff*.

detail the required qualifications for a teacher who can clarify and explain those training rules to a student.

23 Much of the material in the *vibhaṅga* does not even claim to have been spoken by the Buddha, and so the *vibhaṅga* was dubbed by Oldenberg as the 'Old Commentary'. As a commentary, its purpose is not to change the meaning of the rule, but to help in aiding understanding of the rules. And often this is just what the *vibhaṅga* does. But in some cases, the rules and *vibhaṅga* conflict, or at least the *vibhaṅga* makes concrete interpretations which the rules may not define so exclusively.

24 How are we to explain this situation? I believe that the *pāṭimokkha* rules were laid down by the Buddha himself: who else could have had the authority to lay down rules binding on the entire monastic community, without dispute or divergence? The existence of frequent revisions of the rules shows the Buddha's flexibility. But after his death the rules became frozen. It seems that the Sangha could not agree on making any changes, even when these had been authorized by the Buddha, as implied by the curious discussion of the 'lesser and minor rules' during the First Council.[14]

---

[14] The question of the 'lesser and minor rules' (*khuddānukhuddakāni sikkhāpadāni*) is sometimes invoked in the context of bhikkhuni ordination. If the Buddha allowed changing the rules, why can we not do so to make bhikkhuni ordination possible? This argument has a number of flaws: firstly, it wrongly assumes that the Vinaya needs to be changed to allow bhikkhuni ordination; and secondly it assumes that it is possible for the modern Sangha to change anything, which anyone familiar with Sangha workings would know is out of the question. I have elsewhere argued that the question of the lesser and minor rules should be seen, not so much as a legalistic allowance, but as a literary device tying the narrative of the Mahāparinibbāna Sutta to the agenda of the Second Council. Nevertheless, as a legal problem it is not insoluble. The allowance is for the abolition of lesser and minor 'training rules' (*sikkhāpada*), which are among those recited at the *uposatha* (bhikkhu *pācittya* 72: *kiṁ panimehi khuddānukhuddakehi sikkhāpadehi uddiṭṭhehi...*). All of the Elders at the First Council agreed that these terms stood for particular classes of offence; and while they disagreed as to the exact classes, a tacit agreement is often better than an explicit one. The *thullaccayas*, *dukkaṭas*, and *dubhāsita* are not recited at the *uposatha*, and since, it seems, at the early stage the *sekhiyas* and *adhikaraṇasamathas* were also not recited (see Introduction, note 18), the most minor classes of offence that were recited are the *pācittiyas* and *pāṭidesanīyas*. And in the Pali Vinaya we find that the *pācittiyas* are indeed referred to as *khuddaka* at the end of the *pācittiya vibhaṅga* for both the bhikkhus (Pali Vinaya 4.174) and the bhikkhunis (Pali Vinaya 4.345), as well as the Parivāra (Pali Vinaya 5.147). It seems, then, that the *pācittiya* rules are the *khuddaka* and the *pāṭidesanīyas* are the *anukhuddaka*.

25 But monastic life could not stand still, and new developments must be accounted for. These developments were incorporated in the Suttavibhaṅga, which form a uniquely valuable record of the practices as accepted in the diverse schools of ancient Indian Buddhism. Eventually, however, the Suttavibhaṅgas gained canonical status, and could not be further changed. I would therefore attribute the composition of the Suttavibhaṅga to the discussion held among the monastic community, and the increasing need to compile a systematic treatise on discipline to hold together the Sangha. Such discussions would have, of course, begun within the Buddha's lifetime, and would have taken a more systematic form in the generations following the Buddha's passing away.

26 The traditional approach to interpretation is 'synthetic', in the sense that it takes pre-existing elements and treats them as one coherent textual substance. The rule and its explanation (as indeed the whole Vinaya and its commentaries) are assumed to be a consistent system, and are interpreted so as to make them harmonize. This approach is like the rationalist or Platonic tendency in philosophy. Convinced that the universe was constructed in a perfect, rational manner, the search for knowledge became an attempt to discover the actual underlying unity that is assumed to exist. If, for example, the planets do not seem to orbit in their expected perfect circles, this is because our measurements or reasoning is faulty, not because the orbits are in fact not circles.

27 A more realistic interpretative approach might be called 'analytical', based on discerning different parts of a text and investigating their relationship. This has more affinity with an empiricist approach to knowledge. Unity is not assumed, and aberrations or variations are treated as facts just as true as any other. Variations in the texts may well be simple contradictions, arising from misunderstandings, or because different editors had different ideas.

28 These two paradigms in turn stem from two different sets of ideas about where the texts came from. One coming from a synthetic approach would argue that the texts stem from the All-Awakened Buddha, hence must be perfect and consistent. The analytical approach would point to the very many divergences within the existing texts, and would prefer to understand these in terms of the known principles of textual transmission. Like

those who would investigate biological evolution, empiricists assume that the forces that shaped texts in the past are similar in principle—though different in detail—to those that may be observable in the present. This method follows on from the Buddha's own epistemology, where he instructed to first understand the principles at work in the present moment, then to infer from that to the past and future.[15]

29 Such a method departs from the more traditional synthetic approach, which sees the omniscience of the Buddha as a singular, unrepeatable phenomenon, radically different from any epistemological means available to us at the present time. Basing an argument on an unprovable assumption of omniscience is comparable to Christian theology, which imagines the creation of the world as a singular, unrepeatable event, which cannot be reduced to the principles of evolution as observed in the present.[16] Crucially, however, just as the literalists assert that the Bible is the infallible word of God, yet the Bible itself makes no such claim, and is clearly the work of highly fallible humans, the Tipiṭaka makes no claim to the literal omniscience of the Buddha. In many cases the facts are plain wrong: there is no Mount Sineru, there are no creatures thousands of miles long in the seas, there is no northern country of Uttarakuru, there never were past ages with huge sized humans living for thousands of years, the state of technology and society in the deep past was not always constant. If the texts were ignorant of simple physical facts of times and regions just beyond their own boundaries, how could they be expected to understand the conditions in our times? That is a cruel and unjust expectation to force upon the texts.

30 The analytical approach I have just described has come under criticism as resulting in 'Protestant Buddhism'. Armchair scholars, dealing with nothing more challenging than comparing textual versions, decide for themselves that they can reinvent a world religion, ignoring or deriding the foolish superstitions of those who actually follow the religion. They

[15] E.g. SN 42.11, SN 12.33–34.

[16] This is not, of course, to say that all Christians deny evolution. But even those Christians, or other theists, who accept evolution as an explanation of how the world can change and adapt, still posit a unique event as the source of the universe itself. Darwinism, of course, makes no pretence to explain the origin of the universe (although certain recent developments in quantum cosmology are trying to take this step).

end up with a nothing, an army of inferences and speculations about unknowable things, a Buddhism that corresponds neither to the actual texts as they are, nor to Buddhism as it has ever been lived. As to whether we can know anything about 'original Buddhism', the 'obsession' with origins is just another intellectual fad. Living Buddhism cannot be reduced to a pristine pure teaching, subject to degradation and decay in later times.

31 To which I would say: what's wrong with Protestantism? The alternative, surely, is Catholic Buddhism: privileging the existing traditions for no better reason than the sheer fact that they and their works survived. Given the incredible corruption of the Roman Church of the Renaissance, could anyone seriously imagine that modern Christianity would be better off without the Protestant rebellion? The Protestant movement resulted in massive diversity in Christianity; bad for the Roman Catholics, no doubt, but creating a vibrancy that has, in the long run, revitalized the whole religion—including (at least to some degree) the Catholics themselves. Similarly, where would Buddhism today be without the critical inquiries of the 'Protestant Buddhists'—Rhys-Davids, Oldenberg, *et al.*—whose work has inspired reforms and reinvention all over the Buddhist world, by people who have never even heard of them? I could not count the times I have been told, as a monk, by traditional Buddhists, that 'real' Buddhism is hardly to be found in their country any more. And, to be frank, they are quite right. Traditional Buddhism is rank with superstition and magic of the most banal kinds. If such matters merely remained a bit of harmless hocus-pocus, it would not be such a problem. But the reality is that in many areas, not least the treatment of women, the monolithic, unassailable authority of the tradition results in terrible injustice. A bit of 'Protestant' reformation is just what the doctor ordered.

32 To resist the findings of text critical work, to insist—whether out of traditional values or postmodern methodological skepticism—that we must only deal with the texts 'as they are', is a profoundly conservative principle. It not only stifles innovation, it perpetuates ancient injustice for no better reason than that it is ancient. The texts are never 'as they are'—this is an utterly un-Buddhist notion. They are 'as they have become' (*yathābhūta*), arrived to us in their existing form because of the conditions of the past, in particular because of certain editorial decisions by certain monks at cer-

tain times and places. Why should their decisions be privileged forever? Why can they not be questioned, and why, if we have reasons, should we not make other decisions? The religion we are investigating is called 'Buddhism' for a reason: it is, at its heart, the spiritual path taught by the Buddha. To look for inspiration in his words is not a 19th century intellectual dead end, but the basis of all authentic Buddhist practice. It is by example of the Buddha's own Awakening that we seek the truth in ourselves. We merely apply modern, critical methods to this quest, just as Buddhists in every age and every place have reformed Buddhism in terms of their own culture.

33 In Vinaya studies, despite the forbidding complexities of the texts, we are fortunate that the textual strata have been kept reasonably distinct by the legalistic redactors. In interpreting the rules, it seems reasonable to see the rules themselves as, in the main, the words of the Buddha, and the *vibhaṅga* as the explanation of those rules according to the perspective of the schools. Our needs are essentially pragmatic. We need to understand the rule well enough to grasp its ethical core and to know how it should be understood in our time. Often enough, the rule itself is clear and simple, and in such cases there is no need to even worry about the *vibhaṅga*. If we seek clarification, the *vibhaṅga* is there to offer friendly advice, but can only serve to clarify the rule, not adjust or change its scope.

34 This principle might seem self-evident, but the converse approach has been used by Bhikkhu Ṭhānissaro in his *Buddhist Monastic Code*. This book has become the *de facto* guide to Vinaya for most English-speaking Theravādin bhikkhus, and so its interpretive principles must be carefully considered. Ṭhānissaro argues that, where the *vibhaṅga* and the *pāṭimokkha* differ, the *vibhaṅga* should take precedence. His argument (which by a strange coincidence is based on a discussion between the Buddha and Mahāpajāpatī) runs as follows.[17]

> 35 As far as discrepancies between the Vibhaṅga and the rules are concerned, the following passage in the Cullavagga (X.4) suggests that the Buddha himself gave preference to the way the bhikkhus worked out the rules in the Vibhaṅga:

---

[17] ṬHĀNISSARO Bhikkhu, *The Buddhist Monastic Code I*, pp. 11–12. www.accesstoinsight.org/lib/authors/thanissaro/bmc1/bmc1.intro.html.

> 36 As she was standing to one side, Mahāpajāpatī Gotamī said to the Blessed One: 'Venerable sir, those rules of training for the bhikkhunīs that are in common with those for the bhikkhus, venerable sir: What line of conduct should we follow in regard to them?'
>
> 37 'Those rules of training for the bhikkhunīs, Gotamī, that are in common with those for the bhikkhus: *As the bhikkhus train themselves, so should you train yourselves'*.... (emphasis added [by Ṭhānissaro]).
>
> 38 'And those rules of training for bhikkhunīs that are not in common with those for bhikkhus: What line of conduct should we follow in regard to them?'
>
> 39 'Those rules of training for the bhikkhunīs, Gotamī, that are not in common with those for the bhikkhus: Train yourselves in them as they are formulated.'

> 40 This passage implies that already in the time of the Buddha the bhikkhus had begun working out a way to interpret the rules that in some cases was not exactly in line with the way the Buddha had originally formulated them...
>
> 41 Because this development eventually led to the Vibhaṅga, we can be fairly confident that in adhering to the Vibhaṅga we are acting as the Buddha would have us do.

42 It is altogether improbable that a critical point in interpreting the bhikkhus' Vinaya should be left up to an encounter between the Buddha and Mahāpajāpatī, as an inferred byproduct of a discussion in how to interpret the bhikkhuni Vinaya. Surely we can find better grounds than this for such a crucial matter. This is a classic case of overinterpreting a text, taking it as a ruling for something that it was never about in the first place.

43 The Vinaya passage cited by Ṭhānissaro says nothing about the historical evolution of the rules versus the rule explanation. It is concerned with a quite different matter, that is, the relationship between the bhikkhu and bhikkhuni Vinayas. Certain rules are shared in common between the two Sanghas. These were laid down originally for the bhikkhus, and later the rules were applied to the bhikkhunis as well. In other cases, rules were laid down for the bhikkhunis alone, and are not shared by the bhikkhus.[18]

[18] The third case also exists, but is not relevant for this passage: some rules are kept by the bhikkhus alone, not shared with the bhikkhunis. The earliest discussion of this matter in the Pali literature is in the Parivāra (Pali Vinaya 6.146–8).

44 Mahāpajāpatī wants to know how the bhikkhunis should practice regarding these two types of rules. The Buddha's reply has nothing to do with a distinction between rule and explanation. The bhikkhus have already had the rule laid down for them. As we have already seen, the bhikkhus were supposed to train in accordance with the training rules as laid down, and would not transgress them for the sake of life. This passage, and many like it, make it quite explicit that the Buddha wanted the Sangha to practice the *training rules* as laid down. That is why the passage refers exclusively to the training rules, and says nothing about any *vibhaṅga*.

45 The two terms do not suggest a distinction between text and commentary, but rather refer to two different kinds of events: an initial setting out of the rule, and the subsequent practice in accordance with that rule. The bhikkhunis were not present when the rules for the bhikkhus were laid down, so they must learn these subsequently, from how the bhikkhus 'train' in them (where 'training' encompasses both study and practice of the rule). On the other hand, the bhikkhunis obviously cannot learn the rules that are unique for bhikkhunis from the way the bhikkhus are training; instead, they would be present when the rules are laid down, and should practice accordingly.

46 Ṭhānissaro acknowledges that the *vibhaṅga* as it exists today had not yet developed in the time of the Buddha, and assumes the Buddha is referring to an ancient precursor. No doubt he is correct in assuming that the discussions on interpretation among the Sangha, starting in the Buddha's own lifetime, evolved to become the *vibhaṅgas* as we know them. However, given that the *vibhaṅgas* of the schools differ greatly, we can say little about how much of our current *vibhaṅgas* might have existed in the time of the Buddha. Far from being 'confident' that in privileging the existing *vibhaṅga* over the rule itself we are acting as the Buddha would have wanted, to do so is to favor the sectarian interpretations introduced in the Vinayas, by persons unknown, over a period of several hundred years, over the words of the Buddha himself.

47 Ṭhānissaro has this to say about the importance of this interpretive principle:

> 48 And when we check the few places where the *vibhaṅga* deviates from the wording of the rules, we find that almost invariably it has

> tried to reconcile contradictions among the rules themselves, and between the rules and the Khandhakas, so as to make the Vinaya a more coherent whole. This is particularly true with rules that touch on Community transactions. Apparently, many of these rules were formulated before the general patterns for transactions were finalized in the Khandhakas. Thus, after the patterns were established, the compilers of the Vibhaṅga were sometimes forced to deviate from the wording of the original rules to bring them into line with the patterns.[19]

49 He therefore sees the difference as merely a matter of 'tidying up' the Vinaya. Such a process has no doubt occurred, and would indeed account for certain differences between the rules and analysis. This itself is an important historical observation. But in this book we shall see several cases where the rule and the rule explanation differ seriously, in ways that impact in a major way on the lives of the bhikkhunis. This seems to have happened to a greater degree in the bhikkhuni Vinaya. Indeed, one of the major cases we shall investigate is the development of the form of the bhikkhuni ordination procedure, the most important 'Community transaction' (*saṅghakamma*). As Ṭhānissaro suggests, the form originally laid down in the *pāṭimokkha* rules has been adjusted in the *vibhaṅga* to conform with the later developed scheme of the Khandhakas.

1.4 What is a Tradition?

50 Related to these textual problems is an even thornier issue: how should we, as contemporary Buddhist monastics, practice? It was hard enough in the days of dogmatic slumbers, when we rested in the assurance that the Pali was the One And Only Way. Even then we had disagreements, variant interpretations and attitudes. But with the inclusion of vast quantities of authentic Vinaya material, the questions multiply. Unfortunately the habit of ignoring Chinese and other versions of the Vinaya persists, not only in monks who have an understandable institutional investment in Pali orthodoxy, but also in scholars, who rather lamely try to argue that consideration of the Chinese texts would probably not make much of a

---

[19] ṬHĀNISSARO, p. 12.

difference after all. Our body of knowledge in English remains lamentably slim, and largely confined to specialists.

51 Do we stick to just one tradition? This was the classic posture of the traditions that have come down to us. Even the Chinese, with their wealth of Vinaya material, declared that they would follow the Dharmaguptaka, at least in theory, although they continued to study and refer to the other Vinayas. But this is problematic in practice: in certain cases, information is supplied in one Vinaya that is lacking in another.[20] Also, we cannot accept that just one Vinaya supplies a complete picture when we know that each Vinaya differs. Moreover, within, say, the Pali tradition, we find ourselves frequently turning to the commentaries for help when the Vinaya is obscure; but surely a canonical Vinaya must rank as a higher authority than a late commentary.

52 Another approach would be to examine each Vinaya, do some text-critical hocus-pocus (confident in the knowledge that almost no-one will take the time to seriously evaluate what we have done), and bow with reverence to the 'Original Vinaya' that emerges pristine from the crucible. But then what to do when our friends, altering the ingredients of the magic mixture, come up with a different 'Original Vinaya'? The search for an 'Original Vinaya' is, moreover, in its infancy, so that the quantity of textual work required to achieve such a thing is as yet only dreamt of. Nevertheless, the idea should not be written off, as in certain cases it is possible to agree with confidence on what the original version of a text must have been.

53 But perhaps we would be better to abandon such grand schemes and just juggle our texts as best we can. Each case is different, and truth is best arrived at by experimenting with different approaches as seems best for that case. We won't know what really works until long afterwards, and so it is premature to rule out any interpretive approach.

54 We cannot go back. We cannot make ourselves un-know. Critics often deride textual criticism as 'speculative'. But the traditional belief that all the canonical texts were spoken by the Buddha, or even the weaker claim that all the texts were assembled at the First Council is not merely specula-

[20] As, for example, in the decision that a bhikkhuni may not re-ordain, discussed in chapter 4.66–4.68.

tive but plain wrong. It cannot possibly have been the case. The existence of differing versions of the same events proves this beyond reasonable doubt. The claim that a massive body of texts has been passed down unchanged for 2500 years is an extraordinary one, and extraordinary claims require extraordinary evidence. That evidence is not forthcoming. In such a situation, all approaches are hypothetical. Hypothesis is not speculation: speculation invents ideas on a whim, while hypothesis draws inferences based on data. It is not necessary, and usually not possible, to prove that a given hypothesis is 'correct'. Since the traditional point of view is manifestly incorrect, the burden of proof lies with the traditionalists. All we can establish for the time being is whether a given way of looking at the textual and other evidence is *reasonable*. Hypotheses are always subject to revision, and are always partial. They can be falsified by finding new texts or more precise readings of known texts; and they help us make sense out of a complex array of textual data. With the dismantling of the traditional perspective, we need new ways to find meaning in our texts.

55 When we begin to hold the Vinaya up for examination, conservative Buddhists start to get a bit nervous. What are we going to reveal? Will we undermine the very basis for the monastic life? What of the simple purity that comes with faith in a tradition? Doesn't it mean that everyone will just fall back on their own opinions and speculative theories? But we must come to grips with the incontestable fact that the traditional belief—that the Vinaya has been handed down unchanged since the Buddha—is wrong. Insisting on known falsehoods is not, I contest, a principled path.

56 Our notion of a 'tradition', moreover, needs an injection of reality. Patrick Kearney, an Australian meditation teacher, once said that a tradition is not a fixed set of received doctrines, but is more like a family argument. Each Christmas (or Chinese New Year or Songkran...) we gather with our beloved family to renew our old connections. The meal starts off wonderfully, and there's laughs and jokes all around. But during the evening, someone mentions politics—or religion—and the old tensions flare up again. By the end of the night, you find yourself arguing about the same things you argued about last year. And that's what makes you a family. You care enough about the same things to bother arguing about them. We argue about *samatha*

and *vipassanā*, or about the authenticity of the Abhidhamma—or about bhikkhunis—precisely because we care.

57 In supporting the pan-sectarian movement for the establishment and growth of the bhikkhuni Sangha, one constantly hears that this will threaten, even destroy, the foundations of Theravāda Buddhism, and that such a movement can never find acceptance in Theravāda circles. Even if we do not buy into such scare tactics, there is a legitimate concern for the stability and continuation of the Buddhist tradition, which in Theravāda is often said to encompass not only the canon but also the commentarial literature. Here are some remarks from Bhikkhu Bodhi:[21]

58

> ... in almost all Theravāda circles, actual Vinaya practice is determined not by the canonical text alone but by the canonical text as interpreted by the commentary and Ṭīkās [sub-commentaries]. Thus it would be a bold and somewhat controversial move to reject the commentarial interpretation here and stick solely to the word of the canonical Vinaya, arguing for a position counter to that of the commentaries. Vinaya practice is not merely a matter of personal interpretation but of communal consensus, and when most Theravāda communities hold that on this point the commentary is to be followed, the decree of the commentary then functions as law... At a time when the Theravāda bhikkhuni order is still in its infancy, my personal advice is to avoid taking controversial positions that challenge mainstream Theravāda interpretations (except, that is, on the validity of bhikkhuni ordination!)

59 This advice by one of the most esteemed Elders of the Theravāda must be taken seriously. Nevertheless, I feel it is not a sufficient description of the diversity of understandings within Theravāda. Perhaps this is because Bhikkhu Bodhi's ordination was within a lineage that treated the commentaries with great deference. My experience, in the Thai Forest Tradition, has been quite different. Of course the commentaries are, in theory, given weight, but in practice the most important thing is neither canon nor commentary but the opinions and practices of the contemporary Masters.

60 Let me give an overview of the tradition as received in Theravāda, to try to convey some idea of the complexities involved. At the root is the Pali Vinaya, which may or may not be available in any particular monastery,

---

[21] Private communication.

and which may or may not be available in translation. This is universally regarded as the theoretical basis of practice, and yet is little read. On top of the canon lie the classic commentaries, especially the Samantapāsādikā of Buddhaghosa, which is accepted in all Theravādin countries. But the Samantapāsādikā is not a unitary text. It was compiled and edited by Buddhaghosa in the 5th century from several ancient commentaries, and represents the distilled wisdom of centuries of teachers' traditions. It frequently mentions discussions and differences of opinions on specific points, and before the time of Buddhaghosa the opinions that he prefers were by no means universally accepted, even within the fraternity of the Mahāvihāra. Moreover, at that time there were at least two other schools active in Sri Lanka, and several more in South-east Asia. Buddhaghosa's opinions, at the time he wrote them, represented a certain position in the spectrum of possible opinions of one of the Southern schools.

61 Due to Buddhaghosa's tremendous vitality and erudition, his commentaries, it seems, soon became authoritative within the Mahāvihāravāsin circles, and series of sub-commentaries were written. Unlike the commentaries, the sub-commentaries do not stem from a very ancient tradition, but were composed afresh by their authors. There are very many of these; and the existence of an ongoing living tradition is testament to the need for the Sangha to continually revisit its tradition in new contexts. It is usually understood that the sub-commentaries take Buddhaghosa's work as authoritative and do not deviate from his opinions, but seek to clarify and extend his work. I have, however, seen no serious scholarly work that considers whether the sub-commentarial Vinaya tradition is in fact in complete agreement with Buddhaghosa. Also, it is unclear how widely distributed the sub-commentaries were, and it seems likely that much of the Theravādin world has had little exposure to them. Many of them may be local Burmese traditions. Indeed, in many traditional monasteries, the teaching tradition was passed down through little texts called *nissayas*, which are little more than a collection of lecture notes by a senior local teacher. Often these would be the only scriptures available in a monastery.

62 The composition of Vinaya texts was revitalized in modern times. The Pubbasikkhāvaṇṇanā was composed in Thailand by Phra Amarabhirakhit, a student of Prince Mongkut, in 1860. This formed the basis for modern

Thai Vinaya practice, especially in the Forest Tradition, where it is still read as an authoritative text. This marks a critical juncture in the evolution of Theravāda: breaking the tradition of 1500 years, the key Vinaya text is composed in a local language, not Pali, and hence can only be read by Thai bhikkhus. It is unknown in other Theravādin lands, which use other localized modern works for their Vinaya textbooks. The Pubbasikkhā is a difficult text, and for the purpose of the basic monastic curriculum, Vajirañāṇavarorasa composed the *Vinayamukha* in the early 20th century, which is still used as part of the official Thai monastic educational curriculum. Charmingly, whenever a difficult topic is raised, the *Vinayamukha* declares, 'May the Vinaya experts make a decision on this matter.' If the monk, a prince of Thailand, who wrote the textbook is not a Vinaya expert, there would be few who are willing to step forward in such a role. But this saying, while indicating a wise humility in avoiding unnecessary disputes, is also evidence of the diversity of views among the Thai Sangha. The *Vinayamukha* is a work of independent spirit, which frequently disagrees with the commentaries, and even with the Suttavibhaṅga.

63 The latest in this tradition of practical guides to Vinaya is Ṭhāṇissaro's *Buddhist Monastic Code*, which is used very widely in the English-speaking world, and which offers a lucid contemporary interpretation. In addition, within the Ajahn Chah tradition, an unfinished set of Vinaya notes by Ajahn Brahm is used. Both of these works use a conservative analytical approach, which endeavors to find unity whenever possible, but is open to the possibility of contradiction within the tradition.

64 So much for the textual heritage. Even this brief and incomplete survey shows that the situation is complex and there are a multitude of possible perspectives. But we have omitted the most important thing, the monastics themselves. In all ages, Vinaya has been practiced and discussed among the monastics, and they will invariably have different positions. I do not know even two monks who would agree on every detail of Vinaya. Practically, Vinaya practice within a particular community is largely determined by the authority of the abbot as mediated within the community. The abbot may or may not have any knowledge of the texts we have been discussing. Similarly, the texts may or may not be found in the monastery, and if they are there, there may or may not be anyone who reads them. In the vast

majority of cases, decisions about what is 'Vinaya' or not will be based on the local and contemporary sources, either books or the opinions of the teachers. Even among those teachers who are, in theory, committed to upholding the traditional commentarial Theravāda, there are many differences of opinion. And in traditional Theravādin countries, there are many influential monks who question or reject the authority of the commentaries, not to speak of the later texts. Such individualizing forces are constantly acting as a counterforce to the centralizing, harmonizing tendencies of the 'authoritative' texts.

65 In addition to the individual opinions of the teachers, there are factors such as the laws of the land. In Thailand the Vinaya is complemented by a Sangha Act, which lays down certain laws for the Sangha, and appoints a Council of Elders to decide matters of importance in managing the Sangha. While such instruments are, in theory, supposed to uphold the Vinaya, in practice they have as much to do with political and economic imperatives. There are, further, local customs, beliefs, and rituals, which constantly influence the Sangha life. For example, while the Vinaya and statements in the Suttas forbid practice of non-Buddhist rituals, quasi-magical rituals such as making holy water, or tying sacred string, are universally performed by the Sangha. Reform movements will often try, with varying degrees of success, to eliminate such practices, and Buddhist practitioners in traditional lands will regularly decry what they see as 'Brahmanical' intrusions into Buddhism; but it is a losing battle.

66 Let me give just one example of how such forces played out as I have witnessed it. In 1995 I was staying at a branch monastery of Ajahn Chah, run by a monk called Luang Por Hom. He was an old monk, ordained fairly late in life, and come from a simple rural background, but with a shrewd mind. A visiting monk arrived. He had ordained in Dhammayuttika circles, and as such, he was regarded as a semi-outsider, but was still accepted in the Sangha. He confessed a *saṅghādisesa* offense. Luang Por Hom did not have experience in managing the procedure for *saṅghādisesa*, so he asked me to invite a senior Western monk from my home monastery of Wat Pah Nanachat to help with some advice. Meanwhile he read up on the matter in the Thai translation of the Vinaya Piṭaka, which is printed together with the commentary. When the Western monk came for the discussion, Luang

Por Hom said that he had never had to do the *saṅghādisesa* procedure; then he slyly asked the Western monk if he had experience with it. He said yes, to Luang Por's amusement. They discussed the procedure, with the Western monk contributing his knowledge of the texts and practices as understood within the English-speaking Sangha. When it came to one point—I think it was on the question of where the monk undergoing probation should sit while the Sangha recited *pāṭimokkha*—Luang Por Hom remarked that when he was a young monk at Ajahn Chah's monastery, they did it a certain way; but from his reading of the text, it seems it should be another way. The Western monk agreed. Later, before the monk had formally entered the period of probation, Luang Por Hom made him sit at the end of the line of monks, and on the floor, not on the raised platform for the monks. I said to Luang Por that I thought that the offending monk should not undergo such penances until he had formally entered the probationary period. Luang Por agreed, but said that he was doing it to cut his pride and stubbornness.

67 So in this one little case, we see a number of issues at play. The basic framework for the whole event was the Vinaya, which all accepted as authoritative. The commentaries and sub-commentaries were not consulted, unless they were read in the Thai edition along with the root text, but their influence was felt, mediated through later works. The practice at Ajahn Chah's monastery was influential, which was itself largely influenced by the Pubbasikkhā, as well as Ajahn Chah's personal study of the Vinaya and living for many years within the Thai Forest Tradition. The fact that the practice, even of such an esteemed Vinaya master, might deviate from the canonical texts was discussed and accepted (I cannot remember how we actually did the procedure in the end.) In this case, even a relatively uneducated forest monk was quite happy to return to the Vinaya source for the procedure, and to dialogue in a critical way with his tradition. But at the same time, he imposed personal punishments, cheerfully accepting that it was extra to the requirements of the Vinaya, simply because he felt it was important for the spiritual growth of his student.

68 Such is the complexity of interacting influences in one case. In every case the scenario plays out differently, but there will always be an intersection and a dynamic tension between the different authorities.

69 It is, therefore, simplistic to treat the Theravādin tradition as a monolithic entity, an unreflective instantiation of the classical commentarial orthodoxy. The questions we ask in this book are nothing new, even if our methods may be to some degree unconventional. People are people, and Buddhism is a religion for adults. Monastics are mature enough to make up their own minds, and do not need to imagine a false sense of conformity in order to recognize our kinship as human beings who are following the Buddha's path.

70 In the case of bhikkhuni ordination, conservatives often claim that bhikkhunis can never take their place in 'Theravāda'. The reality, of course, is much more complex. Bhikkhunis were a part of 'Theravāda' for over a thousand years. The existence of the bhikkhunis was taken for granted by Buddhaghosa. The question of the revival of the bhikkhuni order is a modern problem, and as Bhikkhu Bodhi has shown, a modern Pali work by Jetavana Sayadaw indicates that there have been opposing and supporting voices through the 20th century. Bhikkhunis who live in Thailand today tell me that they have the personal support of many bhikkhus, despite their lack of acknowledgement by the authorities. The claim that there is a monolithic opposition to bhikkhunis by the Theravādin Sangha is no more than a piece of rather desperate, sad rhetoric.

Chapter 2

PRINCIPLES TO BE RESPECTED

THE GARUDHAMMAS ARE A SET OF RULES, which, according to the traditional narrative, were laid down by the Buddha as the pre-conditions before he reluctantly consented to the ordination of his aunt and foster-mother Mahāpajāpatī Gotamī as the first bhikkhuni. The *garudhammas* as such do not appear in the list of *pāṭimokkha* rules, being outside the normal framework of the Suttavibhaṅga. My *White Bones Red Rot Black Snakes* examines the narrative background in some detail. Here I would like to look more closely at the rules themselves. The rules vary slightly between the traditions, but I focus on the Mahāvihāravāsin version, referring to the others in important cases. A detailed treatment of all variations in the dozen or so versions of these rules would be ponderous and unnecessary.

2 The term *garudhamma* has suffered much in the hands of modern translators. *Garu* literally means 'heavy', and in some places in the Vinaya 'heavy' offenses are contrasted with 'light' offenses.[1] So modern scholars have called these the 'heavy' or 'severe' or 'strict' rules. Countless interpreters have seen the *garudhammas* as an imposition of control by monks over nuns. The idea that the *garudhammas* are essentially about control seems to be influenced by the Christian virtue, in both monasteries and weddings, of 'obedience'. Obedience is an appropriate virtue in an ethical system founded on 'Thou shalt', issued by a Lord on High. Buddhism, however, is based on the ethical principle 'I undertake the training…'. This assumes a

---

[1] E.g. Pali Vinaya 1.68: … *lahukaṁ āpattiṁ na jānāti, garukaṁ āpattiṁ na jānāti…*

mature, responsible relationship with one's ethical framework, and does not rely on a relationship of command.

3 The word *garu*, when used in the Vinaya, normally has quite a different meaning: respect. And the *garudhammas* themselves says this 'rule (*dhamma*) should be revered, respected (*garukatvā*), honored, and worshiped for the rest of your life, not to be transgressed'. Clearly, *garudhamma* means 'Rules to be Respected'. This is confirmed by the standard Chinese rendering, 八敬法 (*ba jing fa*), literally 'eight respect dhammas'. The rules themselves primarily relate to the ways that the bhikkhunis should pay respects to the bhikkhus.

4 The Mahāvihāravāsin Vinaya does not have a detailed analysis (*vibhaṅga*) of the *garudhammas*. Hence we must seek out contexts from elsewhere that might help to illuminate the problems raised by the rules. Certain Vinayas, such as the Lokuttaravāda, do offer detailed analyses of the rules; but by the very fact, and the nature of those analyses, the text is considerably later than the Pali, so must be used with caution.

2.1 Garudhamma 1

> 5 Though a bhikkhuni be ordained for a hundred years, she should bow down, rise up, make anjali, and behave properly towards a bhikkhu ordained that very day.

6 This rule startles with its abruptness, its immediate and total exclusion of the possibility for any other way in which the male and female monastic communities might relate to one another. It stands in stark contrast with the Buddha's reasoned and balanced approach throughout the rest of the Vinaya, where he refuses to lay down a rule until it is needed. This is why we respect the Vinaya and wish to follow it: it is reasonable, a contingent and pragmatic means for people to live in community and develop good behavior. When the Vinaya appears unreasonable, we must ask ourselves: is this our problem, or the text's? Must we abandon our 'modern' conditioning, see through the way that 'feminism' has twisted our perceptions, and realize that this rule is no less than an expression of Awakened Wisdom, the authoritative decree of the Buddha, issuing from his incomprehensible grounding in the Unconditioned? Or does the

problem lie somewhere else entirely? Is it possible that our ancient texts do not issue unsullied from the penetration into perfect wisdom, but result from a lengthy and complex historical process, a process that involved both good and bad, wisdom and folly, compassion and cruelty?

7 Unlike most of the other *garudhammas*, this rule lacks a direct counterpart in most of the *pāṭimokkhas*. That is to say, in most of the Vinayas, the rule only appears here, and has no independent corroboration. We shall look at the exceptions to this later.

8 There is, however, another passage in some Vinayas that reinforces the message of this rule, and which extends it to a general principle that monks should never bow to any women. The Mahāvihāravāsin Vinaya elsewhere in the Khandhakas has a group of 10 *avandiyos* (those who should not be bowed to), which includes women.[2] But the context the rule appears in raises doubts as to the formation of this passage. It follows the well-known story of the partridge, the monkey, and the elephant, where the three animals lived harmoniously by respecting the eldest among them.[3] This story is found in all Vinayas.[4]

9 However the different Vinayas each follow this story with a very different text. The Pali appears, on purely internal criteria, to be an originally independent passage. It changes from the specific list 'bow down, rise up, make anjali, and behave properly' mentioned in the story, to the general term 'not bow'. Not only that, but the content sends a completely different message: the whole point of the three animals story is that we should respect elders, but now we are being told to not respect women, even if they are elder. Taken together, these suggest that the sequel is not intrinsic to the story.

10 The Dharmaguptaka follows the story with a long section, listing quite different individuals than the Pali, although also including women.[5] For example, the Dharmaguptaka includes a matricide, patricide, arahant killer, schismatic, etc., none of which are mentioned in the Pali. The Dharmaguptaka also lists those to whom different people such as novices, trainees, etc., should pay respect, and adds that one should also pay respect in the

---

2 Pali Vinaya 2.162.

3 Pali Vinaya 2.161–2.

4 See FRAUWALLNER, *Earliest Vinaya*, pp. 122–3 for references.

5 T22, № 1428, p. 940, b1: 一切女人不應禮

same way to their stupas; the emphasis on stupas is characteristic of this Vinaya, and evidence of the lateness of this section.[6]

11 The Mahīśāsaka,[7] Sarvāstivāda,[8] and Mahāsaṅghika[9] all say nothing in this place regarding bowing to women.[10] Thus the fact that the injunction against paying respects to women in this case uses a different terminology from the preceding passage; that it is based on a principle of gender rather than age; that it is absent from most of the Vinayas in this place; and that where it is present in the Dharmaguptaka it speaks of stupas, all adds up to a clear conclusion that the passage is a late interpolation.

12 Returning to the *garudhamma* and the specific injunction not to bow to a bhikkhuni, the Mahīśāsaka and Dharmaguptaka Vinayas include the rule as a *pācittiya* ('expiation'—a rule which, when transgressed, can be cleared through a confession), and the Sarvāstivāda has a related rule. Here is the rule from the Sarvāstivāda Vinaya Suttavibhaṅga.

> 13 The Buddha was staying at Sāvatthī. Now at that time the Elder Mahākassapa, putting on his robes before midday, taking his bowl, went to a householder's home for almsround. Then at the place he stopped there was a layman's wife. Seeing Mahākassapa in the distance, she got up and greeted him. But Thullanandā was at that place first. Seeing Mahākassapa in the distance, she did not rise to greet him. Then that layman's wife bowed with her head at the feet of Elder Mahākassapa. She washed her hands and taking his bowl, offered plenty of rice, with curry over it. Mahākassapa received it and left.
>
> 14 The lay woman went to Thullanandā and said: 'Are you aware that was the Elder Mahākassapa, the Buddha's great disciple, who is greatly revered by the deities as a virtuous field of merit? If you were to rise and greet him, what harm would come of that?'

---

[6] T22, № 1428, p. 940, b7: 如是等人塔一切應禮

[7] T22, № 1421, p. 121, a25: 如是奉行

[8] T23, № 1435, p. 242, c13–17: 有三人不如。何等三。一切未受大戒人。不如受大戒人。一切下座不如上座。一切受事説非法人雖作上座。不如下座。不受事人説如法者。一切受大戒人。勝不受戒人。一切上座勝下座。佛勝衆聖

[9] T22, № 1425, p. 446, c2–3: 若見上座來。不起迎和南恭敬者。越毘尼罪

[10] Incidentally, although this rule is sometimes said to be a 'Theravāda' rule, the '[Yogacāra] Bodhisattva Precepts' say one should pay respects to neither a woman nor a lay person. T40, № 1814, p. 683, c15–16: 不應禮白衣。一切女人不應禮

15 Thullanandā said: 'Mahākassapa was originally practicing another religion, [i.e.] Brahmanism. You greatly reverence that, but I do not respect it.'

16 The lay woman was annoyed and scolded: 'These bhikkhunis say, "If you do what is good you will get merit", but when they see bhikkhus coming they do not rise, as if they were women from another religion.'

17 When the bhikkhunis of few wishes, contented, keepers of ascetic practices heard about this they were not pleased. They went to the Buddha and told him everything. For that reason the Buddha summoned the two-fold Sangha together.

18 Knowing, he asked: 'Is it true that you did that thing, or not?'

19 She answered: 'It is true, Blessed One.'

20 The Buddha for this reason in many ways scolded: 'How can this bhikkhuni see a monk coming and not rise?' Having in many ways scolded for that reason, he said to the bhikkhus: 'For the sake of ten benefits, I lay down this precept for bhikkhunis. From today onwards that precept should be taught:

21 'Should a bhikkhuni, seeing a bhikkhu coming, not rise, this is an offense of *pācittiya*.'

22 '*Pācittiya*' means: burn,[11] boil, smear, obstruct. If not confessed, it will obstruct the path. This is the offense: if a bhikkhuni sees a bhikkhu and does not rise, this is a *pācittiya*; straightaway seeing and not rising, straightaway at that point there is *pācittiya*.'[12]

23 A few notes are in order. Thullanandā (Fat Nandā) was Mahākassapa's nemesis, and accordingly, a great fan of Ānanda. Her misbehavior and, in particular, animosity towards Mahākassapa are well attested in the Suttas and Vinaya, and elsewhere she repeats her allegation that Mahākassapa had previously been a non-Buddhist.[13] Thus her behavior on this occasion is just deliberate rudeness towards a revered Elder. Notice that this rule concerns only rising for a bhikkhu when one sees them, and does not mention bowing and the other acts mentioned in the *garudhamma*. We also notice that the criticism by the laywoman specifically invokes the accepted

[11] This explanation is derived from a folk etymology connecting *pācittiya* with *pacati*, to cook. Unfortunately, this play on words is sometimes interpreted literally, and students are informed that if they break *pācittiya* rules they will burn in hell. Needless to say, the early texts contain no trace of such an idea.

[12] Sarvāstivāda Vinaya, bhikkhuni *pācittiya* 103 (T23, № 1435, p. 324, b29–c22).

[13] SN 16.11/ SĀ 1144/ SĀ2 119.

cultural standards of conduct expected of women. In context, then, this rule is perfectly reasonable, merely formalizing the respect due to Elders of the community. However, when the *garudhammas* extend this to form a rule requiring that all bhikkhunis must rise for bhikkhus, the reasonable context is lost, for respect should also be shown to the bhikkhunis for their practice and wisdom.

24 Let us look now at the second appearance of this rule in the *pāṭimokkhas*, this time the Vinaya of the Mahīśāsakas. The rule here is similar to Dharmaguptaka *pācittiya* 175, but in that case there is no proper origin story. It is merely said that the Buddha laid down the rule (as a *garudhamma*) while at Sāvatthī, but the bhikkhunis did not keep it, so he laid it down again as a *pācittiya*.[14] The Mahīśāsaka offers more detail, so we will use that version.

> 25 Now at that time bhikkhunis did not bow to monks, did not greet them, did not receive them, did not invite them to a seat. The bhikkhus were annoyed, and did not return to teach. Then the bhikkhunis were foolish, without knowledge, and not able to train in the precepts. The senior bhikkhunis saw this, looked down on it, and scolded in many ways. The matter was therefore told to the Buddha. For that reason the Buddha summoned together the two-fold Sangha.
>
> 26 He asked the bhikkhunis: 'Is this true or not?'
>
> 27 They replied: 'It is true, Blessed One.'
>
> 28 The Buddha in many ways scolded them: 'Did I not already teach the eight *garudhammas* as suitable etiquette regarding bhikkhus? From today onwards, that precept should be thus recited:
>
> 29 'Should a bhikkhuni, seeing a bhikkhu, not rise up, bow down, and invite him to a seat, this is an offense of *pācittiya*.'
>
> 30 For trainees and novices, it is an offense of wrong-doing. If sick, if previously there is anger and suspicion, with no shared speech [recitation?], there is no offense.'[15]

31 Here there is no developed story, only a formulaic background that is very similar to the backgrounds for several of the other *pācittiya/garudhammas* we shall see below. There is no common ground between this origin story and the Sarvāstivāda version, and hence no basis to infer that either of them have any genuine historical source.

---

[14] HEIRMANN, *Rules for Nuns*, p. 955.

[15] Mahīśāsaka Vinaya, bhikkhuni *pācittiya* 179 (T22, № 1421, p. 97, c20–28).

32 There is a valid reason for the rule in the context: it is a good thing to respect one's teachers. This rule is not an arbitrary imposition, but came from a genuinely problematic situation. One might question whether the monks were being a little precious in refusing to teach; but any teacher knows how hard it is if the students don't display a positive attitude. In ancient India, as indeed throughout Asia today, bowing to one's teachers was a simple and universally observed sign of respect and gratitude. It is, however, true that the rule as it stands does not specifically mention teaching. Like the previous example from the Sarvāstivāda Vinaya, the context of the background story has been extended beyond its reasonable application. A rule requiring bhikkhunis to rise and pay respects to their teachers would have been justifiable, but as it stands the rule is a straightforward example of discrimination. One might have expected, in fact, that it would be more important to establish a rule requiring bhikkhunis to respect their own bhikkhuni teachers; in traditional societies today, nuns will habitually defer to monks, and it is hard to convince them to respect other nuns in the same way. It should also be noted that monks should not give the teaching desiring worldly benefits such as receiving homage, and it is an offense (*pācittiya* 24) for a bhikkhu to accuse another bhikkhu of doing this.

33 The story refers to the *garudhammas* as already existing. There is, however, no question of an offense arising from them. It is as if the status of the *garudhammas* at the time this rule was formulated was of some recommended trainings in etiquette, like, say, the *sekhiya* rules, with no specific penalty attached. Our discussion of *garudhamma* 5 will address the problem of the penalty arising from the *garudhammas*.

34 Now that we have discussed these *pācittiya* offenses related to the first *garudhamma*, let us return to our discussion of the *garudhamma* itself.

35 The Pali version of the *garudhammas* describes the acts of respect that must be shown by the bhikkhunis to the bhikkhus in this way: *abhivādanaṁ paccuṭṭhānaṁ añjalikammaṁ sāmīcikammaṁ*, which I render as 'bow down, rise up, make anjali, and behave properly'. This phrase occurs twice elsewhere in contexts crucial for understanding the *garudhammas*. First is when the Sakyan princes, including Ānanda, asked for Upāli, the former barber and Vinaya expert-to-be, to ordain first, so they can reduce their

Sakyan pride by 'bowing down, rising up, making anjali, and behaving properly' to him.[16] Elsewhere, we are often told of the problems caused in the Sangha by the Sakyans and their pride: Nanda, who famously went forth on account of 500 pink-footed celestial nymphs, and who wore make-up as a monk; Channa, the Buddha's incorrigible charioteer, who on the Buddha's deathbed was given the 'Supreme Punishment' (i.e., the silent treatment); Upananda, who constantly harassed the lay supporters for fine requisites; and of course Devadatta, who tried to kill the Buddha. Tradition says that pride caused the Sakyans to grievously insult Viḍūḍabha, king of Kosala, who in revenge destroyed the Sakyan republic and scattered the clan. Thus the Sakyan pride has become a byword in Buddhist culture. This suggests that the purpose of emphasizing bowing in the *garudhamma*, just as for the Sakyan princes, was to reduce pride. Given that it was Mahāpajāpatī and the Sakyan ladies who were seeking ordination, we might be forgiven for thinking that it was specifically Sakyan pride that is at issue here.

36 The second time this phrase is relevant for understanding this *garudhamma* is even more specific. In the Dakkhiṇāvibhaṅga Sutta the Buddha says to Mahāpajāpatī that it is not easy to repay one who has given the gift of Dhamma through 'bowing down, rising up, making anjali, and behaving properly'.[17] This was part of a discussion that arose when Mahāpajāpatī approached the Buddha and tried to offer him a set of robes. He suggested that rather than offer them to him personally, she make the offering to the Sangha as a whole, going on to explain that offerings to the Sangha were of greater benefit than an offering to any individual, even the Buddha. The message is clear enough. Mahāpajāpatī, who is still a laywoman, is personally attached to the Buddha, her son, and has not learned to respect the Sangha. We now have two contextual reasons for creating this rule: the curbing of Mahāpajāpatī's Sakyan pride, and her personal attachment to Siddhattha.

37 Mahāpajāpatī herself confirms that this particular rule was hard for her to keep. After accepting the *garudhammas*, she says she will treasure them like a youth would bear an adornment of flowers. Hardly has she gone, however, when she exhibits yet another womanly weakness, changing her

---

[16] Pali Vinaya 2.183.

[17] MN 142.4.

mind and getting Ānanda to ask a special privilege from the Buddha: that they forget this rule, and allow paying respect according to seniority. The Buddha refuses.

38 Now, the Buddha is supposed to have said that the acceptance of these rules was Mahāpajāpatī's full ordination. Sometimes what is omitted is ignored, and yet may have a decisive importance, so I must bodily lift the next fact into consciousness: nowhere in this narrative are the bhikkhunis explicitly told that they have to keep these rules. The rules are laid down for Mahāpajāpatī. It is true that the rules are phrased in the general sense of all bhikkhunis, and elsewhere the Vinaya expects the bhikkhunis to keep these rules. But in the core of the primary narrative, it is never directly said that these rules are a part of general bhikkhuni ordination. Nor is the adherence to these rules a part of the ordination procedure in the Mahāvihāravāsin Vinaya, or indeed the procedures of other Vinayas. Since the text explicitly says that the *garudhammas* are intended to be Mahāpajāpatī's ordination, and since there are plausible reasons why they should be relevant for her, there seems every reason to think the *garudhammas* were originally laid down for Mahāpajāpatī alone.

39 When the Buddha refuses Mahāpajāpatī's request to rescind this rule, he explains, rather oddly, that other, badly expounded religions do not allow paying respects to women, so how could he?[18] If badly taught religions do not allow respect for women, I would have thought this was a good reason for well taught religions to encourage it. In any case, it seems the Buddha was quite correct, for this exact rule is in fact found in Jain scriptures. The following is taken from the Yuktiprabodha with the Svopajñavtti of the Svetambara Upadhyāya Meghavijaya. Dated from the 17th century, this presents an argument on the status of women between the two main Jain sects. The work is from the Svetambara perspective, although here we hear the voice of the Dīgambara opponent. The work that is quoted, the Svetambara text Upadeśamālā, appears to date from around the 8th century:

40 > #18: Moreover, when nuns and other women greet a monk, a blessing is uttered by him in such words as: 'Let there be meditation; let your *karmas* be destroyed'; they do not engage in the etiquette of mu-

[18] Pali Vinaya 2.258.

> tual reverential greeting that takes place between monks. If indeed, as you believe, nuns do assume the *mahavratas* [great vows], then how is it that between your monks and nuns there is no mutual reverential greeting of one another according to rank [as there is between monks]? Indeed, this has been prohibited even in your scripture. As is said in the Upadeśamālā:
>
> 41 "Even if a nun were initiated for a hundred years and a monk were initiated just this day, he is still worthy of being worshiped by her through such acts of respect as going forward in reverential greeting, salutation, and bowing down."'[19]

42 The identical wording makes it obvious that here we are seeing not just a generic similarity but a direct copy. While Jainism is older than Buddhism, the Jain texts are, as here, typically younger; so it is not easy to decide whether this rule, as it stands, was copied by the Buddhists from the Jainas or vice versa. Nevertheless, the main point remains: this rule is one that, as claimed by the Buddha, is found among other Indic traditions. The key thing to notice is that the Buddha specifically invokes contemporary social conventions to justify his position, in exactly the same way as the laywoman in the Sarvāstivāda Vinaya story.

43 This raises the contentious issue of the degree to which Vinaya rules and procedures may be adapted according to time and place. As a practicing bhikkhu, I believe that, in general, the essential aspects of the Vinaya remain as true and relevant today as they were 2500 years ago. I do not think we should use, as a blanket excuse, changes in social customs to justify abolishing or ignoring Vinaya rules, even if they may be inconvenient, or we don't understand their purpose. But in instances where the text specifically invokes contemporary social conventions to justify the rule, and where that convention has demonstrably changed, we must question whether such a rule should be kept. And when, in addition, the rule causes unnecessary suffering, I think it's unjust and cruel to insist on keeping it.

44 Here we would do well to remind ourselves of the fundamental ethical principles embodied in the United Nations 'Declaration on the Elimination of Discrimination against Women':

---

[19] JAINI, chapter 6 #18. The Yuktiprabodha, as well as insisting on the ritual humiliation of women, argues that they cannot be enlightened because of their wanton, crooked nature, as well as the vile impurities of their bodies, especially menstruation.

45 **Article 1:** Discrimination against women, denying or limiting as it does their equality of rights with men, is fundamentally unjust and constitutes an offense against human dignity.

46 **Article 2:** All appropriate measures shall be taken to abolish existing laws, customs, regulations and practices which are discriminatory against women, and to establish adequate legal protection for equal rights of men and women...

47 **Article 3:** All appropriate measures shall be taken to educate public opinion and to direct national aspirations towards the eradication of prejudice and the abolition of customary and all other practices which are based on the idea of the inferiority of women.

48 This *garudhamma*, and some others, are manifestly 'laws, customs, regulations and practices which are discriminatory against women'. Discrimination against women is 'fundamentally unjust and constitutes an offense against human dignity.' If bhikkhus wish to maintain the ethical standards expected in our international community, they must take 'all appropriate measures' to abolish these practices.

49 There are those who would wish to argue that such provisions are a 'Western' imposition on Buddhist cultures, and do not represent the values of Buddhist peoples themselves. But when Buddhist peoples are given the chance, they too show that they adhere to such values. For example, here are some excepts from the draft Thai Constitution of 30th April, 2007.

Part 2: Equality

50 **Section 30:** All persons are equal before the law and shall enjoy equal protection under the law.

51 Men and women shall enjoy equal rights.

52 Unjust discrimination against a person on the grounds of the difference in origin, race, language, sex, age, physical or health condition, personal status, economic or social standing, religious belief, education, or constitutional political views, shall not be permitted.

Part 3: People's Rights and Liberties

53 **Section 37:** A person shall enjoy full liberty to profess a religion, a religious sect or creed, and observe religious precepts or exercise a form of worship in accordance with his or her belief.

Chapter IV : Duties of Thai People

54 **Section 70:** Every person shall have the duty to defend the country and obey the law.

55 According to this document, Thai people, including all Thai monks and Western monks living in Thailand, have the duty to obey the law of Thailand.[20] The fundamental law of the nation, superseding all others, is the Constitution. Under the Constitution, men and women have equal rights, and unjust discrimination, such as that expressed in *garudhamma* 1, is illegal. Thai women have the right to 'observe religious precepts' in accordance with their beliefs, which includes taking ordination as bhikkhunis and practicing the bhikkhuni Vinaya as they see fit. In addition, Thai monks, according to this constitution, are permitted to practice their religion according to their beliefs, and this would include performing ordination for bhikkhunis. Prohibiting Thai monks from performing bhikkhuni ordination would transgress one of their basic rights according to the Thai constitution.[21]

56 Perhaps this is why, despite the widespread belief that bhikkhuni ordination is forbidden in Thailand and opposed by the Thai Sangha, the Council of Elders who rule Thai Buddhism (Mahatherasamakhom) have not made any pronouncement regarding bhikkhunis. The Thai Sangha Act

---

[20] This was emphasized by VAJIRAÑĀṆAVARORASA: 'Although monks are already subject to the ancient law contained in the Vinaya, they must also subject themselves to the authority which derives from the specific and general law of the State.' Quoted in MCDANIEL, p. 103.

[21] The tension between a progressive social movement and conservative religious forces is negotiated in various legal contexts. For example, the New South Wales Anti-Discrimination Act 1977 (amended 6 July 2009) section 56 provides a blanket exemption for religious bodies from the anti-discrimination laws that apply to everyone else. The fact that such an exemption was considered legally necessary implies that if it were not present the discriminatory practices of the Church could be considered illegal and subject to prosecution. Here is the relevant section.

> **Section 56 Religious Bodies.** Nothing in this Act affects: (a) the ordination or appointment of priests, ministers of religion or members of any religious order, (b) the training or education of persons seeking ordination or appointment as priests, ministers of religion or members of a religious order, (c) the appointment of any other person in any capacity by a body established to propagate religion, or (d) any other act or practice of a body established to propagate religion that conforms to the doctrines of that religion or is necessary to avoid injury to the religious susceptibilities of the adherents of that religion.

defines its sphere of concern as the bhikkhus, and has no jurisdiction over bhikkhunis.

57 So now the rude shock of this rule has been softened a little. This *garudhamma*, if it is authentic at all, is best seen in context as a curb for the pride of Mahāpajāpatī. The status of this as a rule in general for the bhikkhunis is dubious, since it is only occasionally found in the *pāṭimokkhas*, and where it is found it is in very different forms and settings. But those stories do at least demonstrate a reasonable context within which such a rule might have arisen. In the current form, however, the rule is clearly discriminatory and contravenes accepted national and international principles of equity. Following the basic Vinaya principles that the Sangha should not act in ways that contravene the laws and customs of their culture, and should not act in a way that leads to harm, this rule should be rejected by the contemporary Sangha.

2.2 Garudhamma 2

58
> A bhikkhuni should not spend the *vassa* [rains residence] in a monastery where there are no bhikkhus.

59 This rule is equivalent to the Mahāvihāravāsin bhikkhuni *pācittiya* 56. According to the background story for that rule, some bhikkhunis spent the *vassa* without bhikkhus, so were unable to get teachings. The good nuns complained, and the Buddha responded by requiring they spend *vassa* with bhikkhus.

60 There is no mention that this rule had already been laid down as a *garudhamma*. If the *garudhamma* was already in place, the text would say the case should be dealt with 'according to the rule', which is the standard procedure in such cases. Since this clause is lacking, we can only conclude that the relevant *garudhamma* did not exist at the time this *pācittiya* was laid down. It must therefore have been added in the Mahāpajāpatī story at a later date. A similar logic applies to the other cases where a *garudhamma* is found in the *pācittiyas*; that is, *garudhammas* 2, 3, 4, 6, and 7.

61 'Living without bhikkhus' is defined by the Mahāvihāravāsin Vinaya as 'not able to teach, or not able to go into communion [for the fortnightly *uposatha*]'. This suggests that the bhikkhus need only be close enough for

the bhikkhunis to travel to them for teaching. In pre-car days, this would have been a few kilometers, but now it would apply over a large distance. A more liberal interpretation would allow for a contact via phone or email, since this would still allow the essential teaching to be transmitted.

62 As always, there is no offense for the first offender of the *pācittiya* rule, confirming the point we made earlier: when the *pācittiya* was laid down, the *garudhamma* did not exist.

2.3 Garudhamma 3

63
> Each fortnight the bhikkhunis should expect two things from the bhikkhu Sangha: questioning regarding the *uposatha* [observance], and being approached for teaching.

64 This is identical to Mahāvihāravāsin bhikkhuni *pācittiya* 59. There, the origin story is merely a back-formation from the rule. This time it is the monks who complain. The Dharmaguptaka Vinaya origin story says that the nuns had heard that the Buddha had laid down a rule requiring the fortnightly teaching.[22] Just below, the same thing is said of the requirement for the invitation at the end of the rains residence.[23] Obviously, then, these rules cannot have been laid down at the start of the bhikkhuni order. As always, this is confirmed when the text says that there is no offense for the first offender.

65 This rule, like the previous, was intended to ensure the proper education of the bhikkhunis: it is about what the monks should do for the nuns. We have already seen that this was one reason given for the paying respects to monks, so that they would return to give teaching.

66 There is a corresponding rule in the monks' *pācittiya* 21.[24] This was prompted by the group of six who, for the sake of gains, went to teach the bhikkhunis. But after just a little Dhamma talk, they spent the rest of the day indulging in frivolous chit-chat. When asked by the Buddha whether the teaching was effective, the nuns complained about the monks' conduct (as shown below, this is just one of many places that show that the

[22] HEIRMANN, *Rules for Nuns*, p. 869.
[23] HEIRMANN, *Rules for Nuns*, p. 873.
[24] Pali Vinaya 4.49–53.

bhikkhunis were quite able to criticize monks, despite the *garudhamma* that apparently forbids admonition). The Buddha then laid down a rule ensuring that the bhikkhu who was to teach the bhikkhunis was competent, especially noting that he must also be liked and agreeable to the bhikkhunis.[25]

67 The various Vinayas differ greatly in what they understand 'teaching' to involve in this context. The Vinayas of the Vibhajjavāda group[26] and the Puggalavāda [27] agree in defining 'teaching' as the *garudhammas*. Apparently the most edifying thing these Vinayas can imagine for the bhikkhunis is that they be told, again and again, of how they must be subservient to the bhikkhus. According to the Pali, only if the bhikkhunis are already keeping the *garudhammas* are they to be taught anything else. Bhikkhunis who do not toe the line have their access to Dhamma knowledge switched right off. However, the Mahāsaṅghika Vinaya says that the instruction should be regarding Abhidhamma or Vinaya;[28] the Mūlasarvāstivāda says it should be on ethics, samadhi, and wisdom;[29] and the Sarvāstivāda Gautamī Sutra says the bhikkhunis are to learn 'Sutra, Vinaya, and Abhidhamma'.[30] As an example of correct teaching, the Lokuttaravāda gives the famous verse known as the 'Ovāda Pāṭimokkha':

68 'Not doing any evil,
undertaking the skillful,
Purifying one's own mind—
This is the teaching of the Buddhas.[31]

69 The bhikkhu is then supposed to inform the bhikkhunis that they are to have some discussion about this teaching. Whoever wishes may stay and listen. In all of these cases, the bhikkhunis are expected to obtain a

---

25 Pali Vinaya 4.51: *yebhuyyena bhikkhunīnaṁ piyo hoti manāpo.*

26 Pali Vinaya 4.52; Dharmagupta T22, № 1428, p. 649, a1–2; Mahīśāsaka T22, № 1421, p. 45, c8.

27 T24, № 1461, p. 670, c8–9.

28 T22, № 1425, p. 346, a23–24.

29 T23, № 1442, p. 798, b1.

30 T01, № 26, p. 606, a17: 比丘尼則不得問比丘 經律 阿毘曇. The mention of the Abhidhamma implies its developed sense as one of the three baskets of the Tipiṭaka, and hence is a clear sign of lateness.

31 Roth, p. 67 § 99.

full education, not just into the basics of etiquette, but in the subtle and advanced details of Buddhist philosophy.

70 If we were to take this rule literally as interpreted by the Vibhajjavāda group, we would expect that the monks would be approaching the nuns each fortnight and telling them to bow to monks. Surely this constant activity would have left some remnant in the texts. But what does the evidence tell us? The Nandakovāda Sutta features Venerable Nandaka going for the fortnightly teaching of the nuns.[32] When he gets there he tells them that he will teach by questioning. If they understand, they are to say so, if they do not understand, they are to say so. The respectful manner in which the teaching is introduced, which is similar to the Lokuttaravāda, reminds us that this was meant for the benefit of the nuns, not for their subjugation. The nuns are happy with this mode of teaching, so Nandaka proceeds to give a profound exposition on the six senses. The nuns are delighted, and so is the Buddha: he tells Nandaka to return and teach the nuns again. Nandaka is so clever at teaching the nuns that he is appointed the foremost in that category.

71 This is, so far as I am aware, the only passage in the Pali Suttas that depicts the fortnightly exhortation. Other occasions when the nuns were taught include a time when Ānanda visited the nuns and they didn't wait for a teaching, but told him of their success in *satipaṭṭhāna* meditation.[33] Another time he taught four things to be abandoned: food, craving, conceit, and sex.[34] On a further occasion, Ānanda recalls having been approached by a bhikkhuni named Jaṭilāgāhiyā, who is unknown elsewhere. She asks him regarding a samadhi that is neither led astray nor led back, not actively constrained, freed, steady, content, without anxiety: of what is that the fruit? Ānanda replies that it is the fruit of Awakened knowledge.[35] Another time, Mahākassapa teaches the nuns, the subject is not specified, but it is a 'talk about Dhamma' rather than Vinaya.[36]

72 These are the only examples I can find in the Pali Suttas of the monks teaching the nuns, and the *garudhammas* are conspicuously absent. So

---

[32] MN 146/ SĀ 276.

[33] SN 47.10/ SĀ 615.

[34] AN 4.159/ SĀ 564.

[35] AN 9.37.

[36] SN 16.10/ SĀ 1143/ SĀ2 118.

it would seem that the Mūlasarvāstivāda preserves the most reasonable tradition on this point: the bhikkhunis are to be taught ethics, samadhi, and wisdom. When this definition of the exhortation is changed to the eight *garudhammas*, a rule intended to ensure support for bhikkhunis' education becomes trivial, if not repressive.

73 This is one case where the cultural context is clearly relevant. Traditional cultures usually make little provision for women's education, and some, like certain of the Brahmanical scriptures, prohibit it. Even today, nuns in many traditional Buddhist countries are often illiterate and uneducated. Thus this rule can be seen as an 'affirmative action' provision to ensure that the bhikkhus share their knowledge with the bhikkhunis.

74 It should not need emphasizing that the cultural circumstances have changed dramatically. In many countries today, women have education levels that are equal to those of men. In our monastery, the monks can barely muster up a tertiary degree between them, while most of the nuns have a Master's or a Phd. To insist on maintaining the old educational norms in such an environment is obviously inappropriate. The rule would be better formulated in non-gender terms: those members of the Sangha who have education and knowledge should share this with the less fortunate members of the Sangha. In the context the Buddha was working in, the division between educated and non-educated would have coincided to a large degree with the line between men and women; and in the case of uneducated monks, they could be expected to pick up learning from the other monks, which was difficult for the separate nuns' community. In any case, no matter what one might think the rule should mean, the reality will be that nuns will take their rightful place of equality in the field of Buddhist education.

2.4 Garudhamma 4

75
> After the *vassa*, the bhikkhunis should invite [*pavāraṇā*] both Sanghas regarding three things: [wrong-doings that were] seen, heard, or suspected.

76 This rule refers to the *pavāraṇā* ceremony that is held at the end of each rains retreat. Instead of the usual *uposatha*, the Sangha gathers in harmony,

and invites each other for admonition regarding any wrong-doing that may be in need of forgiveness. This is a way of clearing the air among those living in close community. The bhikkhus perform this ceremony among themselves, but the bhikkhunis are expected to do it both in front of the bhikkhus and the bhikkhunis.

77 The *garudhamma* is equivalent to Mahāvihāravāsin bhikkhuni *pācittiya* 57. The origin story echoes *pācittiya* 56. Again, the rule is laid down in response to the bhikkhunis' complaints. There is a non-offense if they seek but cannot find [a bhikkhu Sangha to invite].

78 In addition to its inclusion in the *pācittiyas*, this rule is also found in the Bhikkhunikkhandhaka, together with various cases and a description of the procedure.[37] Another origin story is given; but this time the Buddha declares they should be dealt with 'according to the rule'. This is a stock phrase referring back to an already-established rule, in this case presumably the *pācittiya*.

79 This rule establishes a link between the two Sanghas, based on the humility of requesting guidance. It only occurs once a year, and is usually treated in a formalistic manner. It is not so much the actual ceremony that matters, as the attitude of mind it engenders. While the rules as they stand are clearly unbalanced, still there is no rule preventing the bhikkhus from inviting the bhikkhunis to admonish them.

2.5 Garudhamma 5

80
> On transgressing a [heavy offense], a bhikkhuni must undergo *mānattā* penance for a half-month before both Sanghas.

81 This is not included in the *pācittiyas*. I put the offense itself here in square brackets, as there are crucial differences between the traditions. It is an important statement, since the performance of *mānattā* is a serious and inconvenient penalty, involving temporary suspension from one's status, exclusion from normal activities, and requiring a Sangha of 20 for rehabilitation. Normally *mānattā* is the rehabilitation procedurefor *saṅghādisesa*, which is the second most serious class of offense. The Mahāvihāravāsin here, however, says that a bhikkhuni must perform *mānattā* if

[37] Pali Vinaya 2.275.

she has trangressed a '*garudhamma*': thus this rule appears to be saying that the *garudhammas* are equivalent in weight to *saṅghādisesas*. In this respect, the Lokuttaravāda is in agreement,[38] as is the Puggalavāda.[39] But the Dharmaguptaka,[40] Mahīśāsaka,[41] Sarvāstivāda,[42] and Mūlasarvāstivāda[43] Vinayas all say in this rule that a bhikkhuni should perform *mānattā* if she commits a *saṅghādisesa*. These rules say nothing of a disciplinary procedure for one who has transgressed a *garudhamma*. The Mahāsaṅghika, on the other hand mentions both *saṅghādisesa* and *garudhamma*.[44] In addition, two other (probably Sarvāstivāda) Sutta versions of the story, the Gautamī Sūtra at MĀ 116 and T 60,[45] also say *saṅghādisesa*. One Sutta of uncertain affiliation just says 'transgressing precepts', without further explanation.[46] Thus the overwhelming weight of tradition here has it that the bhikkhunis must be rehabilitated from *saṅghādisesas* before both communities, which is the normal situation for nuns in the *saṅghādisesa* procedure. The important consequence of this conclusion is that there was no penalty for breaking a *garudhamma*, as suggested by the fact that *pācittiya* rules often cover the same ground as the *garudhammas*.

82 There are a few places in the Vinaya that mention a bhikkhuni who has transgressed a *garudhamma*, and who therefore must undergo *mānattā*.[47] This would seem at first sight to confirm that *mānattā* is indeed the appropriate penalty for a *garudhamma*. But a closer examination leads to the opposite conclusion. In the Vassūpanāyikakkhandhaka, a list of reasons is given why a bhikkhuni may need to request the presence of bhikkhus to come, even though it is the rains retreat. These include if she is ill,

---

[38] ROTH, p. 17 § 13.

[39] T24, № 1461, p. 670, c9–11.

[40] T22, № 1428, p. 923, b10–11.

[41] According to HEIRMANN (*Rules for Nuns*, pp. 97–8 note 12) the term 麁惡罪 used in the Mahīśāsaka here (T22, № 1421, p. 185, c27), though ambiguously meaning 'heavy offence', probably refers to a *saṅghādisesa*.

[42] T23, № 1435, p. 345, c10–12

[43] T24, № 1451, p. 351, a20–22.

[44] T22, № 1425, p. 475, a8–13. HEIRMANN, *Rules for Nuns*, p. 97–8.

[45] MĀ 116 is Sarvāstivāda; T 60 is of uncertain affiliation, but it is so similar it may well be an alterative translation of the same text.

[46] Zhong ben qi jing, T4, № 196, p. 158, c27–29: 七者比丘尼。自未得道。若犯戒律。當半月詣眾中。首過自悔。以棄憍慢之態

[47] E.g. Pali Vinaya 2.279.

suffering dissatisfaction, etc. One of the reasons is if she has transgressed a *garudhamma* and needs to do *mānattā*.[48] But, although our passage is evidently striving for completeness, there is no mention of the case where a bhikkhuni has fallen into *saṅghādisesa* and requires bhikkhus for a *mānattā*. This glaring omission would be easily explained if *garudhamma* had been substituted for *saṅghādisesa*.

83 Indeed, the use of *garudhamma* here for the bhikkhunis is nothing but a copy of a passage, a few paragraphs previous, which declares that a bhikkhu who has fallen into a *garudhamma* must do the *parivāsa* penance, which is the standard procedure for a bhikkhu who has fallen into a *saṅghādisesa* offense.[49]

84 This usage recurs occasionally in unrelated Vinaya passages where it refers to bhikkhus. For example, there is a case where the *upajjhāya* (mentor) has transgressed a *garudhamma* and is deserving of probation.[50] Here again, *garudhamma* obviously refers to a *saṅghādisesa*.

85 It seems that *garudhamma* in this sense is a non-technical term that would occasionally substitute for *saṅghādisesa*; the usage probably fell out of favor with the rise of the more specialized use of *garudhamma* to refer to the eight rules of respect for bhikkhunis. But this would explain why there is an ambiguity in the *garudhammas* themselves as to the meaning of the term.

2.6 Garudhamma 6

86 > A trainee must train for two years in the six precepts before seeking full ordination (*upasampadā*) from both Sanghas.

87 This is parallel to Mahāvihāravāsin bhikkhuni *pācittiya* 63. The origin story speaks of nuns who ordained without training and were therefore unskilled and uneducated. The good bhikkhunis complained, and so the Buddha laid down a two year training period. While all the schools include a similar training allowance, they differ considerably as to the content of

48 Pali Vinaya 1.144: *Idha pana, bhikkhave, bhikkhunī garudhammaṁ ajjhāpannā hoti mānattārahā.*

49 Pali Vinaya 1.143: *Idha pana, bhikkhave, bhikkhu garudhammaṁ ajjhāpanno hoti parivāsāraho.*

50 Pali Vinaya 2.226. *Sace upajjhāyo garudhammaṁ ajjhāpanno hoti parivāsāraho.*

the 'six rules'.[51] In the *garudhamma* itself the six rules are undefined. Since they are not a standard group, appearing nowhere but in this context, how could the nuns have known what was meant? Clearly, the laying down of the *garudhammas* was dependent on the explanation as provided in the bhikkhuni *pācittiya vibhaṅga*, and hence could not have happened at the start of the bhikkhuni Sangha.

88 If this rule was really followed as usually understood in the *garudhamma* story, ordination would have been impossible. The nuns need to train for two years, and then receive ordination; but if they are all trainees, from whom can they get ordination? This rule clearly presupposes the existence of a bhikkhuni Sangha, and a developed ordination procedure, neither of which is possible if the rule was really laid down at the start of the bhikkhuni Sangha's existence.

89 We will be examining the historical provenance of this rule more closely in chapter 7.

2.7 Garudhamma 7

90 Bhikkhunis should not in any way abuse or revile bhikkhus.

91 Equivalent to Mahāvihāravāsin bhikkhuni *pācittiya* 52. The origin story is at Vesālī. An elder of the group of six nuns dies. They make a stupa for her, and hold a noisy mourning ritual. Upāli's preceptor, Kappitaka, who was living in the cemetery, was annoyed at the sound, and smashed the stupa to bits—somewhat of a distasteful overreaction, one might think. Anyway, the group of six nuns say: 'He destroyed our stupa—let's kill him!' Kappitaka escapes with Upāli's help, and the nuns abuse Upāli, thus prompting, not a rule against noisy funerals, or smashing stupas, or attempted murder, but against abusing monks. Other Vinayas tell the story differently. Again, the end of the rule specifies that there was no offense for the original transgressor.

92 This origin story has much of interest, and has been exploited by Gregory Schopen in his essay 'The Suppression of Nuns and the Ritual Murder

[51] 'Six Precepts' (https://sites.google.com/site/sikkhamana/6rules). See discussion in chapter 7.10–18.

of Their Special Dead in Two Buddhist Monastic Codes',[52] an essay which delivers almost as much as the title promises. It should be noted that abusive criticism of anyone by a monk or nun is already covered by bhikkhu *pācittiya* 13, which would seem to make this rule redundant.

93 This rule is similar to the next, and evidently the Mahāsaṅghika/Lokuttaravāda tradition has collapsed the two together, and created an extra *garudhamma* to make up the eight: the bhikkhus should get the best lodgings and food. This development is typical of the generally late character of these Vinayas.[53]

2.8 Garudhamma 8

94 From this day on, it is forbidden for bhikkhunis to criticize bhikkhus; it is not forbidden for bhikkhus to criticize bhikkhunis.

95 This rule appears to have no counterparts in the *pācittiyas* of any school. It also appears to be absent from the *garudhammas* of the Mūlasarvāstivāda, unless this is their *garudhamma* 5.[54] It is, however, found in the *garudhammas* in most of the Vinayas, as well as the Sarvāstivādin Gautamī Sūtra.[55]

96 The operative word here is *vacanapatha*, which I have translated as 'criticize'. It is often interpreted as 'teach', and in Thailand and other places it is assumed that a bhikkhuni can never teach a monk. But this has no basis whatsoever. I find it difficult to believe that any Pali scholar could actually think that *vacanapatha* meant 'teaching', since it is never used in that way.

97 Etymology is of little help here: *vacana* means 'speech' and *patha* literally is 'path', hence 'ways of speech'.

98 But the usage is clear and consistent, and allows us to easily understand the purport of the *garudhamma*. *Vacanapatha* appears in only a few passages, the most common being a stock list of things that are hard to endure. Here is a typical example from the Vinaya:

---

52 SCHOPEN, *Buddhist Monks and Business Matters*, pp. 329–359.

53 See my 'Mahāsaṅghika—the Earliest Vinaya?' https://sites.google.com/site/sectsandsectarianism/

54 ROCKHILL, pp. 61, 62.

55 According to HEIRMANN (p. 96, note 8) this rule is absent from the Pali, Mahāsaṅghika, Lokuttaravāda, and Sarvāstivāda Vinayas. Here, however, she has gone astray, for the rule is in fact found in most or all of these texts.

> 99 'Monks, a person of less than 20 years of age is not able to accept cold, heat, hunger, thirst, contact with flies, mosquitoes, wind & sun, creeping things, abusive & hurtful *vacanapathas*, arisen bodily painful feelings that are sharp, racking, piercing, displeasing, unenjoyable, deadly; he is not the type that can endure such things.'[56]

100 A similar usage is found, for example, in the Lokuttaravāda Vinaya, where a Paccekabuddha is abused while on almsround.[57]

101 In the Kakacūpama Sutta,[58] the monk Moḷiya Phagguṇa was accused of associating too much with the bhikkhunis, so much so that whenever anyone criticized them (*avabhāsati*) he was angry and attacked the one who was criticizing. Later on, the Sutta explains five *vacanapathas*, hearing which one should endeavor to practice loving-kindness: *vacanapathas* that are timely or untimely; true or untrue; gentle or harsh; associated with the good or not; spoken with a heart of love or with inner hate. The structure of the Sutta clearly refers these *vacanapathas* back to the initial criticism that so upset Moḷiya Phagguṇa, so we are justified in equating *vacanapatha* with *avabhāsati*, i.e. criticism.

102 The formulation of this *garudhamma* in the Lokuttaravāda/Mahāsaṅghika reinforces the association with this Sutta. This rule is a little confusing, for this school does not have an equivalent to the *garudhamma* prohibiting a bhikkhuni from abusing bhikkhus. Rather, they seem to have collapsed that rule into the present one, so while the rule formulation seems to deal with criticism, the explanation deals more aggressively with abuse:

> 103 'It is not allowed for a bhikkhuni to aggressively speak to a bhikkhu, saying: 'You filthy monk, you stupid monk,[59] you childish monk,[60] you wicked,[61] doddering, unintelligent incompetent!'

---

[56] Pali Vinaya 4.130; *cf.* MN 2.18, AN ii.117, AN v.132, etc.

[57] ROTH, p. 132. Other references in EDGERTON's *Buddhist Hybrid Sanskrit Dictionary*, Vol 2, under *dur-āgata*, p. 266.

[58] MN 21.

[59] ? Reading *avaidya*. HIRAKAWA adopts the meaning 'doctor' [quack].

[60] *Cūḷa* = Pali *cūḷa* small; but also the tonsure performed on boys of 1–3 years of age; see MONIER-WILLIAMS, p. 401.

[61] Following ROTH, p. 23, note 22.6; except he has misunderstood the next term *mahalla*, for which see STRONG, *The Legend and Cult of Upagupta*, pp. 68–69.

104 The rule itself, in clear distinction from the Pali, says that a bhikkhuni is forbidden to criticize a bhikkhu about what is true or untrue (*bhūtena vā abhūtena vā*), while a bhikkhu is forbidden to criticize a bhikkhuni about what is untrue, but may criticize about what is true. The terms 'true or untrue' clearly link up with the Kakacūpama Sutta.[62] While the phrasing of the rule clearly discriminates against the bhikkhunis, the rule explanation mitigates this, for the actual explanations of how criticism is to be done by monks and nuns to each other is effectively the same. Both are permitted to admonish a close relative in a gentle and encouraging way, but are not permitted to use abusive language.[63]

105 While *vacanapatha*, then, occurs fairly infrequently, the usage is consistent and relevant in the *garudhamma* context. It is something whose main aspect is that it is hard to endure; thus it would seem to be stronger than 'admonishment'. On the other hand, it may be done fairly and kindly, so it is weaker than 'abuse'. This justifies my choice of rendering as 'criticism'.

106 The fact that this rule starts with 'from this day on... ' is most curious. This is the only *garudhamma* to be formulated in this way. It is scarcely possible to make sense of this without accepting the implication that *before this time* it was allowable for bhikkhunis to admonish bhikkhus. But of course, if this was the case, there must have been bhikkhunis to do the admonishing, and so once again the origin story of Mahāpajāpatī cannot represent a literal history. There is, however, no mention of 'from this day on' in the Dharmaguptaka,[64] Mahīśāsaka,[65] or Sarvāstivāda.[66]

107 The Mahāsaṅghika abbreviates the story of Mahāpajāpatī's request, then prefaces the detailed description of the *garudhammas* by having the Buddha declare that: 'From this day forward, Mahāpajāpatī sits at the head of the bhikkhuni Sangha: thus it should be remembered.'[67] This again seems highly unusual, without precedent that I am aware of in the bhikkhu

---

[62] Indeed, given the similarity of the themes, and the rare involvement of the bhikkhunis in a mainstream Sutta, one might be forgiven for wondering whether this rule is in fact derived from this Sutta.

[63] See HIRAKAWA, p. 82–83; ROTH p. 58–61 § 83–8.

[64] T22, № 1428, p. 923, b6–7: 比丘尼不應呵比丘。比丘應呵比丘尼

[65] T22, № 1421, p. 185, c25–26: 比丘尼不得舉比丘罪。而比丘得呵比丘尼

[66] T01, № 26, p. 606, a20–21: 比丘尼不得說比丘所犯。比丘得說比丘尼所犯

[67] T22, № 1425, p. 471, a27–28: 從今日大愛道瞿曇彌比丘尼僧上坐。如是持

Vinaya. Who was sitting at the head of the bhikkhuni Sangha before this? If Mahāpajāpatī was the first bhikkhuni—as the traditions assert, but which I do not believe—then it would be assumed she was always sitting at the head of the bhikkhunis.

108 The mainstream position of the Suttas and Vinaya on admonishment is that an admonisher should be seen as a gem; one should always follow them and never leave. The two *aniyata* rules found in the bhikkhu *pāṭimokkhas* establish a protocol enabling a trustworthy female lay disciple to bring a charge of serious misconduct against a bhikkhu, which must be investigated by the Sangha and the appropriate punishment levied. This protocol is only established for the female lay disciples, not the male. Are we to believe that the Buddha made one rule supporting admonishment by lay women, and another prohibiting it by nuns?

109 *Saṅghādisesa* 12 lays down a heavy penalty for bhikkhus or bhikkhunis who refuse to be admonished, saying: 'Thus there is growth in the Blessed One's following, that is, with mutual admonishment and mutual rehabilitation.'[68] *Garudhamma* 8 directly contradicts this, and stands in sad contrast with the broad stream of the Buddhist teachings on admonishment.

110 Nevertheless, though we cannot ethically acquiesce with this rule in any form, it is possible that its original meaning was much more restricted. We have seen that the bhikkhunis were to approach the bhikkhus every fortnight to request teaching, and that this should be seen as a pro-active measure to ensure the nuns received education. When they came to the bhikkhus, they did so as students. Perhaps the bhikkhus, if they knew of offenses of the bhikkhunis, were to formally inform the bhikkhunis of these, and were to leave the bhikkhunis to carry out their own disciplinary measures. Thus it may be the case that this rule was meant to apply solely to a formal procedure within the Sangha, whereby the experienced bhikkhus could bring necessary matters to the attention of the nuns. If the bhikkhunis were so unscrupulous as to not clear up their offenses as required each fortnightly *uposatha*, this would show they did not have the proper attitude necessary to receive the teaching.

[68] All the Vinayas agree on this point. Here, for example, is the Dharmaguptaka: 如是佛弟子眾得增益。展轉相諫。展轉相教。展轉懺悔 (T22, № 1429, p. 1016, c20–21).

111 There seems little evidence that Buddhist communities through history felt that it was wrong for a bhikkhuni to teach or even justly criticize a bhikkhu. I have elsewhere gathered a series of stories that present nuns as criticizing monks in various ways, and nowhere is this rule brought up.[69] While these stories may not all be strictly historical, they tell us about how Buddhist monastics interpreted the rules at different times. Given the nature of actual relationships between groups of people, the rule prohibiting admonishment of bhikkhus by bhikkhunis can never have been anything other than a dead letter. That the rule books tell a different story is unsurprising. Rule books, ancient and modern, tell us what the rule-writers wanted, not what was actually done. What is perhaps more remarkable is that I cannot find a single example where a nun is criticized or disciplined for admonishing a monk. The conclusion seems inescapable that either this rule was an alien interpolation, or its original scope was very narrow. In any case, the mainstream of the traditions tells us that it is perfectly okay for a bhikkhuni to teach, exhort, or admonish a bhikkhu in a way that is gentle and kind. In doing so, she will be not merely keeping the letter and the spirit of the Vinaya, she will be fulfilling her practice of right speech as part of the noble eightfold path.

2.9 The Garudhammas—an Assessment

112 Bearing in mind our serious reservations about the rules regarding bowing and admonition, these 'heavy rules' are not as heavy as all that. They are either simple principles of good manners, or procedures for ensuring the proper education and support for the nuns. They are certainly not a charter for domination of the nuns by the monks. The nuns are left to rely on their own discretion in making most of their everyday lifestyle choices: how to build their monasteries; when to go for alms; how is the day structured; what meditation to pursue; and so on.

113 The *garudhammas* make provision for points of contact between the bhikkhu and bhikkhuni Sanghas at key Vinaya junctures: *upasampadā*, *saṅghādisesa*, *pavāraṇā*, *vassa*, and *uposatha*. None of these occasions give

[69] 'How Nuns May Scold Monks'. http://santifm.org/santipada/2010/how-nuns-may-scold-monks/

the bhikkhus authority to control the bhikkhunis. Both the bhikkhus and the bhikkhunis are under the overarching authority of the Vinaya, and the Vinaya determines what happens at these times. No power of command is involved, just a shared responsibility to respect and follow the Vinaya.

114 The Vinaya is an ethical system requiring the mature and responsible co-operation of the members of the Sangha. There is, as a rule, no power of command by any individual over another. And so, when the Vinaya omits to grant the bhikkhus power of command over the bhikkhunis, it makes a clear statement, which starkly transgresses against the norms of ancient Indic culture.[70]

115 There is, however, one passage in the Bhikkhunikkhandhaka that might seem to grant this power of command, especially if one were to read it in I.B. Horner's English translation. The bhikkhunis are forbidden from stopping the bhikkhus' *uposatha*, and *pavāraṇā*, from making *savacanīya*, from *anuvāda*,[71] from taking leave, criticizing, and reminding [bhikkhus about their faults]. The bhikkhus, however, are permitted to do all these things to the bhikkhunis. Obviously this passage is discriminatory, and it is hard to imagine how it might have applied in practice. The list of acts is stock, and is part of the things that are prohibited for a bhikkhu who has undergone various formal acts, such as (*tajjaniyakamma*),[72] dependence (*nissayakamma*), expulsion (*pabbājanīyakamma*), or suspension (*ukkhepaniyakamma*).[73]

116 Unfortunately, Horner has chosen to render *savacanīya* as 'command' and *anuvāda* as 'authority'.[74] But when we look closer, these translations are either incorrect or at best of limited application. *Savacanīya* only seems to occur in this context, and is never explained in the text. The commentary, however, says it is speech that is intended to prevent a bhikkhu from leaving the monastery until the dispute is settled, or to summon a bhikkhu

---

[70] The Brahmanical Dharmaśāstras repeat, almost every time they speak of women, that a woman must never be independent, that she must always be subject to her father, her husband, or her son. E.g. VĀŚIṢṬHA 5.1–2; BAUDHĀYANA 2.2.3.44–45; VIṢṆU 25.12–13; MANU 9.2–3.

[71] Pali Vinaya 2.276: *Tena kho pana samayena bhikkhuniyo bhikkhūnaṁ uposathaṁ hapenti, pavāraṁ hapenti, savacanīyaṁ karonti, anuvādaṁ pahapenti, okāsaṁ kārenti, codenti, sārenti.*

[72] Pali Vinaya 2.5.

[73] Pali Vinaya 2.22.

[74] *Book of the Discipline* 5.381.

to go together to find a Vinaya expert to settle the matter.[75] It is unclear to me whether the commentary's opinion of the meaning of *savacanīya* should be followed, as it seems likely that this is just another term referring to 'criticism' or 'rebuke', rather than specifically involving the notion of 'command'. There is no need to resort to the commentary to define *anuvāda,* as it is one of the four kinds of 'legal issue', where it is said to be 'censure' (*anuvāda*) regarding a defect in virtue, conduct, view, or livelihood.[76] Neither of these cases have anything to do with a general power of 'command' or 'authority'. Rather, they apply in the specific, limited context of arisen legal issues.

117 Returning to the procedures outlined in the *garudhammas,* we must bear in mind that, while these are significant Vinaya procedures, they do not happen very often. *Upasampadā* normally happens once in a bhikkhuni's life; *saṅghādisesa* happens rarely if ever in the career of most monastics; *pavāraṇā* and *vassa* happen once a year; *uposatha* is once a fortnight.

118 Taking these rules as the entrance point, most writers have concluded that the bhikkhuni Vinaya is generally discriminatory against the nuns. But a closer look reveals that this is not the case. Yes, the nuns have many more rules. But many of these rules are required for the monks also, except they are not counted in the *pāṭimokkha*, so the appearance of extra rules is largely illusory. This is the case, for example, in the ordination regulations. Or take the *pāṭidesanīyas*, where the four rules for monks are expanded to eight for nuns. But these eight are simply a prohibition against asking for eight kinds of fine foods, except when sick. Similar rules apply elsewhere to the monks. But the monks' *pāṭidesanīyas* don't appear to apply to the bhikkhunis. Thus while the bhikkhunis appear to have more *pāṭidesanīyas*, in practice they have less.

---

[75] Samantapāsādikā 6.1163: *Nasavacanīyaṁ kātabbanti palibodhatthāya vā pakkosanatthāya vā savacanīyaṁ na kātabbaṁ, palibodhatthāya hi karonto 'ahaṁ āyasmantaṁ imasmiṁ vatthusmiṁ savacanīyaṁ karomi, imamhā āvāsā ekapadampi mā pakkāmi, yāva na taṁ adhikaraṇaṁ vūpasantaṁ hotī'ti evaṁ karoti. Pakkosanatthāya karonto 'ahaṁ te savacanīyaṁ karomi, ehi mayā saddhiṁ vinayadharānaṁ sammukhībhāvaṁ gacchāmā'ti evaṁ karoti; tadubhayampi na kātabbaṁ.*

[76] Pali Vinaya 2.88: *Tattha katamaṁ anuvādādhikaraṇaṁ? Idha pana, bhikkhave, bhikkhū bhikkhuṁ anuvadanti sīlavipattiyā vā ācāravipattiyā vā diṭṭhivipattiyā vā ājīvavipattiyā vā.*

119 More important are *saṅghādisesas* 3 and 4, which are serious offenses for lewd speech. The bhikkhunis do not have any corresponding rules. There is instead a special *pārājika* offense for bhikkhunis for speaking lewdly with a man: but in that case, both the bhikkhuni and the man must be overwhelmed with lust, which presupposes a much more advanced stage of developing an intimate relationship. A bhikkhu, on the other hand, can fall into a *saṅghādisesa* simply through an offhand lewd comment provoked by lust. Another example is the first bhikkhus' *saṅghādisesa*, for masturbation, which is treated much more mildly as a *pācittiya* in the nuns' Vinaya.

120 Some of the bhikkhunis' rules which are understood as draconian may be questioned on the textual evidence. This is clear, for example, in our discussion of the *saṅghādisesa* rule regarding travel for a nun.[77]

121 In addition to these, there are several other rules that deal with particularly feminine issues, such as pregnancy and menstrual hygiene. Others provide for the safety and education for the nuns.

122 Several of the bhikkhus' rules, moreover, are not for the exploitation, but the protection of the nuns. For example, it is an offense for a bhikkhu to treat a bhikkhuni as a domestic servant, having them sew and wash robes, and so on. It is also an offense for a bhikkhu to accept food from a bhikkhuni, a rule that was prompted by the difficulty for women to get alms. Curiously enough, many modern Theravāda nuns spend most of their days cooking, shopping, cleaning, sewing, and washing for the monks. Despite the bhikkhus' avowed commitment to the Vinaya, and insistence that this is the real reason for opposing bhikkhunis, for some reason most bhikkhus don't seem to see this as a problem. This is, however, not always the case, for some respected Theravādin teachers, such as Ajahn Chah, insisted that the monks actually practice these rules, and not treat the *mae chis* (eight precept nuns) as domestic servants. Such care for the well-being of the nuns is a sign that balanced perspective of the four-fold Sangha is not entirely lost to Theravāda, and that a movement towards equality may have already begun.

---

[77] Chapter 3.

Chapter 3

TOWNS, RIVERS, JOURNEYS

WALKING FROM VILLAGE TO VILLAGE, from town to town, Buddhist monks were one of the most distinctive sights of old India. Yet on some readings of the Vinaya, the nuns would have been forbidden from enjoying the wandering lifestyle or the seclusion in the forest that is the hallmark of the contemplative life. In this chapter I will focus more closely on one important problematic rule in the bhikkhuni Vinayas. The rule is an offense of *saṅghādisesa* that concerns a bhikkhuni who travels and stays alone. The seriousness of the offense, in matters that are part of everyday life and are in no way blameworthy, makes this rule one of the most difficult and complex issues in bhikkhuni Vinaya. The aim of this study is to clarify the content of the texts, consider their interrelationships, investigate how they relate to the life of bhikkhunis, and to consider how the rule might be applied in the present day.

3.1 Some Preliminaries

2 The rule is found in all available Vinayas. These naturally fall into three groups of schools: Vibhajjavāda, Mahāsaṅghika, and Sarvāstivāda. The Vibhajjavāda is represented by the Mahāvihāravāsin and Dharmaguptaka, which in this case are identical in content, and the Mahīśāsaka, which differs in certain respects. The Mahāsaṅghika and Lokuttaravāda represent the Mahāsaṅghika group, and they are, as usual, very similar. The

Sarvāstivāda and Mūlasarvāstivāda, while sharing certain similarities, are not identical.[1]

3 The rule we are to consider belongs to a class of rules called *saṅghādisesa*. This is the second most serious class of Vinaya offenses, after the *pārājikas*, which entail immediate and permanent expulsion from the Sangha. The Buddha said that for monastics *pārājika* is like death while *saṅghādisesa* is like deadly suffering. A bhikkhuni who has fallen into such an offense must request a period of fifteen days' probation from the Sangha, during which time her seniority is removed, she must confess each day to the entire Sangha, and various other penalties are imposed. Following this, she can be rehabilitated by a Sangha of no less than twenty bhikkhus and twenty bhikkhunis. This complex and somewhat embarrassing procedure is inconvenient for all. Thus we should normally consider that *saṅghādisesas* fall only for offenses that are very serious, but from which rehabilitation is still possible.

4 The problem with our current rule is that it seems to fall for everyday activities, which no-one today would consider blameworthy. This is, however, not all that dissimilar to the bhikkhus' *saṅghādisesas*, as one of them deals with building a hut for oneself that is too large. Given the apparently small size of the allowable hut, this would not generally be regarded as blameworthy today. But given the serious consequences of committing a *saṅghādisesa*, we must carefully consider the various sources, their contexts and interpretations before drawing conclusions.

[1] The Sarvāstivāda textual tradition is slightly peculiar. In their *pāṭimokkha* there is only the final of the four cases that I present below (6d), which I have tried to translate with fidelity to the oddness of the Chinese phrasing. It seems that this is a result of a partial attempt to assimilate the four cases together as one rule, as found in the Mahāvihāravāsin, etc. But the rule as presented in the *vibhaṅga* presents each of the first three cases quite independently. Thus we have, not separate rules as in the Mahāsaṅghika and Mūlasarvāstivāda, nor a series of additions to a rule, as the Vibhajjavāda schools, but separate cases, subsumed within one rule, with a partial attempt to combine them. It is possible that the Indic (presumably Sanskrit) original made use of abbreviations which are not fully clear in the Chinese. As a result, one cannot clearly understand the rule just by reading the Sarvāstivāda *pāṭimokkha*. However, the situation becomes clear when the *vibhaṅga* is taken into consideration. So below I present, not just the final rule formulation as presented in the *pāṭimokkha*, but each of the four cases as they appear in the *vibhaṅga*.

5 The word *saṅghādisesa*, like many other technical Vinaya terms, is controversial and uncertain in meaning, and hence best left untranslated. *Saṅghādisesas* are of two kinds. One class of *saṅghādisesas* requires a series of three warnings at a formal meeting of the Sangha before the bhikkhu or bhikkhuni falls into an offense (*yāvatatiyaka*). Others are effective immediately on transgressing the rule (*paṭhamāpattika*). The current rule is of this kind, which I render as '"immediate-offense" *saṅghādisesa*'.

3.1.1 What does 'alone' mean?

6 Each clause of this rule says that the bhikkhuni is 'alone' (*ekā*). This would seem intuitively obvious: alone means with no-one else. But here the tension between the rule and the *vibhaṅga* becomes acute. For in different places the rules and the *vibhaṅgas* leave 'alone' undefined, while elsewhere 'alone' is said to mean 'without a companion bhikkhuni'. This interpretation, if applied throughout, would severely restrict the movement and activities of the bhikkhuni. Such restriction was a normal part of life in ancient India, where even male Brahmanical students were prohibited from traveling alone.[2]

7 In the modern context, for example, a bhikkhuni traveling on a bus or plane is clearly not 'alone'. However, if this is interpreted to mean she must have a bhikkhuni companion, that would greatly expand the scope of the rule, and provide strict limits on how a bhikkhuni might arrange for her travels. Some argue that this is a protection and an encouragement to practice contentment, while others contest that this is an obstructive restriction on a basic right.

8 The Vinayas of the Sthavira group never specify a companion bhikkhuni in the rule itself. The *vibhaṅgas* vary. Sometimes they specify a bhikkhuni companion, sometimes they say nothing. The Mahāvihāravāsin specifies a bhikkhuni companion in the clauses for spending a night and lagging behind a group; the Mahīśāsaka only for lagging behind a group; the Dharmaguptaka for all cases; the Sarvāstivāda mentions a bhikkhuni companion especially in the context of staying the night, but also includes it in the

[2] E.g. VIṢṆU 63.2.

general non-offense clause; while the Mūlasarvāstivāda does not mention the bhikkhuni companion at all.

9 In contrast, the Mahāsaṅghika group specifies a bhikkhuni companion in the rule itself. These Vinayas do not additionally specify a bhikkhuni companion in the *vibhaṅga*, presumably because that is already clear. It is likely that the mention of the companion in the rule has been absorbed from the *vibhaṅga*, and hence is a sign of lateness in the rule formulation.

10 How one is to understand this situation, then, becomes a matter of interpretation. One might argue that whenever the companion is defined, she is always a bhikkhuni, so this should be extended to cover those cases where there is no clear definition. On the other hand, one might argue that the meaning of 'alone' is straightforward and does not require explanation. The additional requirement for the companion to be a bhikkhuni, then, would apply only in those cases where it is explicitly mentioned, and if one chose to follow the *vibhaṅga* in those cases.

11 In the Mahāvihāravāsin text, the requirement for the companion to be a bhikkhuni is only found in the *vibhaṅga* for the final two clauses of the rule. The question then arises whether this explanation should be applied to the first two clauses, including the one about traveling 'between villages'. This becomes another matter for interpretation, where the assumptions that we bring to bear will affect our outcome.

12 If we follow a 'synthetic' interpretation, we would see 'alone' as having the same meaning in all cases, and interpret it here as implying there must be a bhikkhuni companion. If we take the 'analytical' approach, we would observe that there is no consistent definition of the term in the rule itself, and infer that 'alone' was meant to be understood in the ordinary sense.

13 The two approaches would result in a very different guide for modern practice. If a companion bhikkhuni is required, then travel would always need to be co-ordinated among the bhikkhuni community. This would restrict the ease of movement of the nuns. Many nuns' communities, whether Buddhist or Christian, do in fact follow such guidelines. If 'alone' just meant without any other person, then most means of modern transport would not be covered by this rule, except perhaps for driving a car or motorbike by oneself.

14 Vinaya explanations sometimes begin life in a particular context, and their application is gradually extended over time as the Vinaya becomes ever more complex and definitive. It is plausible to think of the requirement for a bhikkhuni companion as an example of such a process. In the beginning the rule simply referred to the bhikkhuni who was alone. At some later date, during the period of compiling the *vibhaṅga*, it became understood that in certain cases the companion should be a bhikkhuni. Quite possibly this originated in the context of staying overnight outside the monastery. Be that as it may, the idea that 'not alone' means 'with a companion bhikkhuni' gradually colonized the *vibhaṅgas* of the various clauses, and in the Mahāsaṅghika group came to be included in the rules themselves.

3.2 The Rule

Mahāvihāravāsin

15 **Saṅghādisesa 3:** Should a bhikkhuni [a.] go between villages alone, or [b.] cross a river alone, or [c.] spend the night apart alone, or [d.] lag behind a group alone, this bhikkhuni too has transgressed a rule that is an 'immediate-offense' *saṅghādisesa* involving being sent away.[3]

Dharmaguptaka

16 **Saṅghādisesa 7:** Should a bhikkhuni [a.] cross water alone, or [b.] go into a village alone, or [c.] spend the night alone, or [d.] lag behind while walking alone, this bhikkhuni too has transgressed a rule that is an 'immediate-offense' *saṅghādisesa* involving being sent away.[4]

---

[3] Pali Vinaya 4.229: *Yā pana bhikkhunī ekā vā gāmantaraṁ gaccheyya, ekā vā nadīpāraṁ gaccheyya, ekā vā rattiṁ vippavaseyya, ekā vā gaṇamhā ohīyeyya, ayampi bhikkhunī paṭhamāpattikaṁ dhammaṁ āpannā nissāraṇīyaṁ saṅghādisesaṁ.*

[4] T22, № 1431, p. 1032, b23: 若比丘尼。獨渡水 獨入村獨宿獨 在後行。是比丘尼犯初法應捨僧伽婆尸沙. Tsomo translates this rule as : 'If a bhikṣuṇī crosses water alone, enters a village alone, sleeps, lives, or walks alone, then that bhikṣuṇī commits a *saṅghāvaśeṣa* unless she refrains from her misconduct after her first offense' (p. 31). There are a couple of mistakes here. First, the rule is clearly divided by the character 獨, 'alone', into four clauses, not five as suggested by Tsomo's rendering. The mistake comes from taking 在 in its literal sense of 'living', whereas here it merely qualifies the following character

Mahīśāsaka

17 **Saṅghādisesa 6:** Should a bhikkhuni [a.] travel alone, [b.] stay the night alone, [c.] cross a river alone, or [d.] during a journey stay behind alone, with desire and lust for a man, except with reason, that bhikkhuni has fallen into an 'immediate-offense' *saṅghādisesa* entailing confession. The reasons are: a time when the journey is dangerous; a time when one is old, sick, exhausted, and so cannot reach a companion; water is narrow and shallow; there is a place with bridge or boats; it is a place where there is danger from men—that is the reason.[5]

Mahāsaṅghika

18 **Saṅghādisesa 5:** Should a bhikkhuni, without having a bhikkhuni companion, step outside a village boundary, except at the proper time—here the proper time is this: no lust, or illness, this is the proper time—there is an 'immediate-offense' *saṅghādisesa*.[6]

19 **Saṅghādisesa 6:** Should a bhikkhuni spend one night apart from bhikkhunis except at the proper time—here the proper time is this: no lust,[7] a time of illness, or a time when the town is surrounded

---

後 'behind', i.e., 'stays behind'. The more serious mistake is the basic description of the rule, which is repeated in all parallel rule formulations (i.e. Dharmaguptaka *saṅghadisesas* 1–9, Tsomo pp. 30–31). A literal rendering of the Chinese is: 'That bhikkhuni violates (犯) first (初) dhamma (法, i.e. rule) should-be (應) given-up (捨) *saṅghādisesa*.' This corresponds closely with the Pali '*ayaṁ bhikkhunī paṭhamāpattikaṁ dhammaṁ āpannā nissāraṇīyaṁ saṅghādisesaṁ*', which I have rendered as: 'this bhikkhuni has transgressed a rule that is an "immediate-offence" *saṅghādisesa* involving being sent away'. The character 捨 can stand for a large variety of Indic terms, including *nissaraṇa*, which is what the Pali has here. Thus there is no support for Tsomo's implication, which she does not appear to mention or explain elsewhere, that the Dharmaguptaka allows a bhikkhuni to escape these *saṅghādisesas* if they refrain after the first offence.

5 T22, № 1421, p. 80, b4–8: 若比丘尼獨行獨宿獨渡水。於道中獨在後染著男子除因緣是比丘尼初犯僧伽婆尸沙可悔過。因緣者。恐怖走時。老病疲極不及伴時。水狹淺有橋船處。畏男子處。是名因緣. Note: the Mahīśāsaka bhikkhuni *pāṭimokkha*, evidently by mistake, differs from the *vibhaṅga* in omitting the phrase 'walking alone'. (T22, № 1423, p. 207, b21–24.)

6 T22, № 1427, p. 557, b6–8: 若比丘尼。無比丘尼伴行不得出聚落界。除餘時。餘時者。不欲病是名餘時。是法初罪僧伽婆尸沙

7 This is repeated in the *vibhaṅga*. The text above says: 佛言。不欲無罪 (T22, № 1425, p. 519, a14); and below says 不欲病世尊說無罪 (T22, № 1425, p. 518, b19).

by robbers, this is the proper time—there is an 'immediate-offense' *saṅghādisesa.*[8]

20 **Saṅghādisesa 9:** Should a bhikkhuni, at a boat crossing place, cross the river alone, there is an 'immediate-offense' *saṅghādisesa.*[9]

Lokuttaravāda

21 **Saṅghādisesa 5:** Should a bhikkhuni, without bhikkhunis, travel along the road, even between villages, except for the proper occasion—here the proper occasion is this: the bhikkhuni is without lust, or illness, this is the proper occasion here—this rule too is an 'immediate offense'.[10]

22 **Saṅghādisesa 6:** Should a bhikkhuni, without bhikkhunis, spend even one night apart, except for the proper occasion—here the proper occasion is: [the bhikkhuni is without lust],[11] the bhikkhuni is ill, the city is endangered, this is the proper occasion here—this rule too is an 'immediate-offense' *saṅghādisesa.*[12]

23 **Saṅghādisesa 9:** Should a bhikkhuni, without bhikkhunis, cross a river, this rule too is an 'immediate-offense' *saṅghādisesa.*[13]

Mūlasarvāstivāda

Saṅghādisesa 6

24 **(Tibetan):** If a bhikkhuni leaves her dwelling [and goes out] alone at night, then she commits a *saṅghādisesa* on the first offense.[14]

25 **(Chinese):** Again, should a bhikkhuni leave the bhikkhuni monastery and go to another place to spend the night alone, this is a *saṅghādisesa.*[15]

---

8 T22, № 1427, p. 557, b9–11: 若比丘尼。離比丘尼一夜宿。除餘時。餘時者。若病時賊亂圍城時。是名餘時。是法初罪僧伽婆尸沙

9 T22, № 1427, p. 557, b17–18: 若比丘尼。離比丘尼一夜宿。除餘時。餘時者。若病時賊亂圍城時。是名餘時。是法初罪僧伽婆尸沙

10 Roth, p. 110 § 143. Text omits *saṅghādisesa.*

11 Not in the final rule formulation, but mentioned in the *vibhaṅga* just above, Roth p. 134 § 157, line 6.

12 Roth, p. 135 § 157.

13 Roth, p. 142 § 163.

14 Tsomo, p. 84.

15 T24, № 1455, p. 509, b22–23: 若比丘尼。離比丘尼一夜宿。除餘時。餘時者。若病時賊亂圍城時。是名餘時。是法初罪僧伽婆尸沙

Saṅghādisesa 7

26 **(Tibetan):** If a bhikkhuni leaves her dwelling [and goes out] alone in the daytime, then she commits a *saṅghādisesa* on the first offense.[16]

27 **(Chinese):** Again, should a bhikkhuni leave the bhikkhuni monastery in the daytime and go to a lay family alone, this is a *saṅghādisesa.*[17]

Saṅghādisesa 8

28 **(Tibetan):** If a bhikkhuni goes along the road alone, then she commits a *saṅghādisesa* on the first offense.[18]

29 **(Chinese):** Again, should a bhikkhuni walk on the road alone this is a *saṅghādisesa.*[19]

Saṅghādisesa 9

30 **(Tibetan):** If a bhikkhuni crosses a river alone, then she commits a *saṅghādisesa* on the first offense.[20]

31 **(Chinese):** Again, should a bhikkhuni swim across the river alone this is a *saṅghādisesa.*[21]

Sarvāstivāda

Saṅghādisesa 6

32 **a.** Should a bhikkhuni spend the night alone, even just for one night, that is a rule which is an 'immediate-offense' *saṅghādisesa* entailing confession.[22]

33 **b.** Should a bhikkhuni, whether at night or day, go into a lay person's home alone, that is a rule which is an 'immediate-offense' *saṅghādisesa* entailing confession.[23]

34 **c.** Should a bhikkhuni, whether at night or at day, travel to another village alone, that is a rule which is an 'immediate-offense' *saṅghādisesa* entailing confession.[24]

---

[16] TSOMO, p. 84

[17] T24, № 1455, p. 509, b23–24: 若復苾芻尼獨從尼寺晝向俗家者。僧伽伐尸沙

[18] TSOMO, p. 85

[19] T24, № 1455, p. 509, b24–25若復苾芻尼獨在道行者。僧伽伐尸沙

[20] TSOMO, p. 85

[21] T24, № 1455, p. 509, b25–26: 若復苾芻尼獨浮渡河者僧伽伐尸沙

[22] T23, № 1435, p. 308, a7–8: 若。比丘尼一身獨宿。乃至一夜是法初犯僧伽婆尸沙可悔過

[23] T23, № 1435, p. 308, b6–7: 若比丘尼。若夜若晝。一身獨行到白衣家。是法初犯僧伽婆尸沙可悔過

[24] T23, № 1435, p. 308, c5–7: 若比丘尼。若夜若晝。一身獨行往餘聚落。初犯僧伽婆尸沙可悔過

35 **d.** Should a bhikkhuni, whether at night or at day, if [going to] another village, if [going to] another region, if she crosses the river to the further shore and spends the night alone, that is a rule which is an 'immediate-offense' *saṅghādisesa* entailing confession.[25]

36 These may be tabulated as follows, although given the ambiguities of the rules, any attempt at classification can only be provisional. In fact the rules are frequently ambiguous and overlapping, as we shall see, and need to be approached from various angles.

Table 3.1: Towns, Rivers, Journeys: sequence of clauses

	Travel	Cross river	Spend night	Lag behind	Out in day
Mahāvihāra	3a	3b	3c	3d	
Dharmagupta	7b	7a	7c	7d	
Mahīśāsaka	6a	6c	6b	6d	
Mahāsaṅghika	5	9	6	[5 *vibhaṅga*]	
Lokuttaravāda	5	9	6	[5 *vibhaṅga*]	
Mūlasarv	8	9	6	[8 *vibhaṅga*]	7
Sarvāstivāda	6c	6d	6a		(6b)

3.3 Sectarian Group Similarities

37 The rules in both schools of the Mahāsaṅghika group are identical in sequence, and similar in wording. This group is also similar in having only three clauses, while all of the Sthavira schools have four clauses. The extra clause is 'lagging behind a group alone'. This is the final clause in all the texts of the Vibhajjavāda group. In the Sarvāstivāda and Mahāsaṅghika groups, this clause is not found in the rule itself, but is discussed in the rule analysis. This suggests that the clause may have been added later, after the Vibhajjavāda had separated from the Mahāsaṅghika and Sarvāstivāda, which would place us in the post-Aśokan period. Alternatively, the clause may have been included in the earliest text, and subsequently lost due to

[25] T23, № 1437, p. 480, b14–16: 若比丘尼。若夜若晝。若異聚落若異界。若度水彼岸一身獨宿。是法初犯僧伽婆尸沙可悔過

textual corruption in the same period. It is unlikely that the difference stems from geographical or cultural factors, as the clause is shared between the Mahāvihāravāsins of Sri Lanka and the Dharmaguptakas of Gandhāra, as well as the Mahīśāsakas, who were located in central-south India.

38 Like the Mahāsaṅghika group, the Sarvāstivāda group also share an identical sequence of clauses. The rules themselves are similar, although not identical.

39 As noted above, the Vibhajjavāda group mentions lagging behind a group in the final clause of the rule. Apart from this, there is no particular similarity in the rule sequence. In terms of content, the Dharmaguptaka and Mahāvihāravāsin are similar, while the Mahīśāsaka is divergent.

40 The most likely explanation for these differences is that the rule was established in the early period, before the schisms. Yet the exact wording, implications, and structure of the rule was not fixed. Some of the variations may have been present since the earliest times, with the rule understood in different ways in different communities; in other cases variation may have arisen through editorial alteration, accident, or misunderstanding in the process of textual transmission.

41 The Mahāsaṅghika group and Mūlasarvāstivāda are similar to each other in that they split the rule into its components. It must be admitted that this is a rational move, since the rule addresses several quite distinct offenses. But these versions, while similar in that respect, differ in other details. Thus it seems likely that in this case the move to split the rule into its components came about not due to a shared tradition between the Mahāsaṅghika and Mūlasarvāstivāda, but due to a parallel effort to present the rule in a more explicit form.

42 This raises another critical issue: to what extent are the clauses of this rule to be considered as operating within a single context, and to what extent are they separate rules?

43 The texts do not give a consistent answer to this question. There is clearly a certain degree of integration in the rule, as implied by the grammar, by some of the background stories, and by the similar content of certain clauses, as for example the clause regarding 'traveling' and those regarding 'lagging behind a group', or 'crossing a river', which must obviously occur while traveling. Yet the Mahāsaṅghika and Mūlasarvāstivāda,

in their different ways, each divide the clauses into separate rules. Various texts also combine or divide the rules along different lines.

44 We have already seen how the interpretation of the critical term 'alone' is determined by this issue. If the rule is interpreted in accord with the *vibhaṅga*, and if it is further understood 'all of a piece', then 'alone' comes to mean 'without a bhikkhuni companion'.

45 Another fundamental question is whether the rule is meant to apply at all times, or only while traveling on a journey. We have noted that several of the clauses suggest such a context. Yet the clause on 'sleeping alone' might be understood to apply in a monastery, which would imply that bhikkhunis could never spend a night alone. This interpretation is in fact followed in some modern monasteries. Again, the rule itself does not answer our question. We are left with the uncertain witness of the *vibhaṅga*—which speaks of spending the night alone while on a journey outside the monastery—inferring from the relationships within the rule clauses, and our own sense of reasonableness.

3.4 Traveling

46 Now let us take a closer look at the rule/s with the help of the *vibhaṅga* in the various traditions. I will examine each rule clause by clause, and then discuss possible interpretations.

47 **Mahāvihāravāsin 3a:** A nun who was a pupil of Bhaddā Kāpilānī, having quarreled with nuns, goes off to a family of her relations in the village. The other nuns, when they found her, wondered if she had been raped. Though she was safe, they still complained about her behavior, and the Buddha laid down the rule. The full offense falls in putting both feet over the village boundary.

48 **Dharmaguptaka 7b:** Bhikkhuni Khemā, who had many pupils, goes in to the nearby town to visit her relatives because she had little to do. The householders rumored that she was looking for a man. Compared with the Mahāvihāravāsin, the rule itself is identical, while in the background story the name of the nun is different, the offender is the named nun, not her student, the reason for going into town is different, and those who complain are the lay people rather than the bhikkhunis. The rule analysis

is fairly detailed. In a significant extension of the rule, the rule analysis adds that if she travels alone in a wilderness area for the distance of the sound of a drum, this too is a *saṅghādisesa.*

49 **Mahīśāsaka 6a:** Many bhikkhunis were traveling along the road. Lay people saw them and teased them, saying they were probably going to have sex. Then they traveled together with a group of merchants. Bhikkhuni Thullanandā stayed behind the group out of lust and desire for a man. The *saṅghādisesa* falls after traveling, in wilderness, half a *yojana*; in inhabited areas, the distance from one village to the next.[26]

50 The background is curious in that, while the clauses dealing with 'traveling' and 'lagging behind a group' are the first and last clauses of the rule, the story treats them as following after one another. Additionally, there is the odd fact that it is a group of bhikkhunis traveling, not one who is alone. Thus the rule and the analysis do not agree.

51 The Mahīśāsaka is also unusual in that it omits any phrase corresponding to 'between villages'. The clause has only two characters, meaning 'alone goes'. The Sarvāstivāda (6b) has the identical characters for 'alone goes' then adds 'into a lay person's home'. Perhaps, then, the Mahīśāsaka version has been formed through a textual omission. The Pali phrase here is *ekā vā gāmantaraṁ gaccheyya*. If the Mahīśāsaka clause was originally similar, the dropping of the Indic term in the Mahīśāsaka equivalent to the Pali *gāmantara* would leave just the phrase *ekā vā gaccheyya*, which is exactly what the Mahīśāsaka rule has now.

52 **Mahāsaṅghika and Lokuttaravāda 5:** These rules, with some interesting exceptions, are almost identical and should be examined together. They tell the story of Rāṣṭrā bhikkhuni, whose younger sister was married and went away to another village. Falling ill, she called for her sister to come and look after her. But the sister died before the bhikkhuni arrived. The husband, refusing to look after the son, suggested the bhikkhuni do so, at which the bhikkhuni was afraid he intended violence. Pretending to go outside, she fled back to the monastery. The Buddha laid down a rule forbidding traveling along a road by oneself.

53 A second case is given, where a young, attractive bhikkhuni drops behind a group while walking so that she can go to the toilet. Some merchants

[26] T22, № 1421, p. 80, b8–9.

come up and proposition her. After a confrontation she returns to the monastery, where she worried about what had happened and confessed it. The Buddha said there was no offense since she did not desire it.[27]

54 In a third case, the bhikkhuni stays behind the group because she is ill. Again there is no offense.

55 In this way the Mahāsaṅghika group do not mention lagging behind a group in the rule itself, but discuss the situation in their analysis. But for the Mahāsaṅghika group, the point of the example is to give some cases where there is no offense, while for the Vibhajjavāda group the concern is to extend the scope of the rule to cover this additional case.

56 Comparing the final rule formulations, the Lokuttaravāda continues to refer to traveling 'between villages', while the Mahāsaṅghika refers to a bhikkhuni who 'steps outside the village boundary'. This difference is maintained in the respective analyses, which from this juncture proceed in different directions, only to rejoin later.

57 The Lokuttaravāda analysis says 'Traveling along a road, 3 leagues, 2 leagues, 3 leagues [sic], or even between villages'. It then defines 'without desire' (*akāmikā*) as 'obstructed by the corpse of an elephant, a horse, a cow, or a human.' While it might be just possible to construe *kāma* as 'wishing' here, this bizarre explanation obviously disagrees with the background story, where the issue was sexual desire, the normal meaning of *kāma*. There were no corpses in the origin story; and it is hard to imagine how a bhikkhuni could be obstructed by a corpse on her journey. This explanation, without parallels in the Mahāsaṅghika or elsewhere, must stem from some misunderstanding in the Lokuttaravāda tradition.

58 The above sections are absent from the Mahāsaṅghika. But then the two texts rejoin, saying that she does not fall into an offense as long as she travels within a village or town boundary. The next section is obscure, and it seems to me to have prompted some confusion. The Mahāsaṅghika

[27] The textual situation is a little confused, as the Lokuttaravāda text just here says there is an offence, even though without lust. (ROTH, p. 110 § 142, line 4: *Tena hi āpattiḥ akāmikāyeti*). But the Mahāsaṅghika says 'No desire, no offence' (不欲無罪, T22, № 1425, p. 518, b11). And in the reformulation of the rule that occurs twice below the Lokuttaravāda, too, clearly says there is no offence if the bhikkhuni is without lust. (ROTH, p. 110 § 143: ... *anyatra samaye, tatrāyaṁ samayo: akāmikā bhikṣuṇī bhavati, glānikā vā, ayam atra samayo...*). NOLOT, therefore, adopts the correction *anāpatti* (p. 93, note 25).

details the exact moment she falls into an offense when she crosses the village boundary, in accordance with their rule formulation. But the Lokuttaravāda says 'they go between villages or towns, or overstep a dangerous road', thus continuing to think of the rule as a journey between villages. When they leave the boundary, they should stay within arms' reach.

59 It seems that at some stage, the notion of traveling between villages fell out of the Mahāsaṅghika tradition, perhaps as the analysis was being worked out, and the final rule formulation was revised to suit the new understanding. The earlier rule version in the Mahāsaṅghika agrees exactly with the Lokuttaravāda (not to travel alone along a road) and no reason is supplied in the text for the change. So it seems likely that this is a late textual corruption in the Mahāsaṅghika. Hence both the texts of this group can be seen to have textual corruptions, which fall precisely in those places where they diverge.

60 **Mūlasarvāstivāda 8:** Thullanandā stays behind the group for a man. The rule analysis adds little. So, though this Vinaya phrases the rule as if it applied to all journeys, the story suggests that it is meant to apply to lagging behind a group, a rule which is otherwise lacking in the Mūlasarvāstivāda. It is unclear whether this is the result of absorbing two originally separate rules together, or, as I suggested above, the rule about lagging behind was a later addition included in the *vibhaṅga*, but not the *pāṭimokkha*.

61 **Sarvāstivāda 6c:** Thullanandā likes to hang out by the city gates, checking out the guys, whether they are good-looking or ugly. She spots a particularly handsome fellow, and asks where he is going. He says he is off to a certain village, and she asks if she can come along. He says, 'As you please.' Off they go, laughing and joking. He visits several villages and enters them while Thullanandā, having no business, waits outside. Eventually, she returns to the monastery and lies down complaining of her aches and pains. Notice that throughout the story, Thullanandā avoids actually entering the village. The rule analysis explains that in going to another village, there is a *saṅghādisesa* on arriving at the village, but if one turns back before reaching it, there is a *thullaccaya*. Similarly, if in a place with no village, in a wilderness, there is a *saṅghādisesa* for every *krośa* ('call' = ¼ *yojana*), or *thullaccaya* if one turns back before then.

3.4.1 Interpretation

62 The origin stories give us little help, as they share little in common. In the Mahāvihāravāsin and Dharmaguptaka stories, it seems hardly blameworthy to visit one's relatives, whether or not one has been quarreling. The Sarvāstivāda, Mūlasarvāstivāda, and Mahīśāsaka give us stories of genuine bad behavior, but these are such stereotypical tales of Thullanandā that, with no back-up from the other Vinayas, they have little credence as history. And the Sarvāstivāda tells an entirely different story. Only the Mūlasarvāstivāda and the Mahīśāsaka have a similar story—Thullanandā staying behind the group for a man—which might indicate a connection between these Vinayas; or just as likely, each simply back-formed a story from the rule, inserting Thullanandā in her usual 'bad nun' character.

63 Wandering in and out of lay people's houses for the fun of it is not regarded as suitable behavior for a monastic. There are several other rules in the Vinaya, as well as many statements in the Suttas, that address what is felt to be unbecoming or excessive socializing between monastics—both male and female—and lay people. However, this rule does stand out as a serious offense for what we would see as being, at most, a laxity of monastic etiquette. One imagines that there must have been a more serious circumstance that prompted the rule formulation.

64 The rule analyses add little to our understanding. Strikingly, they all deal with totally different issues, and apart from some stereotyped clauses appear to have no common material. The Dharmaguptaka has the most developed analysis, and here we find the drastic extension of this rule to cover any travel outside a village, a clear departure from the original intent of the rule.

65 Perhaps the most confusing aspect of this clause is the basic term *gāmantara*, which is grammatically ambiguous, and has been interpreted in at least three mutually exclusive ways, leading to quite different rules.

66 *Gāmantara* literally means 'village-between'. One possible interpretation is 'inside the village'. This reading was followed by certain modern[28] interpreters. In this case, the rule would forbid a bhikkhuni from stepping inside a village by herself. A village might have been felt to be a worldly

[28] PTS Dict. says that *gāmantara* means 'the (interior of the) village', while NORMAN (p. 125) translates it as '[next] village'.

and dangerous environment for a lone nun. However, the Pali normally uses a more specific idiom to 'enter a village': *gāmaṁ pavisati*.

67 Alternatively, *gāmantara* might be read in exactly the opposite sense: 'the region between the villages'. The offense would therefore fall for a bhikkhuni who stepped *out* of a village. This reading appears to have been followed by the Lokuttaravāda/Mahāsaṅghika tradition. In this case, it could be argued that the wilderness was a dangerous place for a lone nun, who needed the protection of an inhabited region. How easy it is to imagine *post-hoc* rationalizations for utterly contradictory scenarios!

68 Several of the background stories (Mahāvihāravāsin 3a, Dharmaguptaka 7b, Mahāsaṅghika/Lokuttaravāda 5) appear to favor the interpretation of *gāmantara* as 'inside a village', since they deal with a bhikkhuni visiting lay people's families alone. This is also addressed in some of the rules themselves, most explicitly in Sarvāstivāda 6b.

69 The presentation of the rule in the background stories and analyses is typically ambiguous. The bhikkhuni travels, then enters a village or house. It is unclear whether the offense then applies for the traveling or the entering. The Mahāvihāravāsin says that when you put your feet over the village boundary, it is an offense. But this could apply in either context: either it is the entering of the village, or else it is the completion of traveling between villages. In the Mahīśāsaka, it is clear the story does not involve entering a village, but this rule, as discussed later, lacks any equivalent for *gāmantara*. Only the Sarvāstivāda (6c) clearly deals with traveling and *not* entering a village.

70 However, when used in other *pāṭimokkha* rules *gāmantara* clearly means neither 'inside the village' nor 'in the region between villages' but 'the distance from one village to the next'. For example, the bhikkhus have rules which forbid traveling by arrangement with bhikkhunis (*pācittiya* 27), a caravan of thieves (*pācittiya* 66), or women (*pācittiya* 67) 'even between villages'. These rules appear to be closely connected with our current *saṅghādisesa*. A comparison of our current rule in the Lokuttaravāda version should make this clear. I will only give the Lokuttaravāda and compare with *pācittiya* 26 of the Lokuttaravāda and Mahāsaṅghika bhikkhu *pāṭimokkhas*. This will enable direct comparison of the Indic texts, without

filtering through translation. The examples could be expanded indefinitely, but this should be sufficient to establish the similarity.

Table 3.2: Gāmantara in Various Rules

Lokuttaravāda bhikkhuni saṅghādisesa 5	Lokuttaravāda bhikkhu pācittiya 26	Mahāsaṅghika bhikkhu pācittiya 26
yā puna bhikṣuṇī bhikṣuṇīya vinā	*yo puna bhikṣu bhikṣuṇīya sārdhaṁ saṁvidhāya*	*yo puna bhikṣū bhikṣūṇīya sārdhaṁ saṁvidhāya*
adhvāna-mārgaṁ pratipadyeya antamasato grāmāntaram pi anyatra-samaye	*adhvāna-mārgaṁ pratipadyeya antamasato grāmāntaraṁ pi anyatra-samaye pācattikaṁ*	*adhvāna-māgaṁ pratipadyeya antamasato grāmāntaraṁ pi anyatra-samaye pācattikam*
tatrāyaṁ samayo akāmikā bhikṣuṇī bhavati glanikā vā ayam atra samayo	*tatrāyaṁ samayo mārgo bhavati sabhayo sapratibhayo sāśaṁkasaṁmato ayam atra samayo*	*tatrāyaṁ samayo māgo bhavati sabhayo sapratibhayo sāsaṁkasammaṁto ayam atra samayo*
ayam pi dharmo prathamāpattiko		

71 The structure of the rules is identical, and it seems certain that they were intended to apply in similar circumstances. There seems little doubt that this clause dealt with bhikkhunis who were traveling along the road between villages.

72 Once more, this little ambiguity makes a vast difference in practice. How, for example, are we to understand the dozens of cases where a bhikkhuni is depicted as walking into the village for alms, or wandering off into the forest for meditation? Here is one such case, the origin story for *pācittiya* 55 from the Mahāvihāravāsin Vinaya:

> 73 Now at that time a certain nun, walking for alms along a certain road in Sāvatthī, approached a certain family; having approached she sat down on an appointed seat. Then these people, having offered food to this nun, spoke thus: 'Lady, other nuns may also come.' Then that nun thinking, 'How may these nuns not come?' approached the nuns and spoke thus: 'Ladies, in such and such a place there are fierce dogs, a wild bull, the place is a swamp, do not go there!'...[29]

[29] Pali Vinaya 4.312.

74 Here it is quite clear the nun was traveling alone and visiting houses alone. The case is far from unique. In fact, the Vinaya constantly depicts bhikkhunis walking into the village for alms alone, visiting houses alone, or traveling through the countryside alone. In only a cursory survey of the Dharmaguptaka and Mahāvihāravāsin Vinayas, I have counted around thirty such cases, where the bhikkhuni is, or at least seems to be, alone.[30]

75 This is not confined to the Vinaya tradition, for similar situations occur throughout the Therīgāthā. For example, Subhā Jīvakambavanikā is chatted up as she enters Jīvaka's mango grove, being asked: 'What delight is there for you, if you plunge into the wood **alone**?' (*kā tuyhaṁ rati bhavissati, yadi **ekā** vanamogahissasi*).[31] Particularly striking is the case of Jinadattā a 'Vinaya expert', who comes, apparently alone, to a lay household, and sits to take her meal.[32]

76 As a verse collection, the Therīgāthā is light on background details and offers more insight into the psychology of the nuns than their lifestyle. Nevertheless, in most cases where lifestyle is referred to, it sounds as if the nuns are frequenting woods and secluded spots, even if it is not clear that they are alone. For example, we have reference to a nun 'wandering here and there',[33] 'entering inside the wood',[34] going to the mountains for meditation,[35] or, having wandered for alms, sitting at the root of a tree for meditation.[36]

77 The Bhikkhunī Saṁyutta, which consists of 10 short suttas involving bhikkhunis, throughout depicts bhikkhunis dwelling in the solitude of the forest. Each sutta depicts the bhikkhuni walking for alms in Sāvatthī, returning for the day's meditation at the 'Blind Man's Grove'. It seems

---

[30] Dharmaguptaka (page numbers to HEIRMANN, *Rules for Nuns*): *nissaggiya pācittiya* 21 (p. 457), 19 (p. 448), 22 (p. 460), 29 (p. 479, 480), 30 (p. 482, 483); *pācittiya* 82 (p. 617), 83 (p. 618), 84 (p. 620), 99 (p. 701), 105 (p. 735), 106 (p. 737), 115 (p. 755), 119 (p. 762), 120 (p. 764), 161, 162, 163 (pp. 923*ff*). Mahāvihāravāsin (page numbers to HORNER, *Book of the Discipline*, Vol 3): *pācittiya* 15 (p. 270), 16 (p. 273), 25 (p. 292), 35 (p. 311), 36 (p. 315), 48 (p. 335), 55 (p. 350), 61 (p. 361), 62 (p. 363), 96 (417).

[31] Therīgāthā 372.

[32] Therīgāthā 427–428.

[33] Therīgāthā 92.

[34] Therīgāthā 80.

[35] Therīgāthā 27, 29, 48.

[36] Therīgāthā 75.

clear enough that they are alone, both when going for alms and entering the forest. In certain cases this is confirmed: Āḷavikā is said to be seeking seclusion (*vivekatthinī*);[37] Kisāgotamī is taunted for being 'alone in the woods' (*vanamajjhagatā ekā*);[38] Uppalavaṇṇā is teased while 'standing alone at the root of a *sāla* tree' (*ekā tuvaṁ tiṭṭhasi sālamūle*).[39] This evidence is very weighty, for this Saṁyutta is one of the few major early collections of literature concerning the bhikkhunis, and in fact constitutes the major document concerning the bhikkhunis within the four Nikāyas/Āgamas. No doubt these examples could be multiplied by a more thorough sampling of the literature. But the quantity is already enough to raise a serious question mark over the meaning of the rule.

78 According to the first two interpretations of *gāmantara*, we would have to accept that most of the bhikkhunis openly flouted this rule, without so much as a murmur of protest by the bhikkhus. One could always use the counterargument that these cases must have happened before the rule was laid down. This argument, however, is merely an *ad hoc* rationalization. It would only have force if there was independent evidence to suggest

---

[37] SN 1.5. SĀ 1198 has 遠離 (T2, № 99, p. 326, a1); SĀ2 214 has 空靜處 (T2, № 100, p. 453, c10). Both of these Chinese renderings appear to stand for *viveka*, 'seclusion, secluded, empty, or private place'.

[38] SN 1.5.3. SĀ 1200 has 獨坐於樹下 (T2, № 99, p. 326, c1), 'sitting alone among the trees'; SĀ2 216 has 獨處於林中 (T2, № 100, p. 454, a29), 'staying alone in the forest'.

[39] SN 1.5.5. SĀ 1201 has 獨一無等侶 (T2, № 99, p. 326, c27), 'solitary, without an equal companion'. SĀ2 217 has 獨一比丘尼 (T2, № 100, p. 454, b21), 'a solitary bhikkhuni'. The next line has 更無第二伴 (T2, № 100, p. 454, b22), 'with no companion'. There is evident confusion in this line. The corresponding verse in Therīgāthā 230 has 'you have no [male] companion' (*na cāpi te dutiyo atthi koci*) where the Bhikkhunī Saṁyutta reads 'you have no [female] second (*dutiyā* = companion) in beauty', i.e. 'your beauty is unrivalled' (*na catthi te dutiyā vaṇṇadhātu*). Thus for the Pali Bhikkhunī Saṁyutta, *dutiya* is used to extoll Uppalavaṇṇā's beauty, while in the Therīgāthā and both the Chinese versions of the Bhikkhunī Saṁyutta, the term refers to her being alone in the woods. Interestingly, Therīgāthā 230 uses the explictly masculine form *dutiyo*, so the saying does not refer to a bhikkhuni companion, but to a male protector. The Pali commentary to the Therīgāthā, as noted by NORMAN (Elder's Verses II, p. 104), seems to acknowledge both readings, glossing *dutiyo* with both *sahāyabhūto ārakkhako* ('companion, protector') and *rūpasampattiyā vā tuyhaṁ dutiyo* ('or your second in regards perfection of appearance'). However, the Saṁyutta commentary only notices the 'beauty' meaning, as is relevant to that reading.

that all these cases happened at an early period in the dispensation. Such evidence is not forthcoming.

79 If, however, the rule was restricted to the rarer case of an actual journey, rather than the everyday movements of the nuns, such contradictions would be eased. This leads us on to our next uncertainty: what exactly does 'going' mean?

80 The verb that is used to indicate 'going' is the Pali *gacchati*, which is the most common verb for movement, cognate with the English 'to go'. It is applied very broadly, and might be used of just about any sort of movement, literal or metaphorical.

81 However, we should not underestimate the extent to which changes in technology have affected our use of the word 'to go'. In ancient India, travel was almost always by foot, especially for bhikkhus and bhikkhunis, who were forbidden from traveling in a vehicle (although hardly anyone applies that rule literally today).[40] When a bhikkhu or bhikkhuni was said to 'go', it would have been assumed they were walking.

82 Indeed, in important cases 'going' is clearly meant to be walking. For example, the standard description of the four postures is 'going', standing, sitting, lying. These postures are mutually exclusive, and 'going' must mean 'walking'. Travel in a vehicle must be excluded, for then one is usually sitting, or may be standing or lying. If we look at the *pāṭimokkha* rules as a whole, the monks and nuns have other rules that deal with appropriate conduct regarding the opposite sex in the various postures: lying, sitting, standing. It is, therefore, not at all arbitrary to treat this rule, and others involving monks or nuns 'going', as applying specifically to walking.

83 This, then, becomes another question of interpretation. Do we choose to understand the term *gacchati* in its widest possible scope, in which case any sort of transport would be understood under this rule? Or should it be treated in terms of the most direct applicable meaning, where *gacchati* was applied to the context of walking? If the latter case, we are then faced with the question of how the rule should be applied in the context of modern transport.

84 In the case of the rules regarding restrictions of travel by bhikkhus, for example, that a bhikkhu should not travel by arrangement with a

[40] Pali Vinaya 1.191; bhikkhuni *pācittiya* 85 at Pali Vinaya 4.338.

woman, some bhikkhus today do take the verb 'travel' to mean 'walk'. In the bhikkhus' rules the verb is *paṭipajjati*, not *gacchati* as in the bhikkhuni *saṅghādisesa*, although the two terms are clearly referring to the same act. Certainly, a long stroll through a secluded forest would offer more occasion for intimacy than a car journey. This being so, many bhikkhus believe this particular rule does not apply to car journeys, and regularly travel by arrangement with a woman in the car. This interpretation suggests that the Vinaya rules are applied according to posture: if a monk is walking, the rules about 'going' apply, if he is sitting, the rules about 'sitting' apply. In such cases, the bhikkhu should ensure that he is not alone with the woman in the car, in line with the rule forbidding sitting together with a woman in a private place.

85 As a further defense of this interpretation, allow me to make the following analogy. Consider the act of traveling: there are two basic components. One aspect is that you start in one place and end in another. Another aspect is what you do in between the two places. Consider how to apply the Vinaya for a bhikkhu on board the Starship Enterprise who wished to teleport to Earth, accompanied by a woman. They vanish from the spaceship and re-appear on the planet's surface. Would this be a case of 'traveling together'? If traveling means to start at one place and end up in another, then yes, this is traveling. But surely the rule could not apply in this case. It would only be inappropriate if, say, they were teleporting to a secluded place for a liaison; but this would be covered by other rules. This suggests that it is not the fact of being in one place and then another which is the issue. The issue is what happens along the journey. And indeed, it is while going along the journey that the problems arise in the background stories. This suggests that we consider the application of the rules in terms of comparing the situation while traveling: is sitting in a car or bus more like walking along a forest path, or is it more like sitting in a room together? It seems to me that it is clearly the latter.

3.5 Crossing a river

86 **Mahāvihāravāsin 3b:** Two bhikkhunis are traveling together. They reach a river crossing, and the ferryman agrees to take them across one

by one. But while they are separated, he rapes them in turn. Crossing a river is defined as when the lower robe is made wet; when both feet reach the far shore the full offense falls.

87 **Dharmaguptaka 7a:** A bhikkhuni lifted up her robes when wading across a river. A rogue, seeing this, was inflamed with lust and attacked her. The rule analysis defines 'water' as 'water of a river one cannot cross alone', which would seem to be curiously tautological. It then gives elaborate instructions on exactly what to do at each stage of the crossing, waiting carefully for the companion bhikkhuni and so on.

88 **Mahīśāsaka 6c:** Many bhikkhunis cross over to get cow dung. The water rose and they were not able to return. Rogues attacked them. This does not fit the rule, which specifies the bhikkhunis must be alone. The river is defined as being 10 'elbows' [41] deep, or coming up to the hips.

89 **Mahāsaṅghika and Lokuttaravāda 5:** Thullanandā takes off her clothes and swims over the Aciravatī river, sits on the far shore for a little, then swims back again at a place where many women could see it. The rule analysis is negligible.

90 **Mūlasarvāstivāda 9:** Also at the Aciravatī, tells instead of a group of bhikkhunis who arrive at the river, but the boat is on the further shore. One bhikkhuni, seeing that the boat was owned by her former husband, volunteers to swim over and bring the boat back over. But halfway across she becomes exhausted, and despite encouragement from the other bhikkhunis, her strength fails her. As usual, the rule analysis adds little; there is an extra offense of wrong-doing for making a raft.

91 **Sarvāstivāda 6d:** Starts off similarly, but there is no boat involved. A bhikkhuni is chosen because she is fit and strong to test how deep the water is. But after crossing, the river becomes too gushing to be able to return. She stays overnight on the far shore and is, of course, raped. This is not dissimilar to the Mahīśāsaka version. The rule analysis goes into quite some detail. It mentions two cases, one who takes off her robes to cross, one who does not. It then goes on to describe a number of different permutations, if with a companion, or if one bhikkhuni turns back halfway,

[41] T22, № 1421, p. 80, b110.

and so on. There is no offense if using a bridge or a boat.[42] The usual non-offense clauses apply.

3.5.1 Interpretation

92 Here we are really uncertain as to the basic purpose of the rule. Each of the Vibhajjavāda schools tells a completely different story. The Mahāsaṅghika schools are, as usual, very close, and the Sarvāstivāda schools have some similarity. But we are left uncertain whether the rule is in order to prevent bhikkhunis from being raped while crossing on a boat (but the Sarvāstivāda makes it no offense if using a boat), or from unintentionally provoking rogues while wading across, or getting stranded while seeking cow dung, or from making indecent displays of oneself while swimming, or from drowning.

93 It may be relevant that the Jains had strict rules against monastics crossing water. Similarly, the Brahmanical Dharmaśāstras have several rules forbidding Brahman students from crossing rivers, for fear of their safety.[43] Perhaps the confusion in the origin stories is because the rule originated in a non-Buddhist context which was later forgotten. Another relevant context is that the bhikkhus have a *pācittiya* rule against playing in the water. The behavior of Thullanandā in the Mahāsaṅghika versions would count as an extreme version of this rule, which would justify an up-grading of the offense to a *saṅghādisesa.*

94 The Sudassanavinayavibhāsā, which follows the order of the Dharmaguptaka here, remarks only that: 'A bhikkhuni crossing water alone in a boat also becomes guilty of a *saṅghādisesa*.'[44] This suggests that this commentary was commenting on the Dharmaguptaka rule. The Theravāda Samantapāsādikā, on the contrary, has a long and complex comment.

95 A clear-cut interpretation of the purpose, or purposes, of this rule cannot be inferred with any certainty from the texts. Nevertheless, anyone who has spent time in the Ganges valley could never forget the might of Indian rivers. Fed off the melting Himalayan snows, the rivers are massive and unpredictable. Crossing them was an ever-present danger, especially

42 T23, № 1435, p. 309, a11.
43 E.g. VĀŚIṢṬHA 12.45; VIṢṆU 63.44, 46, 50.
44 BAPAT, p. 491.

for wanderers like the bhikkhunis. The safety of bhikkhunis crossing such waters must have been a concern.

3.6 Spending the night

96 **Mahāvihāravāsin 3c:** Many bhikkhunis, while traveling through Kosala, arrived at a village and spent the night. A man there was attracted to one of the bhikkhunis and arranged a separate sleeping place for her. Thinking that this looked like trouble, the bhikkhuni, without informing the other bhikkhunis, went to another house for the night. When the man came in looking for that bhikkhuni, he disturbed the other bhikkhunis, and they concluded that the missing bhikkhuni had been out with the man. The rule analysis defines 'alone dwelling apart' as being more than arm's reach from a companion bhikkhuni at the time of dawn.

97 **Dharmaguptaka 7c:** This follows on from the story in the previous clause of the Dharmaguptaka (7b), concerning traveling. The bhikkhuni Khemā, having traveled alone, then stayed overnight in the village, prompting further rumors. The rule analysis is again quite developed: if bhikkhunis spend the night together, they should remain within arm's reach; if alone, when the side touches the ground it is a *saṅghādisesa*; each time she turns she incurs another *saṅghādisesa*. Then the analysis further explains about when bhikkhunis spend the night in a village. The non-offense clauses are similarly developed.

98 **Mahīśāsaka 6b:** Many bhikkhunis spend a night alone. This appears incongruous, and perhaps the character for 'many' has been inserted by mistake. Anyway, they lose their robes and break their holy life (i.e., have sex).[45] The rule analysis adds little, but clarifies that the full offense falls at daybreak, like the Mahāvihāravāsin but unlike the Dharmaguptaka.

99 **Mahāsaṅghika 6:** Tells the story of the going forth and attainment by a bhikkhuni called Kammadhītā (*jie-mu-zi*). Some of the verses turn out to be similar to those of Subhā Kammāradhītā found at Therīgāthā 338–365. Being taught by Uppalavaṇṇā, Subhā realizes the Dhamma in just eight days, and thereafter, being renowned for her beautiful teaching, she receives many offerings, causing jealousy among the other bhikkhunis.

[45] T22, № 1421, p. 80, a20.

The Buddha goes on to tell a story of seven daughters of a certain King of Benares in the past, all of whom become prominent women in the current dispensation. The text abbreviates, saying it should be expanded as in the 'Seven Women Sutta'. This text is in fact spelt out in detail in the Lokuttaravāda version; the story is also found in Pali Jātaka vi.481 and referred to elsewhere. This whole episode has nothing to do with our current rule.[46] It would seem rather to belong to Mahāsaṅghika *saṅghādisesa* 4, concerning speaking in envy. Immediately after telling us to 'explain in detail as in the "Seven Women Sutta"', it merely says that a bhikkhuni stayed the night away from the company of bhikkhunis, prompting the laying down of the rule.[47] Thus there is hardly any proper origin story for this rule. The analysis adds that within the monastery the bhikkhunis should check each other within arm's length three times each night, in the early, middle and later parts of the night; failure to do so is a transgression of Vinaya (*vinayatikkrama*) each time, and *thullaccaya* if one omits to do this at all.

100 **Lokuttaravāda 6:** Tells the story of Subhā Kammāradhītā in great detail. Subhā's verses at Therīgāthā 364–367 are similar to the verses 1–4 of Roth's edition of the Lokuttaravāda Vinaya.[48] But the Lokuttaravāda calls her 'Śuklā Karmāradhītā', and the following verses 6–7 are indeed similar to the verses of Sukkā at Therīgāthā 54 and 55. Evidently there is some confusion, and, since the names are similar in sound and meaning, it could be that there were two bhikkhunis who were made one, or one split into two.[49]

101 In any case, the text tells a long story (*apadāna*) of the seven daughters of King Kiki of Benares, now reborn as the great disciples Śuklā, Uppalavaṇṇā, Paṭācārā, Kīsa-Gotamī, Mahāpajāpatī, and Visākhā.[50] After closing this, the text abruptly says that Śuklā went from house to house to teach, and ended up staying away from the bhikkhunis, prompting the laying down of the rule. Thus the connection between the *apadāna* and the rule, which is entirely lacking in the Mahāsaṅghika, is made, barely, in the fuller Lokuttaravāda version. It is remarkable that an arahant should occasion the

---

[46] The interpolation is from T22, № 1425, p. 518, b25 to T22, № 1425, p. 519, a5–6.
[47] T22, № 1425, p. 519, a6.
[48] ROTH, pp. 111–112.
[49] ROTH does not notice the connection between Subhā and Śuklā.
[50] ? The text only mentions six.

laying down of a *saṅghādisesa*, underscoring the fact that breaking this rule need not involve a bad intention.

102 Not content with such a drawn-out origin story, the Lokuttaravāda goes on to tell another long story of the ravages of the evil King Virūḍhaka of Sāvatthī. In the Pali, this story is only known in the commentaries. The Lokuttaravāda and the Mahāsaṅghika obviously share a common heritage, with the Mahāsaṅghika as usual abbreviating the stories, while the Lokuttaravāda spells them out in full.

103 But perhaps the most remarkable textual commonality is the exemption for a bhikkhuni without lust. In both Vinayas, this exemption is mentioned, but only in the *vibhaṅga*, and is apparently forgotten in the rule formulation itself.

104 **Mūlasarvāstivāda 6:** The Tibetan and Chinese versions of this rule diverge, in a manner similar to the rule against entering lay homes alone. According to the Tibetan, it is an offense for a bhikkhuni to go out alone from the monastery at night, in contrast with their *saṅghādisesa* 6, which prohibits going out in the daytime. The Chinese, on the other hand, specifies that the offense falls only when spending the night alone. Since, as in the previous case, the Chinese is more consistent with the version found in all the other Vinayas, it seems likely that the Tibetan has suffered textual corruption here.

105 In the origin story as rendered in the Chinese version, the Buddha is at Rājagaha, not Sāvatthī as in most versions, and the story concerns *Sumittā bhikkhuni, who on a groundless pretext defamed Sāriputta, saying in front of the bhikkhus that he had violated his precepts. Then she disrobed, and had a baby who became ill. She had a sister who was a bhikkhuni called Ñāṇamittā. Sumittā, being gravely sick and wishing to kill herself, sent a message for her sister to come and see her. But when she reached home, Sumittā died. The husband cried out when seeing her body, saying 'Who will support my family?' Ñāṇamittā is suggested, but says nothing for fear of bringing disgrace on the baby. When dawn came, she wished to leave. The husband asked where she was going. When he tried to grab Ñāṇamittā, she cried out, then went back to the monastery, where the bhikkhunis asked where she had spent the night. The rule analysis is short,

merely saying that one must be with a companion if staying outside the monastery.

106 **Sarvāstivāda 6a:** Tells of Bhaddā Kapilā. Her sister died and she went to see the family. Night fell and she became afraid of possible dangers on the road back to the monastery, so she stayed the night. The husband thought that she wanted to break her precepts, and repeatedly propositioned her during the night, saying he had much wealth and treasure, and suggesting she could be a mother to the orphaned child. Out of fear she remained silent each time. At sunrise she escaped back to the monastery.

107 The Sarvāstivāda rule analysis mainly concerns itself with the question of the exact period that defines night, whether the early, middle, or late part; in fact it goes beyond this, dividing each of the three watches of the night into a further three—the early, middle, and late sections of the first watch, and so on. At each stage there is an offense of *saṅghādisesa*. There is a standard list of non-offense clauses.

3.6.1 Interpretation

108 The operative word here is *vippavāsa*, to 'dwell apart'. This word is in addition to the usual 'alone', so must have an extra meaning.[51] It is not defined here, so we should see how it is used in the rest of the Vinaya. The most common use in Vinaya of 'dwell apart' is regarding a monastic's duty not to 'dwell apart' from their three robes.[52] The purpose of this rule was so that bhikkhus would not abandon their fundamental requisites, but would take good care of them. For convenience, a special *sīmā* may be established which provides a boundary within which a monk is deemed to be 'not dwelling apart from' his robes. To 'dwell apart' also occurs in the *parivāsa* and *mānattā* duties for bhikkhus, where they lose one day of their probationary period if they 'dwell apart' from other bhikkhus, by going from a residence where there are bhikkhus to a place where

[51] The Pali *vibhaṅga* does not comment separately on the words 'alone' and 'dwell apart', so when it refers to the 'companion bhikkhuni' it is not obvious how she relates to the rule. But this is cleared up by the next clause, lagging behind a group, which also refers to a 'companion bhikkhuni' but does not concern 'dwelling apart'. Therefore, the 'companion bhikkhuni' relates to the term 'alone', not the term 'dwell apart'. 'Dwelling apart', then, does not of itself refer to being away from the companion bhikkhuni.

[52] Pali Vinaya *nissaggiya pācittiya* 2 and 29.

there are no bhikkhus of the same communion, unless accompanied by a bhikkhu who is not on probation, or if there is danger.[53] In these cases, to 'dwell apart' means 'away from the monastery'. Being separated from one's robes is defined in great detail in the *vibhaṅga*; for example, if staying in a town with a unified governance and protected boundaries, one may be anywhere within the village and not separated from one's robes. If the town is unwalled, then one must be within the same house.[54]

109 To 'dwell apart' therefore means 'in a different monastery', 'away from the monastery', 'in a separate building or house', etc. The bhikkhuni, then would 'dwell apart' when she travels from the monastery and stays in a lay person's home or a single unit, etc. It is at such a time that, according to the Pali *vibhaṅga*, she should remain within arm's reach of her companion bhikkhuni at dawn.

110 This reading of *vippavāsa* reminds us that the origin stories all concern cases where the bhikkhuni is traveling, and all the other clauses of this rule also concern a bhikkhuni who is traveling. It is extremely likely that this rule was not intended to apply to a bhikkhuni living in the monastery. It was meant to apply to one who was 'traveling', which in the Buddha's day meant walking from one village to the next. In such a case it would indeed be dangerous for a bhikkhuni to arrive at a village and to stay alone in a house where she had been invited. Even if a group of bhikkhunis were traveling together, they may well be invited to stay the night in individual houses, thus prompting the need for the rule.

111 This rule should be compared with the bhikkhus' *pācittiyas* 5 and 6, forbidding sleeping in the same place as laymen (for more than three nights) or women. The origin story for *pācittiya* 5 tells of the time when the bhikkhus fell asleep in the same place as laymen visiting the monastery. Being inexperienced, they drooled and exposed themselves, prompting the Buddha to lay down the rule. *Pācittiya* 6, against sleeping in the same house as a woman, was prompted by the occasion when Anuruddha stayed in a woman's residence and she tried to seduce him. Thus there were felt to be good reasons to ensure that monastics were restrained and careful in their sleeping arrangements.

---

[53] Pali Vinaya 2. 32–4.

[54] Pali Vinaya 3.200–2.

112 Again we find the origin stories are quite distinct in the Vibhajjavāda schools, with no obvious commonalities. The Mahāvihāravāsin story seems quite artificial. Surely it would be natural for the bhikkhuni, on perceiving the man was cherishing unwholesome intentions, to inform the other bhikkhunis. This incongruity cannot be explained away by the fact that she had separate quarters from the rest of the bhikkhunis. The sleeping places, though separate, must have been close together, because the man later tripped over the group of bhikkhunis while looking for his beloved. We are left with an origin story that fails to convince as a realistic tale. Moreover, the Mahīśāsaka adds a blanket exemption for when a bhikkhuni acts out of fear of a man; surely this is only common sense—Vinaya should not prevent a bhikkhuni from protecting herself. The other Vibhajjavāda Vinayas hardly have any origin story to speak of.

113 By contrast, the Mahāsaṅghika group presents an excessively developed story, with the addition of at least one *apadāna*, although this was subsequently abbreviated in the text that was translated into Chinese. But still, even though there is a definite story, the connection between the story and the rule is only made in a few short words, and the fact that an arahant is involved is quite extraordinary. The Mahāsaṅghika and Lokuttaravāda Vinayas both provide an exception if the bhikkhuni is without lust. This appears incongruous in the context of their origin stories, which deal with an arahant bhikkhuni. But it is not unusual to find Vinaya rules which are formulated or modified in ways that do not exactly agree with the origin story. In some cases, this situation could have come about because of later modifications of the rule by the Buddha. But in this case, because of the strangeness of the origin story being about an arahant, the tenuousness of any connection between the story and the rule itself, and the fact that the origin stories of the other Vinayas are completely different, I think the incongruity is merely a result of the textual history of the rule.

114 The Vinayas of the Sarvāstivāda group, on the other hand, present stories that, while not identical, clearly share common roots, and in addition deal directly with the situation mentioned in the rule. The bhikkhuni does not merely spend the night without other bhikkhunis, but does so in an emotionally fraught situation, together with a single man and a young baby. While her motivation was pure, and her intention compassionate,

still she has inadvertently exposed herself to serious danger. Thus, while it does not seem possible to ascertain which, if any, of the origin stories has any historical credibility, the Vinayas of the Sarvāstivāda group provide us with the most meaningful context within which to appreciate how the rule might have functioned.

3.7 Lagging behind a group

115 **Mahāvihāravāsin 3d:** A group of bhikkhunis are traveling in Kosala. One of them stays behind the group to go to the toilet. Men see her and rape her. The rule analysis explains that when in a wilderness, going out of seeing and hearing of a companion is *saṅghādisesa.*

116 **Dharmaguptaka 7d:** Also set in Kosala, but differs in that this time it is Thullanandā and the group of six bhikkhunis who stay behind the group, because they want to get a man. The rule analysis is similar to the Mahāvihāravāsin, but not identical: there is no mention here of being 'where there is no village, in the wilderness'; and while the Mahāvihāravāsin says in leaving the range of seeing and hearing there is a *thullaccaya*, having left there is a *saṅghādisesa*, the Dharmaguptaka says that when the bhikkhuni is either out of sight but not hearing, or out of hearing but not sight of the companion, this is a *thullaccaya*, but out of both hearing and seeing is a *saṅghādisesa*. Thus for the Mahāvihāravāsins the crucial distinction was the degree of completion of the act of leaving the vicinity, for the Dharmaguptakas it is the different senses.

117 **Mahīśāsaka 6d:** As mentioned earlier, in the rule itself this clause is separated from the clause about traveling, but in the *vibhaṅga* lagging behind a group is treated as part of the same situation: while a group of bhikkhunis were traveling with merchants, Thullanandā dropped behind the group out of desire for a man. The full offense falls when one is out of seeing and hearing.

118 **Mahāsaṅghika and Lokuttaravāda 5 (*vibhaṅga* only):** Follows on from the story of Rāṣṭrā bhikkhuni, whose younger sister was married and went away to another village. Falling ill, she called for her sister to come and look after her. But the sister died before the bhikkhuni arrived. The husband, refusing to look after the son, suggested the bhikkhuni do so, at which the

bhikkhuni was afraid he intended violence. Pretending to go outside, she fled back to the monastery.

119 There is a second story which tells of a bhikkhuni who stayed behind a group to go to the toilet while traveling.[55] She is propositioned by merchants, who try to persuade her to enjoy the pleasures of the flesh while she is young and pretty. This is similar to the Mahāvihāravāsin origin story for this rule. However, the outcome is different, for the Lokuttaravāda uses this as a case where there is no offense.

120 The analysis, echoing the rule formulation, says there is no offense if without lust[56] or ill. It then adds that there is no offense traveling inside a village, but from the village boundary one should remain within arm's reach; past this is *thullaccaya*, past two arms' reach is *saṅghādisesa*.

121 **Mūlasarvāstivāda 8 (*vibhaṅga* only):** Depicts Thullanandā as staying behind the group for a man. The rule analysis adds little. Thus, though this Vinaya phrases the rule as if it applied to all journeys, the story reveals that it is meant to apply, as in the Vibhajjavāda Vinayas, to lagging behind a group. Both this version and the Mahīśāsaka seem to confuse these two situations.

3.7.1 Interpretation

122 As with the previous clauses, this rule reflects concerns also found in the bhikkhus' *pācittiyas*. Specifically, *pācittiya* 27 forbidding bhikkhus from traveling by arrangement with bhikkhunis except in time of danger; *pācittiya* 28 against traveling by boat with bhikkhunis; *pācittiya* 66 against traveling by arrangement with thieves; and *pācittiya* 67 against traveling by arrangement with women. These rules display a striking concern for the propriety of traveling and it is not sure how they are to be interpreted in the context of modern transport.

123 Again, the Vibhajjavāda group have differing origin stories, although there is some similarity in that both the Dharmaguptaka and Mahīśāsaka tell us that it was Thullanandā who stayed behind the group out of desire for a man. While this kind of shameless behavior no doubt deserves a

[55] T22, № 1425, p. 518, b4–9.

[56] See chapter 3, note 27.

saṅghādisesa, the fact that the story so stereotypically involves Thullanandā makes it unconvincing as history. It is not even sure that the similarity of the stories suggests a common origin, for in this case it is quite conceivable that the two traditions could have arrived at such similar stories independently merely through parallel back-formations from the rule. The same consideration applies to the Mūlasarvāstivāda version. In all these cases, the actual circumstances don't really ring true: even if such shameless nuns were really after a man, how could they get one by simply hanging back behind a group?

124 The Vinayas of the Mahāsaṅghika group tell a story that clearly shares a common basis with the (Mūla-) Sarvāstivāda story for the rule against staying overnight. The story seems to fit that context better, since in all versions it was when staying overnight, not when traveling, that the bhikkhuni fell into danger.

3.8 Going out in the Day

125 **Mūlasarvāstivāda 7:** The Tibetan and Chinese versions of this rule show a significant divergence. The Tibetan is more general, making it an offense for a bhikkhuni to go out alone from the monastery in the daytime, while the Chinese specifies that the offense falls only when going alone into the homes of lay families. Since this latter is more consistent with the version found in most of the other Vinayas, it seems likely that the Tibetan has suffered textual corruption here and the Chinese preserves a more accurate memory of the rule. We also note a minor difference, consistently observed throughout the *saṅghādisesas*, that the Tibetan adds the term 'on the first offense', corresponding with the Pali *paṭhamāpattikā*, which is absent from the Chinese translation of this *pāṭimokkha*. The Chinese version of the origin story features Thullanandā going into a village to teach Dhamma to a layman. There is little in the way of rule analysis, just a couple of minor derived offenses.

126 **Sarvāstivāda 6b:** Also features Thullanandā, but this time she spends all morning going in and out of lay peoples' homes for fun. She returns to the monastery in the afternoon, lies down complaining of her aches and pains, and asks the other nuns to give her a massage. They ask her

why she is aching, and she tells them. They ask if she had any duties regarding the Buddha, Dhamma, and Sangha to perform in the houses and she says no. Thus this story, although also featuring Thullanandā, is quite distinct from the Mūlasarvāstivāda version, for there she is going to teach Dhamma, while here she specifically says that she does not have any Dhammic reason. The rule analysis adds little, being mainly concerned with clarifying when is 'day' and 'night', and a standard list of non-offense clauses: if the companion bhikkhuni abandons her precepts or dies, if there is any one of the 'eight difficulties', there is no offense.

3.9 Conclusion

127 The more we investigate this rule, the less sure we are of any definitive reading. The traditions show significant variation even in the basic rule, and there is only occasional agreement in the origin stories. It seems questionable whether any of these stories have any historical basis. Rather, they should be compared with that large class of stories, known as etiological myths, which are invented in later days to explain a pre-existing custom or practice, when the true significance had become obscured. One could imagine that, in the course of teaching the *pāṭimokkha*, teachers would bring or invent examples of how the rule might apply. While these would remain for some time as part of the fluid oral tradition, gradually they would become fixed, and incorporated into the standard explanation of the rule in the Vinaya.[57]

128 The divergence in the origin stories in our current rule is far from an isolated case. For example, if we compare the Mahāvihāravāsin with the Mahāsaṅghika bhikkhuni Vinaya, we find that none of the *pārājika* or *saṅghādisesa* rules share a common origin story. Such similarities as do occur might easily have arisen since they both explain the same or similar rules. Since these two Vinayas stem from schools which separated at the first schism, the total divergence in these origin stories casts doubt on whether there was any commonly accepted tradition for the origin of these rules at the time of the schism.

[57] A similar process may be observed in, say, the Jātaka tales or the Udāna literature. Compare ANĀLAYO, 'The Development of the Pali Udāna Collection'.

129 As for the sectarian tendencies in the rules, the Sarvāstivāda sometimes, but not always, agrees with the Mūlasarvāstivāda. The Vibhajjavāda schools, on the other hand, seem to have little in common as regards the origin stories, suggesting that these were fixed in the traditions independently, probably some time after the schisms. The two Mahāsaṅghika schools, in vivid contrast, are very close, so much so that we might be justified in asking whether we are dealing with two genuinely different schools here, or the same Vinaya, of which the Chinese preserves a translation of a heavily abbreviated text, and the Sanskrit preserves a fuller text. All of these general remarks, it should hardly need saying, stand in need of testing in the light of a broader consideration of the Vinayas.

130 There is no doubt that the origin stories for this rule are sectarian, and are not part of the common heritage of the schools. However, although the explanations arose in the sectarian period, there are no ideologically based differences. The differences are not due to distinct doctrinal perspectives, but simply due to the natural course of explanation and adaption of the texts within the living communities over the several hundred years during which the Vinaya was redacted.

131 A similar situation obtains in the case of the rule analyses. Sometimes they are the same; sometimes they are similar but have important differences; often they have little or nothing in common. In some cases, the different rule explanations simply talk about different aspects of the rule, whereas in other cases the explanations clearly contradict each other.

132 A comparison of the lengths of the rule analyses gives pause for thought. It is difficult to do this exactly, for the Vinayas arrange the material differently, and there are the inevitable variations in how repetitions are handled. Without, then, wishing to make too much of this, I have roughly counted the quantity of characters used in the Chinese translations of the rule explanations for one clause taken at random, that concerning crossing the river. Doing my best to include all comparable material (word analysis, permutations, derived offenses, non-offenses), I have arrived at the following numbers of characters: Mahāsaṅghika 21; Mahīśāsaka 65; Mūlasarvāstivāda 78; Sarvāstivāda 288; Dharmaguptaka 295. Thus the longest two have more than *ten times* the explanatory material of the shortest one.

133 We have also noticed that in several cases the analysis seems to be much stricter than the rule itself. In different ways, the analyses try to extend a rule that covered traveling in certain circumstances to become a general prohibition. This tendency seems to be most advanced in the Dharmaguptaka, one of the longest of all the versions. This suggests that, not only was the rule explanation evolved over time, but the tendency was for a stricter formulation.

134 This process of evolving contextualization of a fixed rule frequently obscures even the basic purpose of the rules. We are left to dimly infer what the original purpose of the rule may have been. There are a number of concerns that crop up regularly. One concern is for physical safety. Several other Vinaya rules address safety while traveling, a concern which is also echoed in the rules for brahman students in the Dharmaśāstras. This concern is most paramount in the case of crossing a river.

135 More obvious is the concern to protect the bhikkhunis from physical assault.[58] There is no doubt that this was a genuine worry, not mere paranoia. While it might seem draconian to enforce a *saṅghādisesa* on the bhikkhuni, it should be borne in mind that such rules were for the regulation of the badly behaved nuns or reckless young nuns. A decision must be made: and the implied judgment of the texts is that it is preferable to impose restrictions, and even the mild penances of the *saṅghādisesa* procedure, rather than risk having any nuns suffer the violence and trauma of rape.

136 Less frequently, the rules express concern that it is not the danger of random attacks, but of the bhikkhunis themselves actively soliciting sexual encounters. But these scenarios, which are stereotypical accounts of Thullanandā's bad behavior, remain doubtful, as any sexual act would be covered by other rules restricting a bhikkhuni's conduct with men. Nevertheless, the Mahāsaṅghika and Lokuttaravāda make some exemptions for the case when a bhikkhuni is without lust, specifically for the clauses concerning traveling and staying the night alone. In addition the Mahīśāsaka specifies that the rule against lagging behind a group only applies in the case of a bhikkhuni who does it out of lust.

---

[58] This concern also lays behind Dharmaguptaka bhikkhuni *pācittiyas* 97 and 98 (T22, p. 747, a1–b15; HEIRMANN, *Rules for Nuns*, pp. 698–700).

137 In developed countries today, it is normal for women to travel alone, and the chances of them being either criticized or attacked are slim. In addition, it should be born in mind that the legal right to free travel for women is asserted in the United Nations 'Declaration on the Elimination of Discrimination against Women'.

> 138 **Article 6: 1.** ...all appropriate measures ... shall be taken to ensure to women, married or unmarried, equal rights with men in the field of civil law, and in particular:
>
> 139 **...(c)** The same rights as men with regard to the law on the movement of persons.

140 The question must be asked: is our current rule in violation of this principle? If the concern is for a genuine regard for the safety of the nuns, then surely not, for this must take precedence. But if we are applying a rule whose intent is far from clear, in situations far removed from the original context, and which is susceptible of various interpretations, then we should surely be obliged to seek an interpretation that resolved, as far as possible, any potential conflict between Vinaya and the accepted norms of international ethics.

141 This is not an alteration of Vinaya, for the Vinaya itself is founded on and assumes the principles of ancient Indian law. Throughout, the Sangha operates in a way that conforms with legal and cultural norms, and which meets or exceeds the highest moral expectations of the contemporary culture. The Buddha expected the Sangha to obey the law, and was immediately willing to adjust practices that offended custom.

142 In our more complex legal situation, with the intersection of Vinaya, tradition, national law, and international guidelines, the wisest course is to steer as best as possible in a way that will satisfy all of these requirements, with particular regard for the spiritual welfare of the bhikkhunis.

143 In conclusion, then, I would recommend that as a matter of practice this rule should be followed merely literally, without the various expansions and elaborations suggested by the *vibhaṅgas*. The original context, so far as can be reasonably inferred, concerns a bhikkhuni walking on a journey, at least as far as from one village to the next. In such a case, a bhikkhuni should not walk alone; she should take care to not become separated from her group; and if a river must be crossed, especially if there is a deep river

that must be waded or swam across, she should do so safely, in the company of others. If she must stay overnight while walking on a journey she should not be alone, and if she accepts the interpretation of the *vibhaṅga,* she should have a bhikkhuni companion with her at dawn.

Chapter 4

BHIKKHUNI PĀRĀJIKA 1

THE LIFE OF THE NUNS IS HIDDEN behind that of the monks. The code of rules for Buddhist nuns (*bhikkhunī pāṭimokkha*) contains many rules held in common with the rules for Buddhist monks. These bhikkhuni rules have for the most part been formed by simply changing the gender of the bhikkhus' rules. In most cases, the bhikkhunis' version of the rules are not listed in the canonical Vinayas as we have them. The bhikkhuni Vinayas generally confine themselves to laying out and defining the rules that are unique to the bhikkhunis. It is assumed that many of the bhikkhus' rules also apply, but this is not always spelt out clearly. For example, the Mahāvihāravāsin Vinaya gives no hint as to which of the bhikkhus' rules should be adopted by the bhikkhunis, or how they should be rephrased. The canonical appendix, the Parivāra, lists the number of rules in each class that are shared and unshared, but does not mention the specific rules.[1] That information is found only in the commentaries. Other schools give more information in the canon itself. In particular, the rule we are dealing with now, since it is the first rule in the *pāṭimokkha*, was dealt with in fair detail in some of the Vinayas.

2 This essay briefly highlights one case where it seems that the bhikkhunis' rule could not have been formed by simply changing the gender of the corresponding bhikkhus' rule. The rule itself, the first *pārājika* for

[1] Pali Vinaya 5.146–7.

bhikkhunis, does not appear in standard editions of the Pali canon.[2] This class of offense is the most serious of all monastic offenses, resulting in immediate and permanent expulsion from full communion in the bhikkhu or bhikkhuni Sangha.[3] The first *pārājika* prohibits sexual intercourse. Here is the rule from the Mahāvihāravāsin bhikkhu *pāṭimokkha*.

3 > Should any bhikkhu who is endowed with the bhikkhus' training and livelihood, not having given up the training, not having declared his inability, engage in the act of sexual intercourse, even with a female animal, he is *pārājika*, not in communion.[4]

4 Comparison with the other available versions of this rule reveals that there are no significant variations in the rule formulation across the schools.[5]

5 In the bhikkhuni *pārājika* 1, however, we find a significant difference in the rule formulation. As the rule is not found in the Pali Canon, it is sourced

---

2 The Chulachomklao of Siam Pāli Tipiṭaka, published in 1893, starts the bhikkhuni rules with the 'first *pārājika*', and then proceeds to give what is in fact the fifth *pārājika* (www.tipitakahall.net/siam/3C1). The online edition of the VRI Tipiṭaka and the PTS edition (4.211) similarly list the fifth *pārājika* as the first. Since the PTS edition does not list any variant readings here (4.365) it would seem as if this was the standard practice in the manuscripts. The incoherence of this presentation is clear since at the end of each *pārājika*, the text anounces that 'first' through 'fourth' rules are concluded. Yet on the very next line after the 'fourth' *pārājika*, the text declares that the 'eight *pārājikas* have been recited'. The online 'World Tipiṭaka Edition', on the other hand, lists the first four *pārājikas* in the contents, but the pages corresponding to these are empty (www.tipitakastudies.net/tipitaka/2V/2/2.1).

3 This basic premise of the Vinaya has been questioned by Shayne CLARKE ('Monks Who Have Sex). However, he overinterprets his material. The passages he quote show the setting up of a separate monastic status, the *śikṣādattaka*, which allows a *pārājika* bhikkhu who immediately confesses with remorse to remain living in the monastery. They are partially readmitted into the community, but are carefully excluded from full participation in the central acts of *saṅghakamma*. Hence the *śikṣādattaka* is not, *contra* Clarke, 'in communion'. In fact the Mahīśasaka, Dharmaguptaka, and Sarvāstivāda Vinayas display a nicety of judgement: a *śikṣādattaka* may listen to the *pāṭimokkha*—and hence be reminded of their ethical obligations—but may not make up the quorum. In other words, their presence cannot enable them to have any power of decision over the lives of bhikkhus, for example at an ordination.

4 Pali Vinaya 3.23: *Yo pana bhikkhu bhikkhūnaṁ sikkhāsājīvasamāpanno, sikkhaṁ apaccakkhāya, dubbalyaṁ anāvikatvā, methunaṁ dhammaṁ paṭiseveyya, antamaso tiracchānagatāyapi, pārājiko hoti asaṁvāso.*

5 PACHOW, pp. 71–2.

from the Pali commentary Samantapāsādikā[6] and from manuscripts of the 'Dual pāṭimokkha'. These have been found as palm-leaf manuscripts in various places in Myanmar and Sri Lanka, and were recently published in a modern critical edition.[7] The text is as follows.

6 Should any bhikkhuni willingly engage in the act of sexual intercourse, even with a male animal, she is *pārājika*, not in communion.

7 Here we notice two distinct differences from the bhikkhus' rule. The first is the insertion of the word *chandaso*. This means 'with desire'. The Indic term is the most flexible of the very many Indic words for desire. It is frequently used in a negative sense of sensual or sexual desire. It is also used in a neutral sense of 'consent, willingness', such as when a bhikkhu sends their 'consent' by proxy to an act of the Sangha which he is unable to attend. It is also commonly used in a positive sense as the basis of psychic power consisting of desire, which here means the aspiration for the Dhamma. This last meaning cannot apply here, so we are left with two possibilities. Either the word means 'with sexual lust', or it means 'consenting'. The two may not always be the same. For example, someone may have sex for money, with no lust, perhaps even revulsion in mind. Or they may have a twisted view that performing such services is an act of merit or part of the spiritual path. Thus the occurrence of this word, and its possible interpretation, make a significant difference to the application of the rule.

8 The second difference is the absence of the phrase 'endowed with the bhikkhus' training and livelihood, not having given up the training, not having declared his inability…'. This phrase simply makes explicit what is understood in all the *pārājika* rules anyway: they apply to a fully ordained monk or nun. Thus the absence of this phrase does not significantly affect the application of the rule. However, it is a distinctive and quite recognizable part of the rule which will help us to evaluate parallels and differences in the rule formulation.

9 There is another version of the rule preserved in an Indic language, the Lokuttaravāda in Hybrid Sanskrit.

---

6 Samantapāsādikā 7.1302. This may be the earliest attested version of this rule.

7 PRUITT and NORMAN, pp. 116–7: *Yā pana bhikkhunī chandaso methunaṁ dhammaṁ paṭiseveyya antamaso tiraccānagatena pi, pārājikā hoti asaṁvāsā.*

10 Should any bhikkhuni willingly engage in the vulgar act of sexual intercourse, even together with a male animal, that bhikṣuṇī is *pārājika*, not in communion.[8]

11 Despite a couple of minor differences in phrasing, this version is strikingly similar to the Burmese Pali version we have seen above. The word *grāmya* ('vulgar') is added, but this word is found frequently in similar contexts in the Pali, and does not alter the meaning. In fact it is found in the gloss on *methuna* a little later in the word-analysis of both the *vibhaṅga* to the bhikkhus' *pārājika* 1, as well as the Lokuttaravāda version, so it is quite possible that it has simply crept into the Lokuttaravāda rule from the word-analysis.

12 The Lokuttaravāda, unlike the Pali, is taken from the canonical Vinaya, so as well as the rule itself, we have a word-analysis. This helps us with the ambiguous term *chanda*. The comment in the Lokuttaravāda is: ' "Willingly" means with lustful mind' (*cchandaso ti raktacittā*). Thus the Lokuttaravāda tradition says that a bhikkhuni would only fall into *pārājika* if she had a mind of lust. Unfortunately, the absence of a gloss of the Pali means we do not know whether this interpretation was also followed in the formative years of the Mahāvihāravāsin school.

13 However, the mature Mahāvihāravāsin position is in fact identical with the Lokuttaravāda, as *chandaso* occurs consistently throughout the Mahāvihāravāsin commentarial tradition.[9] For example, the *pāṭimokkha* commentary Kaṅkhāvitaraṇī says that ' "Willingly" means with willingness connected with sexual lust and desire.'[10] Thus the rule and explanation in the Mahāvihāravāsin and Lokuttaravāda are identical, despite the fact that they are not attested in the earliest stage of the Pali canon.

---

[8] ROTH, p. 79 § 117. *Yā punar bhikṣuṇī chandaśo maithunaṁ grāmya-dharmaṁ pratiṣeveya antamasato tiryagyoni-gatenāpi sārdhaṁ iyaṁ bhikṣuṇī pārājikā bhavaty asaṁvāsyā.* There are many spelling variants between this, the final phrasing of the rule, and its previous occurrence at ROTH p. 76 § 114.

[9] Parivāra-aṭṭhakathā:vi aṭṭha.-5 Ro.:7.1302; Sāratthadīpanī-ṭikā-3:vi. ṭī.-3 Mya.:3.114; Kaṅkhāvitaraṇī-aṭṭhakathā:vi. ṭī Ro.:0.1, 0.25, 0.157; Vajirabuddhi-ṭīkā:Vi ṭī Mya.:0.65, 0.355; Vimativinodanī-ṭikā:vi. ṭī. Mya.:2.68: Kaṅkhāvitaraṇī-purāṇa-abhinava-ṭīkā: vi. ṭī. Mya.:0.12; Vinayavinicchaya-uttaravinicchaya:Vi. ṭī. Mya.:0.186. My thanks to Bhikkhu Ñāṇatusita for these references.

[10] Kaṅkhāvitaraṇī 0.157: ' *"Chandaso"ti methunarāgappaṭisaṁyuttena chandena ceva ruciyā ca.*'

14 An examination of the bhikkhuni *pāṭimokkhas* in Chinese translation, however, shows that they have not preserved such a clear distinction between the bhikkhu and the bhikkhuni *pārājika* 1. The Chinese, unlike the Mahāvihāravāsin, preserve lists of the bare *pāṭimokkha* rules in their canon, alongside the full Vinaya. Typically these rules have been extracted from the canonical Vinayas, rather than stemming from an independent textual tradition. Here are the rules.

> 15 **Mahīśāsaka:** Should any bhikkhuni, sharing the bhikkhunis' training rules, not having given up the training rules due to inability, willingly engage in sexual intercourse, even with an animal, that bhikkhuni is *pārājika*, not in communion.[11]

> 16 **Dharmaguptaka:** Should any bhikkhuni engage in sexual intercourse, transgressing what is not the holy life, even with an animal, that bhikkhuni is *pārājika*, not in communion.[12]

> 17 **Sarvāstivāda:** Should any bhikkhuni, having undertaken the bhikkhunis' training, having not given up the precepts, having not got out from the precepts due to inability, engage in sexual intercourse, even with an animal, that bhikkhuni is *pārājika*, not in communion.[13]

> 18 **Mūlasarvāstivāda:** Again, should any bhikkhuni, sharing the bhikkhunis' training rules, not having given up the training rules, not having declared her inability to keep the training, engage in unholy conduct, sexual intercourse, even with an animal, that bhikkhuni also is *pārājika*, not in communion.[14]

> 19 **Mahāsaṅghika:** Should any bhikkhuni, having full ordination in the midst of the two-fold Sangha, not having renounced the precepts, not getting out from the precepts due to inability, engage in sexual intercourse, even with an animal, that bhikkhuni is *pārājika*, not in communion.[15]

20 Thus it seems that the Mahāsaṅghika, Mūlasarvāstivāda, and Sarvāstivāda all preserve rules that are essentially similar to the corresponding bhikkhus' *pārājika* 1, rather than the special bhikkhunis' form as attested

---

[11] T22, № 1421, p. 77, c4–6 = T22, № 1423, p. 206, c29–p. 207, a2.
[12] T22, № 1428, p. 714, a14–15 = T22, № 1431, p. 1031, b16–17.
[13] T23, № 1437, p. 479, b29–c2 = T23, № 1435, p. 333, c29–p. 334, a2.
[14] T24, № 1455, p. 508, c10–12.
[15] T22, № 1427, p. 556, c4–7.

in the Pali and Lokuttaravāda. This cannot be explained by a fault of the translators, for the extant bhikkhuni *pārājika* 1 of the Mūlasarvāstivāda in Sanskrit also reflects the form of the bhikkhus' rule.[16] The case of the Dharmaguptaka and the Mahīśāsaka are less clear.

21 The Dharmaguptaka differs from the bhikkhus' rule in that it lacks any reference to 'disavowing the bhikkhunis' training rules, declaring her weakness'. This could be because it, too, stems from the bhikkhunis' special version of this rule, or it could have happened through simple textual loss. If so, this must have happened before the *vibhaṅga* was formed.

22 Whether this version should be read as a further example of the special phrasing of bhikkhuni *pārājika* 1 depends on how we read the ambiguous characters 婬欲. They could either stand for 'sexual intercourse', or alternatively 欲 might stand for 'desire', which would align this version with those of the Mahāvihāravāsin/Lokuttaravāda.

23 This problem is, however, readily solvable by reference to the corresponding rule in the Dharmaguptaka bhikkhu *pāṭimokkha*. There, the same phrase 婬欲 appears. By universal testimony of all the Vinayas, this cannot stand for 'desire', for a word for 'desire' never occurs in the bhikkhu *pārājika* 1. It must represent the Indic *methunadhamma*, meaning 'sexual intercourse', which is found in every version of bhikkhu *pārājika* 1. This is confirmed since it is followed by characters clearly standing for *abrahmacariya*, which is a synonym of *methunadhamma*. The meaning of 婬欲 in the Dharmaguptaka bhikkhu and bhikkhuni *pārājika* 1, therefore, must be 'sexual intercourse'. Hence the bhikkhuni rule lacks anything that might correspond with the Indic *chanda*, 'desire'. We are therefore unable to definitely conclude whether this version represents a third example of a special formulation of the bhikkhuni *pārājika* 1, or whether it has simply lost some text from the bhikkhus' rule formulation.

24 The situation with the Mahīśāsaka is similarly unclear. This includes both a character meaning 'according to one's desire' (隨意), but also includes the clause about giving up the training. It seems that this version

---

[16] Sanskrit *bhikṣuṇī karmavācanā* 137.11–13 (quoted in Roth, p. 79 note § 117.6): *Yā punar bhikṣuṇī bhikṣuṇībhiḥ sārddhaṁ śikṣāsāmīcīṁ samāpannā ṣikśam apratyākhyāya śikṣādaurbalyam anāviṣkṛtyābrahmacaryam maithunaṁ dharmaṁ pratisevetāntatas tiragyonigatenāpi sārddhaṁ.*

either combines the two other versions together, or perhaps we are just witnessing an ambiguity in the Chinese.

25 Thus it seems that the Mahāvihāravāsin/Lokuttaravāda recension of this rule is not explicitly shared by any other Vinayas, although the Dharmaguptaka, and the Mahīśāsaka have some features in common. This raises the question where the formulation stems from. The Pali version is not found in the Pali Tipitaka, and derives from commentaries and from an extracanonical work found in a manuscript in Burma early in the 20th century. The consistency with which it is presented throughout the commentarial tradition makes it likely there was an older manuscript tradition of the bhikkhuni *pāṭimokkha*, but I am not aware if any actual texts exist. The Lokuttaravāda manuscript, on the other hand, takes us much further back as a physical object, since the manuscript takes us back to around the 11th century.[17]

26 The presence of this variant rule formulation alerts us to the fact there are significant correlations between schools that in terms of sectarian history are relatively separate, which may be even closer than the correlations between closely related schools. More importantly, the *pāṭimokkha* is most important as an oral text. It is recited each fortnight in the midst of the Sangha, and constitutes the key ritual ingredient that affirms the communal identity of the Sangha. Since this would have been recited regularly by the bhikkhunis, not by the bhikkhus, it seems likely that this variant, preserved so tenuously through the ages in far-flung reaches of the Buddhist world, preserves a memory of the bhikkhunis' own liturgical literature. This was passed down, it seems, outside the Councils and hence outside the control of the bhikkhus.

4.1 Can a Bhikkhuni Ordain Again?

27 The persistence of a distinctive version of bhikkhuni *pārājika* 1 is a remarkable instance of textual tenacity. It raises the question as to why the difference arose in the first place. According to the Pali tradition, the difference stems from the differing manner of disrobal in the male and female Sanghas. A bhikkhu may disrobe by means of verbally renouncing

[17] ROTH, pp. xx*ff*.

the training, while a bhikkhuni may only disrobe by physically removing the robes and leaving the monastery with the intention to be no longer a bhikkhuni.

28 To understand the situation more clearly, let us look first of all at how a bhikkhu disrobes in the Pali tradition. This is described extensively in the discussion to bhikkhu *pārājika* 1. A bhikkhu must, being of clear mind, and intending to disrobe, declare that he is disrobing clearly in the present tense to someone who understands. Different cases are discussed where these factors are either present or not. Here is a typical example. Since the bhikkhu's statement is in an optative form ('what if… ') he fails to disrobe.

29 > He says and makes known: 'What if I were to **disavow** the Buddha?' This, monks, is revealing his inability but not **disavowing the training.**[18]

30 For our purposes, the important detail is that, in the initial sentence by the monk, he either speaks (*vadati*) or makes known (*viññāpeti*, 'expresses'). *Viññāpeti* would cover forms of communication similar to speech, e.g. writing or sign language. Both of these acts are covered by the term *paccakkhāti*, which we translate as 'disavow'. The root of this verb is √*(k)khā*, to say or declare. Those familiar with Pali chanting may recognize √*(k)khā* from the standard recollection of the Dhamma: '*sva***kkhā***to bhagavatā dhammo*' ('the Dhamma is well-**proclaimed** by the Blessed One').

31 Now, while this technical discussion makes it very clear what is and is not a correct form of leaving the bhikkhu life, in non-technical passages, a bhikkhu is often said to *vibbhamati*, which we translate simply as 'disrobe'.[19] The basic meaning is to 'go astray', as for example a wandering or

[18] Pali Vinaya 3.24*ff*: '*Yannūnāhaṁ buddhaṁ* ***paccakkheyyan'ti*** *vadati viññāpeti. Evampi, bhikkhave, dubbalyāvikammañceva hoti* ***sikkhā ca apaccakkhātā****.*

[19] E.g. Pali Vinaya 3. 39, 3.40, 3.67, 3.183. Throughout the Mahākkhandhaka *vibbhamati* appears in a list for monks who are unavailable because they have left, disrobed, gone over to another sect, or died. HÜSKEN ('Rephrased Rules', p. 28 note 22) states that *vibbhamati* is used as a synonym for *nāsitā* (expelled) in the *vibhaṅga* to bhikkhuni *pārājika* 1, and hence states that one who is *vibbhantā* cannot re-ordain, whether a bhikkhu or bhikkhuni. However she herself refers to a passage (Pali Vinaya 1.97-8) with a series of cases where a bhikkhu disrobes (*vibbhamati*) and then is allowed to re-ordain. This is hardly an 'exception' as she says; the same usage is found dozens of times in the Samuccayakkhandhaka. Nowhere is it stated that a bhikkhu who is *vibbhanta* may not re-ordain. She is mistaken in saying that bhikkhuni *pārājika* 1 (i.e. *pārājika* 5 if the rules

confused mind. Since this is a non-technical term in the bhikkhu Vinaya, it is nowhere defined. Yet it is this form of disrobal, not the technically defined 'disavowal of the training' which is allowed for the bhikkhunis.

32 Now on that occasion, a certain bhikkhuni, **having disavowed the training, disrobed.** Having later approached the bhikkhunis, she asked for ordination. The Blessed One declared in regard to that matter: 'Monks, **there is no disavowal of the training** by a bhikkhuni. But when she has **disrobed**, at that moment she is not a bhikkhuni.'[20]

33 The purpose of this rule is a little obscure, but the overall sense is clear enough. A bhikkhuni is not permitted to disrobe in the normal manner used by the bhikkhus, that is, by verbally renouncing the training. Rather she is 'not a bhikkhuni' when she has 'disrobed' 'or gone astray'. This seems to refer to the physical act of actually leaving the monastic environment, literally disrobing and putting on lay clothes with the intention to be no longer a bhikkhuni. The Pali commentary affirms that putting on lay clothes is the defining act here. Similarly, the Mahāsaṅghika and Lokuttaravāda Vinayas discuss a case where a bhikkhuni puts on lay clothes as an expedient to avoid being attacked; the Buddha rules that such an act as an expedient is only a minor infringement, for the sake of safety is no offense, but if she does so intending on renouncing the training she is no longer a bhikkhuni.[21]

34 No reason is given to explain why the male and female Sanghas should disrobe in such different ways. But whatever the reason might have been, it clarifies why *pārājika* 1 does not speak of a bhikkhuni as 'disavowing the training'. However, this still does not explain why the extra word 'willingly'

---

taken in common with the bhikkhus are counted) refers to *vibbhamati*; presumably she means *pārājika* 6. The statement there is: *Nāsitā nāma sayaṁ vā vibbhantā hoti aññehi vā nāsitā.* ('Expelled' means: she is disrobed by herself or expelled by others.) This does not state that *vibbhantā* and *nāsitā* are synonyms. It simply states that the term *nāsitā* in this rule covers both cases. One is 'expelled' because the Sangha has good reason to consider a person unsuitable as a monastic. One 'disrobes' for all sorts of reasons, many of which do not imply any misconduct as a monastic.

[20] Pali Vinaya 2.279: *Tena kho pana samayena aññatarā bhikkhunī* ***sikkhaṁ paccakkhāya vibbhami.*** *Sā puna paccāgantvā bhikkhuniyo upasampada yāci. Bhagavato etamattha ārocesu. "****Na,*** *bhikkhave, bhikkhuniyā* ***sikkhāpaccakkhāna;*** *yadeva sā* ***vibbhantā*** *tadeva sā abhikkhunī"ti.*

[21] *Tyaktamuktena cittena.* Mahāsaṅghika Vinaya *Bhikṣuṇī-prakīrṇaka* 20 (T 1425 p. 547); Lokuttaravāda *Bhikṣuṇī-prakīrṇaka* 31 (ROTH p. 316 § 283).

was inserted. Perhaps this merely emphasizes that one must have a lustful mind to be guilty of this offense, given that women are more likely to be forced into sex unwillingly.

35 The Pali Vinaya commentaries, such as the Dvemātikapāḷī, confirm that the difference in disrobal methods is related to the difference in phrasing of *pārājika* 1.

36 > Since there is no disavowal of the training by bhikkhunis, the phrase 'endowed with the training and way of life, not having disavowed the training, not have declared inability' is not recited.[22]

37 In this case even a subtle difference in the rule formulation accurately reflects the inner structure of other portions of the Vinaya, which is impressive testimony to the consistency and care of the compilers. It also makes it very likely that this formulation of the rule is in fact the correct one, not the formulation that sounds more like the bhikkhus' rules. This rule has, it seems, been passed down accurately in the Mahāvihāravāsin, even though for them it is not strictly canonical.

38 There is a similar situation in the Lokuttaravāda Vinaya. As we noted in the discussion of *pārājika* 1, the form of the rule is virtually identical in both the Pali and Lokuttaravāda versions. And, just as the Pali maintains an awareness of the different modes of disrobal for bhikkhus and bhikkhunis, even in unrelated sections of the Vinaya, so, it seems, does the Lokuttaravāda. The extant text of the Lokuttaravāda bhikṣuṇī Vinaya contains the bhikkhuni Suttavibhaṅga, as well as a shorter miscellaneous section for both bhikkhus and bhikkhunis. There we find a list of three things that make one 'not a bhikkhu' or 'not a bhikkhuni'. These lists are identical, except that a bhikkhu is said to, with a mind intent on disrobal, 'disavow the training',[23] while a bhikkhuni is said to have 'fallen away from good conduct'.[24] Similar rules are found in the corresponding sections of the Mahāsaṅghika Vinaya.[25] There is, however, a striking

---

22 *Yasmā ca bhikkhuniyā sikkhāpaccakkhānaṁ nāma natthi, tasmā bhikkhunīnaṁ 'sikkhāsājīvasamāpannā sikkhaṁ apaccakkhāya dubbalyaṁ anāvikatvā'ti avatvā.* My source for this text is the online VRI Tipiṭaka. Unfortunately, this site does not supply individual URLs for each page, nor does it supply page references to the printed editions.

23 ROTH p. 321 § 290 (*Bhikṣuṇī-prakīrṇaka* 46): *Tyakta-muktena cittena śikṣāṁ pratyākhyāti.*

24 ROTH p. 321 § 290 (*Bhikṣuṇī-prakīrṇaka* 47): *Tyaktamuktena cittena ācāraṁ vikopayati.*

25 Mahāsaṅghika Vinaya *Bhikṣuṇī-prakīrṇaka* 37, 38 T22, № 1425 p. 548a, HIRAKAWA p. 411.

difference between the Lokuttaravāda and Mahāsaṅghika in that, whereas for the Lokuttaravāda this ruling is consistent with their formulation of *pārājika* 1, the Mahāsaṅghika, as we noted above, has the bhikkhus' form of *pārājika* 1, which allows that a bhikkhuni may 'disavow the training'. This is not merely an isolated slip-up, but is an important feature of the rule analysis.[26] Clearly the Mahāsaṅghika analysis of this rule is built upon the assumption that a bhikkhuni can disavow the training. The passages discussing this aspect of the rule are absent from the corresponding sections of the Lokuttaravāda text. Thus the Lokuttaravāda consistently maintains that a bhikkhuni does not 'disavow the training', while the Mahāsaṅghika *pārājika* 1 allows that she can, while the *Bhikṣuṇī-prakīrṇaka* assumes that she cannot, but disrobes by literally removing her robes.

39 There is a further rule, found in similar form in all Vinayas,[27] that should be taken into consideration. It is a *saṅghādisesa* offense for a bhikkhuni who, being angry, declares that she 'disavows' the Buddha, Dhamma, Sangha, and the training, and declares that there are other female ascetics of good behavior, who she intends to join. The term for 'disavow' is, in both the Pali and the Lokuttaravāda, the same used for the bhikkhus who 'disavow the training'. If a bhikkhu were to say in such a case 'I disavow the Buddha', then by that much alone he would be disrobed and no longer a bhikkhu. Clearly that cannot be the case for the bhikkhuni who says this. She must still belong to the Sangha, or else she could not have a disciplinary procedure performed against her. Perhaps it might be argued that for the bhikkhu to disrobe he must have a clear intention to do so, whereas for the bhikkhuni in this rule it is a mere outburst of anger. That may be true; and yet the rule is a *yāvatatiyaka*, which requires that the bhikkhuni Sangha admonish the offender up to three times in the midst of the Sangha to relinquish her statement. She must be seriously set in her intention, not just making a moment's angry outburst.

---

[26] See HIRAKAWA pp. 104–7.

[27] Mahāvihāravāsin *saṅghādisesa* 12 (Pali Vinaya 4.235–7); Dharmaguptaka *saṅghādisesa* 16 (T22, № 1428, p. 725, c6–p. 726, c8); Mahīśāsaka *saṅghādisesa* 17 (T22, № 1421, p. 82, c17); Mahāsaṅghika *saṅghādisesa* 19 (T22, № 1425, p. 523, c3–p. 524, a18); Lokuttaravāda *saṅghādisesa* 19 (ROTH p. 159–163 § 172); Sarvāstivāda *saṅghādisesa* 14 (T23, № 1435, p. 311, a3–c1); Mūlasarvāstivāda *saṅghādisesa* 13 (T23, № 1443, p. 937, a4–c5).

40 The most reasonable interpretation of this state of affairs is that this rule was laid down in a context where a bhikkhuni could not disavow the training. No matter how much she verbally abuses the Triple Gem and declares she is leaving the Sangha, as long as she does not actually 'disrobe', she remains a bhikkhuni. This, I would argue, is because the rule, as part of the *pāṭimokkha* itself, harks back to an early period in the Sangha when, as attested by the Pali and Lokuttaravāda Vinayas, a bhikkhuni could not disrobe by 'disavowing' the training. Even though many of the Vinaya traditions later forgot this nuance, it was maintained in the *pāṭimokkha* text, even though this was now inconsistent with the developed position of the school.

41 So far, so good. We have what appears to be a minor technical distinction in practice for bhikkhus and bhikkhunis, which would not seem to have a great impact on their monastic life. But the commentary to the passage that determines the correct manner of disrobal for bhikkhunis goes on to say that having disrobed, a bhikkhuni may not re-ordain.

42 > 'When she has disrobed': because she has disrobed, by her own preference and acceptance has put on white [lay] clothes, therefore she is not a bhikkhuni, not by disavowal of the training is this seen. **She does not get full ordination again.**[28]

43 This comment clearly oversteps the scope of the original text, which says nothing of re-ordination. It seems to have been influenced by the subsequent paragraph in the text, which discusses a second case, that of a bhikkhuni who leaves the bhikkhuni monastery and joins a community of another religion.

44 > Now on that occasion a certain bhikkhuni, wearing her ocher robe, went over to the fold of the non-Buddhist religionists (*tittha*). She returned and asked the bhikkhunis for ordination (*upasampadā*).[29] The Blessed One declared in regard to that matter: 'Monks, a bhikkhuni

[28] Samantapāsādikā 6.1295: *Yadeva sā vibbhantāti yasmā sā vibbhantā attano ruciyā khantiyā odātāni vatthāni nivatthā, tasmāyeva sā abhikkhunī, na sikkhāpaccakkhānenāti dasseti. Sā puna upasampadaṁ na labhati.*

[29] Note the use of *upasampadā* for bhikkhuni ordination. This is a clear marker of a late passage, not one which is part of the early bhikkhuni's own tradition. See chapter 6.

who, wearing her ocher robe, goes over to the fold of the non-Buddhist religionists, on her return is not to be ordained.'[30]

45 Here she is, it seems, still wearing her ocher robe,[31] but has changed religions. It is clearly her acts, rather than her speech, which are relevant. This rule does not apply in the case of a bhikkhuni who has disrobed first. Furthermore, this rule makes it clear exactly what type of bhikkhuni may not be re-ordained: one who has gone over to another sect. The same rule applies for the bhikkhus.[32]

46 The Pali commentary raises the stakes in this equation. Whereas the canonical text says nothing about whether one who 'disrobes' (*vibbhamati*) can re-ordain, and states that one who goes over to another religion while wearing her robe cannot take full ordination again, the commentary states that no disrobed bhikkhuni can re-ordain; one who puts on the white clothes first (in other words, one who *vibbhamatis*) may take novice ordination, but one who goes over to another religion may not even take novice ordination.[33]

47 Why were these new rulings on novice ordination imposed? Remember that the original rulings made a clear distinction between the two cases. A bhikkhuni who disrobes honorably has done no wrong and is deserving of no punishment, whereas one who has gone over to another religion has acted fraudulently and may no longer be trusted, and hence is denied the chance to ordain again. The commentary, however, also denies re-ordination to the one who has disrobed honorably, and so both these cases receive the same punishment, which hardly seems fair.[34] So in order

---

[30] Pali Vinaya 2.279: *Tena kho pana samayena aññatarā bhikkhunī sakāsāvā titthāyatanaṁ saṅkami. Sā puna paccāgantvā bhikkhuniyo upasampadaṁ yāci. Bhagavato etamatthaṁ ārocesuṁ. 'Yā sā, bhikkhave, bhikkhunī sakāsāvā titthāyatanaṁ saṅkantā, sā āgatā na upasampādetabbā'ti.*

[31] The PTS reading is *sakāsāvā* (2.279). The World Tipitaka reads *sakāvāsā*, 'from her own monastery' (http://studies.worldtipitaka.org/tipitaka/4V/10/10.3). But this seems to be a peculiarity of the Burmese tradition.

[32] Pali Vinaya 1.86: *Titthiyapakkantako, bhikkhave, anupasampanno na upasampādetabbo, upasampanno nāsetabbo.* This has nothing to do with the normal case of a bhikkhuni who disrobes.

[33] Samantapāsādikā 6.1295: *'Sā āgatā na upasampādetabbā'ti na kevalaṁ na upasampādetabbā, pabbajjampi na labhati. Odātāni gahetvā vibbhantā pana pabbajjāmattaṁ labhati.*

[34] This anomaly was noticed by VAJIRAÑĀṆAVARORASA, 3.267.

to maintain the original pattern that the one who has acted fraudulently should receive a greater penalty, the commentary invents a new ruling saying that she may not even take novice ordination again. The very artificiality of these extra rulings highlights their difference from the canonical text. In such passages, the 'commentary' is no longer commenting on the text in any meaningful way, but is adding new rulings that had presumably found their way into contemporary practice.

48 In this way the commentary creates a link between two questions which in the original text are unrelated. One concerns the manner of disrobal, the second is ordaining again. The commentarial belief that re-ordination is impossible for bhikkhunis, while of course it is allowed for bhikkhus, is commonly held today. Several of the canonical Vinayas, in fact, say that a bhikkhuni may not re-ordain. The Mahāsaṅghika,[35] and Lokuttaravāda[36] Vinayas ask the candidate prior to bhikkhuni ordination if she has ever taken full ordination before. If she has, she is told to leave, she cannot take full ordination. Vinayas of the Sarvāstivāda group offer more details. Here is the origin story as told in the Mūlasarvāstivāda Vinaya.

> 49 At that time, in the city of Sāvatthī, there lived an elder. Not long after his marriage, his wife became pregnant and gave birth to a daughter. When the child was born, the father passed away. The mother raised the child up and not long after, passed away too.
>
> 50 At that time bhikkhuni Thullanandā went on almsround and came to this dwelling place. On seeing the lady, she asked: 'Which family do you belong to?'
>
> 51 [The lady] replied: 'Venerable, I do not belong to anyone.'
>
> 52 The nun said: 'If this is so, why don't you renounce the homelife?'
>
> 53 The lady replied: 'Who can give me ordination?'
>
> 54 The nun said: 'I can, you may follow me.' In this way the lady followed the nun to her dwelling place and received ordination to become a bhikkhuni. However, being entangled by defilements, she later disrobed. When Thullanandā went for her almsround, she met this lady and asked: 'Young lady, how is your livelihood?'
>
> 55 She replied: 'Venerable, I find it difficult to survive with no one to depend on.'

---

35 T22 № 1425 p. 472, b5.

36 ROTH p. 33 § 35: *Upasampanna-pūrvāsi? anyadāpi yady āha 'upasampanna-pūrvā' ti vaktavyā: 'gaccha nasya cala prapalāhi. nāsti te upasampadā'.*

> 56 (The Nun) then asked: 'If this is so, why don't you renounce the homelife?
>
> 57 'I have already disrobed, who will give me ordination?'
>
> 58 The nun replied that she could. Without delay, the lady received ordination and followed the practice of almsbegging. An elder Brahman saw this, became suspicious and slandered, spreading his suspicion that the Sakyan ladies, on grounds of virtue sometimes ordained to tread the holy life, and sometimes stopped the holy practice to return to the defiled stains of secular life. They follow their sentiments for happiness and this is not virtuous. The bhikkhunis came to hear of this and told the bhikkhus, who then reported it to the Buddha. The Buddha thought thus:
>
> 59 'Because the disrobed bhikkhuni has committed this fault, from now onwards, disrobed bhikkhunis shall not be ordained. The elders of (other sects) find happiness in jeering and destroying my dhamma. As such, bhikkhunis, once they disrobe to return to laylife, should not be re-ordained. If they are given ordination, the *upajjhāya* and teachers commit an offence.'[37]

60 The background story locates the problem in the criticism levelled by critics of Buddhism, especially the followers of other sects. This is not hugely plausible, given that it was normal for wanderers of several sects to regularly alternate periods of ordained and lay life.[38] Nor is any particular reason given as to why the bhikkhunis should differ from the bhikkhus in this regard. Furthermore, the problem here is obviously Thullanandā's behaviour, and by any reasonable standard she would long ago have been forbidden from accepting students for ordination. The student who was encouraged to take ordination was an orphan, living in a precarious situation, who ordained seeking security rather than out of a genuine spiritual urge. She was given ordination immediately (with no apparent training period).

---

[37] T24, № 1451, p. 352, b2–20. This is not an isolated passage. The idea is also found at T24 № 1451 p. 358c1–3 (緣處同前。具壽鄔波離請世尊曰　。大德。若苾芻尼捨戒歸俗重求出家得與出家近圓不佛言鄔波離一經捨戒更不應出家); Mūlasarvāstivāda Bhikṣuṇī Karmavācanā (SCHMIDT 16b2–4: *Kaccit tvaṁ pūrvaṁ pravrajiteti? yadi kathayati 'pravrajitā', vaktavyā: 'ata eva gaccheti'*); T24 № 1453 p. 462a3–4 (汝非先出家不。若言不者善。如言‖我曾出家者。報云汝去。無尼歸俗重許出家). This section of the Mūlasarvāstivāda Vinaya, the Ekottarakarmaśataka is, according to Shayne Clarke (private communication) an anthologized work, which is quite divergent in its Chinese and Tibetan versions.

[38] See MN 89.10, MN 36.6.

In this case, surely the appropriate thing would be to test the sincerity of the applicant, not prohibit all women in the future from re-ordaining.

61 As we have come to expect, the Sarvāstivāda Vinaya offers a completely different origin story.

> 62 The Buddha was at the city of Rājagaha. At that time, the women were suffering from the treatment of the brothers-in-law and sisters-in-law. So they left home and ordained as bhikkhunis. During the time that they were living as students with their *upajjhāya* and Teachers, they were vexed by suffering. They therefore disrobed and returned to wearing the white clothes of the lay person. The lay-devotees scolded and berated saying:
>
> 63 'Those inauspicious and fraudulent women! Previously we were their masters. When they became bhikkhunis, they received our respects. Now we withdraw such respects. They are not stable.'
>
> 64 The Buddha was told, and said: 'Should a bhikkhuni give up the precepts, she is not allowed to receive the going forth and full ordination again.'[39]

65 Compared to the Mūlasarvāstivāda, the city is different, the reason for going forth is different, there is no mention of Thullanandā, and the critics are not the religious, but the lay folk. As usual, these stories record, not the history of how the rule was actually formed, but the inventions of later generations of monks. Here, too, we find no reason given why the bhikkhunis should be treated differently than the bhikkhus.

66 It is clear enough that the Vinayas of the Sarvāstivāda group prohibit a bhikkhuni from re-ordaining. In addition, it is frequently stated that the Dharmaguptaka Vinaya prohibits re-ordination of bhikkhunis,[40] but despite considerable searching and consultation, I have been unable to find any passage that confirms this. The widespread belief that the Dhar-

---

[39] T23, no 1435, p. 291, a10–16. As with the Mūlasarvāstivāda, this prohibition is echoed elsewhere in the Sarvāstivāda Vinaya (T23, № 1435, p. 377, c16). This passage allows an extraordinary exception: a bhikkhuni may reordain if she changes sex and becomes a man. A similar passage is found in the Sarvāstivāda Vinaya Mātṛkā (T23, № 1441, p. 569, a16–9) and the Kathāvastu of the Uttaragrantha of the Tibetan Mūlasarvāstivāda Vinaya (sTog 'Dul ba NA 316b4–317a1).

[40] For example, Wu Yin (p. 144) states: 'According to the Dharmaguptaka Vinaya, a woman may be ordained only once in this lifetime. Regardless of whether she has violated a *pārājika*, once a bhikshuni gives back her vows, she cannot become a bhikshuni again in this life.'

maguptaka Vinaya prohibits bhikkhunis from re-ordaining seems to stem from the remarks by the monk 懷素 (Huai Su) in his famous commentary on the Dharmaguptaka Vinaya.[41] The world of Chinese commentaries is a mystery to me, so I do not know whether this ruling may be found in any earlier texts.

67 The Ten [part] Vinaya (= Sarvāstivāda) has a similar text to the Four [part Vinaya = Dharmaguptaka]. Bhikkhu(s) who disrobe do not face obstructions. Bhikkhunis who disrobe face the fear of being stigmatised as defiled. Therefore, in the Ten [part Vinaya], (she) cannot be re-ordained. Referring to scroll 40...[42]

68 Huai Su goes on to quote the very passages from the Sarvāstivāda Vinaya that we have already reviewed. It seems clear enough from this that there was no explicit statement forbidding re-ordination in the Dharmaguptaka Vinaya, but Huai Su felt that the matter should be treated in line with the rulings of the Sarvāstivāda Vinaya. Finally we have a reason for the discrimination; and it's no surprise that the problem is women's 'defilements'. Since this reason is clearly sexist, and has no basis in the original text, it should be rejected.

69 The Mahīśāsaka Vinaya has so far yielded no passage on this point.

70 In conclusion then, the correct version of *pārājika* 1 for bhikkhunis has been maintained in the Pali tradition, despite the fact that it is not found in the canonical Vinaya itself. This is a rare case of a genuinely early text surviving outside the mainstream redaction process of the Councils. The *pāṭimokkha* is the most important ritual text for the Sangha, and to this day it is recited in full on the fortnightly uposatha day by Theravāda bhikkhus. The ancient Mahāvihāravāsin bhikkhunis would have carried out a similar custom. Thus the bhikkhuni *pāṭimokkha* would have been passed down as an oral text within the bhikkhuni lineage. While the bhikkhunis' sections of the Vinaya have suffered decay, due to the weakening and eventual disappearance of the bhikkhuni Sangha within the later Mahāvihāravāsin tradition, the *pāṭimokkha* has survived into the manuscript and commentar-

[41] Huai Su (625–698 CE) was a disciple of Xuan Zang, who specialized in the study of the Dharmaguptaka Vinaya, and was renowned for his bold challenges to the accepted understanding of Vinaya in his day. A modern retelling of his life story, 'Huai Su' by LIN Sen-shou, is at http://taipei.tzuchi.org.tw/tzquart/2005fa/qf8.htm.

[42] X42, № 735, p. 454, a7–19. This text is not found in the CBETA Taishō edition.

ial tradition, a testament to the bhikkhunis' contribution to Pali literature, and more importantly, a reminder of the vital presence within Theravāda of a female Sangha who were dedicated to learning and practicing Vinaya.

71 In the mainland Vinayas, the situation becomes complex due to the evident contamination of the bhikkhuni Vinaya by the wording of the bhikkhus' *pārājika* 1 in most of the Vinayas apart from the Lokuttaravāda, together with a generally less well understood and articulated form of the bhikkhuni Vinaya, and, we may assume, the lack of the bhikkhuni's voice in making such decisions. Since the bhikkhunis were said to not be able to 'disavow the training', when their version of *pārājika* 1 became similar to that of the bhikkhus, it came to be understood that they could not re-ordain. This process, it seems, happened broadly but not always consistently across the Buddhist schools. The Vinayas of the Sarvāstivāda group developed the most elaborate context. In the Mahāsaṅghika group the prohibition became incorporated in the ordination question. In the Vibhajjavāda schools, the prohibition against bhikkhuni re-ordination was not incorporated in the canonical Vinayas, but was adopted by the commentators. In the case of the Chinese commentator on the Dharmaguptaka Vinaya, this is explicitly said to be under the influence of the Sarvāstivāda Vinaya. We may assume that a similar influence underlies Buddhaghosa's comments here.

4.2 Nuns and Rape

72 In some countries, such as India, nuns have been raped and subsequently forced or encouraged to disrobe, being told that they have broken the basic precept for their celibate life (*pārājika* 1), and can no longer continue to live as a nun. This has caused a tremendous degree of distress and trauma, and moreover creates a climate where nuns fear to report any attacks, which can further encourage would-be rapists. But the Vinaya is not so cruel, and deals with rape in a compassionate way, allowing the nun, who is the victim not the perpetrator, to continue her spiritual path.

73 The position of the Vinayas on this point is quite straightforward, so we will simply present some relevant Vinaya passages from the Vinayas of the three main traditions: the Pali Vinaya of the Theravāda; the Dharmagup-

taka Vinaya as observed in the Chinese and related Mahāyāna traditions; and the Mūlasarvāstivāda Vinaya as observed in the Tibetan Vajrayāna tradition.

4.2.1 Mahāvihāravāsin

74 The Pali version of bhikkhuni *pārājika* 1 specifies that a bhikkhuni only falls into an offense if she acts willingly. This is confirmed by actual examples in the Pali Vinaya where a bhikkhuni is raped:

75 > Now on that occasion a certain student was infatuated with the bhikkhuni Uppalavaṇṇā. And then that student, while bhikkhuni Uppalavaṇṇā had entered the town for alms, entered her hut and sat down concealed. Bhikkhuni Uppalavaṇṇā, returning from alms-round after her meal, washed her feet, entered the hut, and sat down on the couch. And then that student grabbed bhikkhuni Uppalavaṇṇā and raped her. Uppalavaṇṇā bhikkhuni told the other bhikkhunis about this. The bhikkhunis told the bhikkhus about it. The bhikkhus told the Buddha about it. [The Buddha said:] 'There is no offense, bhikkhus, since she did not consent'.[43]

76 Similarly, there are other cases of bhikkhunis who are raped, and in no instance is any offense or blame imputed to the bhikkhuni.[44] This is entirely consistent with the application of the rule for bhikkhus, since whenever a bhikkhu had sexual intercourse or oral sex without his consent he was excused by the Buddha.[45] Indeed, there is a series of cases where bhikkhus, bhikkhunis, *sikkhamānas*, *sāmaṇeras*, and *sāmaṇerīs* are abducted by Licchavī youths and forced to have sex with each other. In each case, if there is no consent there is no offense.[46] This understanding is maintained in the Pali commentarial tradition.[47]

[43] Pali Vinaya 3.35. *Anāpatti, bhikkhave, asādiyantiyāti.*

[44] Pali Vinaya 2.278, 2.280.

[45] E.g. Pali Vinaya 3.36, 3.38, etc.

[46] Pali Vinaya 3.39.

[47] E.g. Dvemātikapāḷī: *Chande pana asati balakkārena padhaṁsitāya anāpatti.*

4.2.2 Dharmaguptaka

77 Unlike the Pali, the rule itself does not specify that the bhikkhuni is acting out of lust. However, this factor is found in the rule analysis, which specifies that a bhikkhuni must consent to penetration with sexual desire.[48] Further, she must experience pleasure at the time of entering, remaining, or leaving in order for there to be an offense.[49] This is made clear in the non-offense clause:

> 78 There is no offense if while asleep she does not know; if there is no pleasure; in all cases where there is no lustful thought.[50]

4.2.3 Mūlasarvāstivāda

79 Like the Dharmaguptaka, there is no specific mention of 'desire' in the rule formulation itself. But the rule explanation makes it clear:

> 80 If she is forced, then if she does not feel pleasure in the three times [i.e., when entering, staying, or leaving] there is no offense. The offender is to be expelled.[51]

4.2.4 Who is to blame?

81 The Vinaya attitude towards rape of a bhikkhuni is uncompromising. A man who rapes a bhikkhuni cannot ever be ordained, and if they are ordained by mistake, they must be expelled.[52] Similarly, a novice who rapes a nun must be expelled.[53] The treatment of a rapist of bhikkhunis is treated in the same way as one who commits one of the 5 *ānantarika* acts (murdering one's mother or father or an arahant, wounding a Buddha, and maliciously causing schism in the Sangha). Thus the rape of a bhikkhuni is regarded as one of the most heinous possible acts, with dreadful kammic repercussions on the offender. When Uppalavaṇṇā was raped, the commentary tells us that the earth, unable to bear the weight of that evil, split

---

[48] T22, № 1428, p. 714, b5–6: 比丘尼有婬心。捉人男根。著三處大小便道及口
[49] T22, № 1428, p. 714, b12*ff.*
[50] T22, № 1428, p. 714, c7–9: 不犯者。眠無所覺知不受樂一切無欲心
[51] T23, № 1443, p. 914, b12: 若被逼者三時不樂無犯。逼他者滅擯
[52] Pali Vinaya 1.89.
[53] Pali Vinaya 1.85.

in two and swallowed up the rapist. Never is the slightest blame attached to the victim of the rape.

82 The Vinayas are clear and unanimous: there is no offense for a nun who is raped. The blame lies with the rapist, not the victim. A nun, whose life is devoted to celibacy and non-violence, will feel shattered and deeply traumatized by rape. At that time she needs support from her friends and teachers in the holy life. As in all the Vinaya cases mentioned above, she need feel no shame or blame in talking about the rape honestly and openly with other nuns, and if need be, with monks as well. The friends and teachers of the victim need to extend the greatest possible compassion and support. They must clearly and consistently reassure the victim that she has done nothing wrong and has not in any way broken her precepts. It is important that the police are told about the rape, so they can try to prevent similar crimes in the future. The Sangha should investigate whether there is any ongoing danger to nuns in that situation, and should take steps to ensure their protection and safety. If necessary, I would suggest that the nuns should be taught self-defense skills to ward off an attacker.

Chapter 5

ORDINATION OF NUNS BY MONKS

THE REVIVAL OF THE BHIKKHUNI SANGHA hinges on the validity of ordination procedure. It is argued that a full bhikkhuni ordination requires a Sangha of bhikkhus and bhikkhunis. Since the ordination tradition has been broken, and there are no Theravādin bhikkhunis, it is impossible to restart the bhikkhuni Sangha.

2 I believe this argument is flawed on a number of levels, and in this chapter I would like to examine the assumptions in the argument as to the nature of *saṅghakamma*, and the import of the textual statements, especially regarding ordination of bhikkhunis by a Sangha of bhikkhus alone. I should emphasize that I am not trying to suggest that this is the best way to perform bhikkhuni ordination. On the contrary, I believe that the sectarian assumptions underlying the conception of 'Theravāda' as a distinct Vinaya lineage are mistaken, and that there is no objection to performing *saṅghakamma* with Dharmaguptaka bhikkhunis from the East Asian tradition, or whose ordination stems from that tradition. I am here giving a supplementary argument: that even if the dual ordination with Dharmaguptaka bhikkhunis is invalid, ordination by Theravādin bhikkhus alone is allowed by the Pali Vinaya.

3 There is a clear and explicit allowance in the Mahāvihāravāsin Vinaya for bhikkhunis to be ordained by bhikkhus only, without requiring the

presence of a community of bhikkhunis. This allowance is granted immediately after Mahāpajāpatī's ordination, when she asks the Buddha what to do about the 500 Sakyan ladies who have followed her in seeking the going forth. Here is the passage from the Bhikkhunikkhandhaka:

> 4 Then Mahāpajāpatī Gotamī approached the Blessed One. Having approached and bowed down to the Blessed One she stood to one side. Standing to one side she said this to the Blessed One: 'Bhante, how am I to practice with regard to these Sakyan women?' Then the Blessed One inspired, roused, uplifted and exhorted Mahāpajāpatī Gotamī with talk on Dhamma, and having bowed down she left keeping her right side towards him. Then the Blessed One having given a Dhamma talk addressed the bhikkhus with regard to that reason, with regard to that cause saying: **'Bhikkhus, I allow bhikkhunis to be ordained by bhikkhus'.**[1]

5 This is perfectly straightforward. There is no detail as to how the ordination was to be performed, so we are left to surmise that it was probably done in just the same way as for male candidates. The text then digresses on a number of other matters before relating the further development of bhikkhuni ordination. Various problems arose among the female ordination candidates, and the bhikkhus were required to question them before the ordination:

> 6 Now on that occasion the bhikkhus ask the bhikkhunis regarding the obstructive things. The women seeking ordination were embarrassed and ashamed and were not able to answer. The Blessed One declared regarding this matter: 'I allow, monks, [a woman] who has been ordained on one side in the bhikkhuni Sangha and is purified [regarding the obstructive things] to be ordained in the bhikkhu Sangha.'[2]

7 This is the allowance for ordination by the bhikkhunis first, then the bhikkhus. Following this are the details for bhikkhuni ordination, the various procedures and statements. From here on, it is assumed that bhikkhuni ordination is normally done on both sides. As an exception to this, we find mention of a bhikkhuni 'ordained on [only] one side':

---

1 Pali Vinaya 2.257. *Anujānāmi bhikkhave bhikkhūhi bhikkhūniyo upasampādetunti.*

2 Pali Vinaya 2.271: *Anujānāmi, bhikkhave, ekato-upasampannāya bhikkhunisaṅghe visuddhāya bhikkhusaṅghe upasampādetunti.*

8 One ordained on one side in the bhikkhuni Sangha, and pure...'[3]

9 This means she has ordination in front of only one of the Sanghas, typically before the bhikkhunis. In the detailed definition of 'bhikkhuni' in the bhikkhuni Vinaya there is, however, no mention of one ordained 'on one side'.[4] The shorter definition of a bhikkhuni in the bhikkhu Vinaya states that she is ordained on 'both sides'.[5] Nevertheless, in the next line, in discussing the offenses falling for exhorting bhikkhunis without permission of the Sangha, there is mention of bhikkhunis ordained on 'one side'.[6]

10 So the bhikkhuni accepted on one side is occasionally acknowledged, but was certainly not mainstream. In all the contexts it appears, it clearly implies she is accepted in the bhikkhuni Sangha (*ekato-upasampannā bhikkhunīsaṅghe, visuddhā...*). I do not believe there is anywhere in the Pali Vinaya, after the allowance for ordination on both sides, that speaks of a bhikkhuni ordained only by the bhikkhus. It seems that the normal process was that one would ordain in the bhikkhuni Sangha, then in the bhikkhu Sangha. Sometimes this process might be interrupted, for example if there were dangers preventing her from traveling to the bhikkhu Sangha for ordination. During this interval she would be ordained on 'one side'.

11 Nevertheless, it remains the indisputable fact that the allowance for ordination by bhikkhus alone is there. The important point is that this allowance is never rescinded. This contrasts with the situation in the bhikkhu ordination procedure. The first allowance is for the going forth and ordination by three refuges:

12 I allow, monks, the going forth and ordination by these three goings-for-refuge.[7]

13 Later this is rescinded:

14 Monks, that ordination by the three goings-for-refuge that I allowed, **from today I rescind**. I allow, monks, ordination by a formal Act with a motion and three announcements.[8]

---

[3] E.g. Pali Vinaya 2.274: *Ekato-upasampannā bhikkhunisaṅghe, visuddhā...*

[4] Pali Vinaya 4.214.

[5] Pali Vinaya 4.52: *Bhikkhuniyo nāma ubhatosaṅghe upasampannā.*

[6] Pali Vinaya 4.52: *Ekato-upasampanna ovadati, āpatti dukkaṭassa.*

[7] Pali Vinaya 1.22: *Anujānāmi, bhikkhave, imehi tīhi saraṇagamaṇehi pabbajjaṁ upasampadaṁ.*

[8] Pali Vinaya 1.56: *Yā sā, bhikkhave, mayā tīhi saraṇagamaṇehi upasampadā anuññātā,* ***taṁ ajjatagge paṭikkhipāmi.*** *Anujānāmi, bhikkhave, ñatticatutthena kammena upasampādetu.*

15 This is explicit; from this point on, it is not possible to perform full ordination by means of the three refuges. A similar clarity is found in a series of rulings in the Bhikkhunikkhandhaka, immediately after the allowance for bhikkhus to ordain bhikkhunis, and before the dual ordination is instituted. The text goes on to describe four similar cases, when the bhikkhus were to perform certain formal Acts on behalf of the bhikkhunis. First was the recitation of the *pāṭimokkha*. The Buddha allowed the bhikkhus to recite *pāṭimokkha* for the bhikkhunis. But this was criticized, so the Buddha rescinded that allowance, then stated that the bhikkhunis should recite their own *pāṭimokkha*.[9] However, the bhikkhus were allowed to teach the bhikkhunis if they did not know how. Then a similar process is described with the confession of offenses: the bhikkhus were to hear the bhikkhunis' offenses, then this was rescinded, and the bhikkhunis heard each others' offenses, but the bhikkhus were allowed to teach them how to do it if they did not know.[10] Exactly the same process occurred for the carrying out of formal acts of the Sangha (*kamma*), as well as for disciplinary issues (*adhikaraṇa*).[11] In each of these four cases, the text allows monks to do the relevant act for the bhikkhunis, then disallows this and has the bhikkhunis do it for themselves.

16 This pattern clearly mirrors the evolution of ordination procedure. Since the ordination procedure is the most fundamental to the existence of the Sangha, the first presented in the text, and presented in the most detail, it seems to me that this was probably the paradigm which the other cases followed. The accumulation of similar situations, each of which does not work, is a classic sign of the artificial nature of the texts. Surely an enlightened Buddha would have realized after making a mistake once or twice that the bhikkhunis had to do things for themselves!

17 It is reasonable to suppose that, at the beginning of the bhikkhunis Sangha, they would have needed support from the bhikkhus to perform such detailed legal procedures. But this is covered in any case by the allowance for the bhikkhus to teach the bhikkhunis when the need arose. Whether or not the bhikkhus actually did all of these things for the bhikkhu-

---

[9] Pali Vinaya 2.360.

[10] Pali Vinaya 2.259–260.

[11] Pali Vinaya 2.260–261.

nis, these passages as they stand do little except reinforce the impression that the bhikkhunis were in all things dependent on the bhikkhus.

18 In all these cases the original allowance was explicitly disallowed when the new procedure was introduced. But the situation with bhikkhuni ordination is less definitive. The allowance for ordination by bhikkhus only is clearly stated and never rescinded, but the text proceeds as if it no longer applied.

19 How one understands this becomes a matter of interpretation. One might argue that the fact that the Buddha rescinded the early allowance in a number of similar cases is a precedent meaning that the allowance should also be rescinded in this case. On the other hand, one might argue that the consistency of the statements rescinding earlier procedures suggests that the text was carefully edited, and the omission in this case must have been deliberate. For some reason, the Buddha or the redactors decided to leave this allowance, perhaps foreseeing exactly such an eventuality as we are facing today.

20 For myself, I would understand this as most likely just a slight editorial sloppiness in treating the bhikkhuni procedure, and would not wish to over-interpret. I doubt very much that those who formulated this rule, whether the Buddha or later redactors, foresaw that this little detail would become the focal point for such a critical issue, such that the future of Buddhism would rest on a textual anomaly. Bhikkhuni ordination by bhikkhus only is not the 'best practice' according to the Pali Vinaya. But it is certainly allowed.

5.1 Vinaya and variability

21 In modern Buddhism, a rigorous scrupulousness in the details of formal Acts of the Sangha, especially ordination procedure, is insisted on. And of course it is important to be careful in how this central rite of the monastic life is carried out. Yet many details of modern practice are not found in the Vinayas, and many things in the Vinayas themselves are much more flexible than modern practice.

22 A good example of this is found in the Uposathakkhandhaka, dealing with the fortnightly recitation of the *pāṭimokkha*. Normally, such recitation

requires a group of four or more monastics, and all those present in the monastery should attend.[12] But there is an extensive discussion of '50 cases of non-offense', where the *uposatha* is carried out by a group of four or more resident bhikkhus, who 'perceive' (*saññī*) that the Sangha is complete, whereas in fact there are other resident bhikkhus not in attendance:

23 > And here, monks, in a certain monastery on the *uposatha* day many resident bhikkhus gather, four or more. They do not know: 'There are other resident bhikkhus who have not come.' Perceiving [that it is in accordance with] Dhamma, perceiving [that it is in accordance with] Vinaya, perceiving that the chapter is in harmony, they perform the *uposatha*, they recite the *pāṭimokkha*. While they are reciting the *pāṭimokkha*, then other resident bhikkhus come, the same number. What is recited is well-recited, what remains should be heard. There is no offense for the reciters.[13]

24 Similar statements recur throughout this section, and are repeated in the Pavāraṇākkhandhaka.[14] Such passages imply that, even in certain cases where the detailed requirements for a *saṅghakamma* have not been formally satisfied, the validity of the act will still stand, as long as those performing the *saṅghakamma* believe they are doing it correctly.

25 This corresponds with a common legal principle, where a clause is often included in corporate constitutions to the effect that, even if the committee is elected incorrectly according to the details of the procedure, the decisions and acts made by that improperly appointed committee still stand. This kind of safeguard is a simple application of common sense. It is not meant to justify sloppiness with procedures, but to acknowledge the reality that procedures are not always followed perfectly, yet associations still need to function.

26 Now, these passages do not occur directly in the context of ordination. But the contexts where they do occur—the Uposathakkhandhaka and the Pavāraṇākkhandhaka—are the two places in the Vinaya where *saṅghakamma* is discussed in most detail. It is normally understood that general requirements for *saṅghakamma* as defined in these places are also required in other places, even where this is not spelled out in the text.

---

[12] Pali Vinaya 1.105.

[13] Pali Vinaya 1.128.

[14] Pali Vinaya 1.165

For example, the requirement for a monastic boundary (*sīmā*) is found in the Uposathakkhandhaka.[15] This chapter follows the Mahākkhandhaka, where the ordination procedure is laid down, but there is no mention of *sīmās* in the context of ordination. Yet the traditions insist very strongly that a properly defined *sīmā* is necessary for ordination, to the extent that sometimes *sīmās* are used solely for that purpose. So if the traditions generalize from the Uposatha- and Pavāraṇākkhandhakas in the case of *sīmās*, why not follow the same principle in other cases?

27 If we look at the passages that directly address the validity of ordination, we see a similar flexibility. For example, the Mahākkhandhaka contains extensive details as to who should and should not be ordained. In so doing, it maintains a clear and consistent distinction between those acts which would invalidate the ordination, resulting in the expulsion of the candidate (*nāsetabba*), and those where an offense of wrong-doing must be confessed by the *upajjhāya* (*āpatti dukkaṭassa*). The heavier rule applies, as one would expect, in the more serious cases.

28 As a partial list of such cases, an ordinand is to be expelled if they are a eunuch (Pali Vinaya 1.86) or hermaphrodite (1.89), one who 'lives in communion by theft' (i.e. a fraudulent pretender to bhikkhuhood, 1.86), one who goes over to another religion while still wearing the robes (1.86), an animal (1.88), a matricide, patricide, or arahant killer (1.88–9), a raper of bhikkhunis, a schismatic, or one who wounds the Buddha (1.89). In each of these cases the text explicitly says they 'should not be ordained. If they are ordained, they should be expelled.'

29 On the other hand, many cases are listed where an offense of wrong-doing is imposed, but there is no mention of expulsion. These include cases where there is no *upajjhāya* (1.89); the Sangha acts as *upajjhāya* (1.89); a group (of two or three bhikkhus) acts as *upajjhāya* (1.89); the *upajjhāya* belongs to any of the categories of those who cannot be ordained, such as those mentioned above (1.89–90); the candidate has no proper bowl and robes (1.90–1); or the candidate has certain medical conditions (1.91).

30 In these cases, as long as those performing the ordination do their best, and believe that everything is in accordance with Vinaya, then the act can stand, even if the procedure is not perfect in every respect. And this

[15] Pali Vinaya 1.105, etc.

is the only reasonable position. There is no bhikkhu alive who is able to prove beyond reasonable doubt that his ordination stems from an unbroken transmission reaching back to the Buddha. We have some knowledge of our own ordination, but beyond that we rely entirely on faith. There is little in Theravāda traditions to record the ordination lineages. This stands in contrast with the bhikkhuni lineages, which are attested for many hundreds of years in written records from China and Korea. But even these are incomplete, and it is simply unreasonable to insist that any ordination lineage stemming literally back to the Buddha actually survives today.

31 And it not as if the validity of Theravāda ordination is beyond doubt: the founding of the modern Thai Dhammayuttika order was precisely because it was feared that standards of Vinaya were so bad that no bhikkhus in Thailand at that time held a valid ordination. If this were true, then 95% of bhikkhus in Thailand (including myself!) would have an invalid ordination, and since most bhikkhus in Sri Lanka also derive from the Thai lineage (Siyam Nikāya), they would be in the same predicament. But the situation is even worse than this, for Vinaya experts of the Mahā Nikāya in Thailand question the validity of the ordinations upon which the Dhammayuttika order was founded, since the *upajjhāya* had less than ten vassas.

32 I don't say these things in order to induce fear in bhikkhus (a *pācittiya* offense!), but to point out how tenuous our very notions of ordination lineages are. This does not mean that things are hopeless, it just means that we have to take a reasonable, common-sense position. All we can do is to do our best. We find a good community of well-practicing bhikkhus, follow the training, and perform the ceremony as well as possible. If it somehow happened that the ordination lineage had been, unknown to us, broken long ago, what difference would it really make? Nobody insists that all bhikkhus must remain as novices forever because we cannot 'prove' that there is an unbroken lineage. Why then should we take such a stand with the bhikkhunis?

Chapter 6

VUṬṬHĀPANA & UPASAMPADĀ

BUDDHIST COMMUNITIES have always told themselves stories about how their scriptures came into being. These stories, codified early on in the canonical Vinaya accounts of the First and Second Councils, are an essential link in the development of a distinctively 'Buddhist' identity. We believe in and adhere to the Dhamma and Vinaya because we believe they were agreed upon by the 500 arahants of the First Council as the essential sum of the Buddha's teachings. But the Councils were run entirely by bhikkhus. There is no mention of the involvement of bhikkhunis, or of lay folk. This is despite the fact that the Buddha encouraged the carrying out of the unified recitation by 'each and every' person to whom he had taught the Dhamma, an embracing principle which was clearly intended to include all the four assemblies.[1] In this, he was evidently envisaging a process that centered around the Dhamma; and indeed, he said that agreement on points of Vinaya was not so important.[2]

---

[1] DN 29.17 Pāsādika: *Tasmātiha, cunda, ye vo mayā dhammā abhiññā desitā, tattha sabbeheva saṅgamma samāgamma atthena atthaṁ byañjanena byañjanaṁ saṅgāyitabbaṁ na vivaditabbaṁ, yathayidaṁ brahmacariyaṁ addhaniyaṁ assa ciraṭṭhitikaṁ, tadassa bahujanahitāya bahujanasukhāya lokānukampāya atthāya hitāya sukhāya devamanussānaṁ.* This passage immediately follows on from an extended discussion of how the Dhamma is only complete because the four assemblies—bhikkhus, bhikkhunis, laymen, laywomen—are present, learned, and skilled in the Dhamma.

[2] MN 104.5 Sāmagāma.

2 The Councils, as they are recorded in the existing Vinaya texts, were very different affairs. They were not purely Dhamma recitations, but involved disciplinary processes of Vinaya as well. This is especially true of the Second Council, which is almost entirely a record of a disciplinary procedure. The recitation of the Dhamma is not even mentioned in the Pali account, and is found only in later sources. But the Vinayas were, it seems, composed following the Second Council; and in particular the Khandhakas, with their massive narrative arc, were put together in order to authenticate the acts of the Second Council. For this reason, the First Council also takes on the cast of a Vinaya procedure, with formal statements and questioning in the manner of a *kammavācā*. The whole enterprise has no precedent or authority in the Suttas or Vinaya, and so it's no surprise that Pūrāṇa, despite his respect for the recitation, preferred to remember the teachings in his own way.[3] No doubt he was not alone.

3 Since the Councils had become a Vinaya proceeding, there was no question of the involvement of bhikkhunis or lay folk. The bhikkhus, of course, always do their disciplinary work in private. So the alternative voices are excluded from the process, which explains the small number of Sutta texts involving bhikkhunis. In this situation it is remarkable that we do preserve some extraordinary teachings from the bhikkhunis. In addition, the Pali commentaries record that one of the ancient collections, the Itivuttaka, was learned from the Buddha by a group of lay women, and later passed on to the bhikkhus.

4 The Councils were not the last word on Buddhist scriptures, however. The process of reciting and developing texts must have been going on all the time, in all places, with de-centering and innovative tendencies in constant tension with the canonizing and conservative function of the Councils. The bhikkhuni community must have had their own tradition

[3] Pali Vinaya 2.290. This event is widely recorded. The Haimavata Vinaya Mātikā (T24, № 1463, p. 819, a3–a29) and Mahīśāsaka Vinaya (T22, № 1421, p. 190, b12–c11) record the actual points of contention. They consist of 7 or 8 points regarding details of Vinaya, such as whether a monastic is allowed to pick up food, to store food indoors, etc. These allowances, it seems, were made in a time of famine. Pūrāṇa learnt them, then travelled to distant areas. While Pūrāṇa was away in the south, according to Kassapa, the Buddha rescinded the special famine allowance. The scenario is very realistic. Such problems must have been happening all the time, and show how the Vinayas would have evolved in their different directions.

of oral texts. Who knows what they may have remembered and passed down?—perhaps an array of teachings by the Buddha intended just for the nuns. Much is lost, and much will never be recovered. But I believe that in the bhikkhuni Vinaya we can recover a few words that are distinctive of the bhikkhunis; words which hint at a different picture of early Buddhist ordination than the accepted version passed down by the bhikkhus.

5 If we are to investigate possible traces of a distinctive bhikkhuni voice in the existing texts, we should start with the bhikkhuni *pāṭimokkha*. This would have been recited among the bhikkhunis each fortnight, with no bhikkhus present. It is an outsider's text, compiled and passed down among the bhikkhunis, and insulated to some degree from the mainstream redaction process of the bhikkhus. To this day, the bhikkhuni *pāṭimokkha* is not found in the canonical Pali Vinaya. And yet, as we have seen in our discussion of *pārājika* 1, the tradition has, it seems, maintained a genuine old memory of distinctive forms for the bhikkhunis.

6.1 Vuṭṭhāpana, Pavattinī, Sahajīvinī

6 There is a set of distinctive terms in the Mahāvihāravāsin bhikkhuni *pāṭimokkha*, which are quite different in form, though similar in meaning, to the corresponding terms found in the bhikkhus' Vinaya.

7 Von Hinüber has noted that two of these terms, *vuṭṭhāpana*[4] and *pavattinī* are used in a similar sense in Jain Vinaya texts, except there they are used of both male and female monastics. Similarly, the Jain texts mention a preliminary 'training' period that recalls the women's *sikkhamānā* training before full ordination.[5] Von Hinüber makes the obvious inference that there may be some connection. However, he follows this useful suggestion with the curious argument that Mahāpajāpatī and the Sakyan ladies who shave their hair and don the ocher robes after being first refused ordination by the Buddha 'look like' a group of non-Buddhist ascetics, and suggests that this was the occasion for the introduction of the Jain Vinaya terminol-

[4] Also see MONIER-WILLIAMS: *upasthāpana*... the act of ordaining (a monk), Jain...

[5] VON HINÜBER, pp. 17-19.

ogy.[6] This argument is unpersuasive,[7] but in any case there are far better candidates to introduce Jain Vinaya into the bhikkhuni Sangha. Prime candidates would include Bhaddā Kuṇḍalakesā, who was called 'Curly-haired': when she ordained as a Jain nun, they pulled her hair out by the roots, and when it grew back it came in curls. She was ordained by the Buddha in Rājagaha using the 'Come, bhikkhuni!' formula, the same method used to give bhikkhu ordination to the early *jaṭila* and *samaṇa* converts. Or else Mahākassapa's former wife, Bhaddā Kapilānī who, according to the commentary, stayed at a non-Buddhist nunnery since she went forth before the bhikkhuni order was established. No doubt there were many more.

8 The cross-over of Vinaya terminology was, of course, the norm rather than the exception, and is by no means confined to the bhikkhunis, for much of the bhikkhus' terminology is also shared with the Jains. We cannot know whether the Buddhists borrowed from the Jains, or the Jains from the Buddhists, or if they both simply used the vocabulary common to the time. Nevertheless, no matter how or where the influence manifested, the fact remains that the connection is there. And as Von Hinüber rightly argues, the idea that specific strands of non-Buddhist monastic terms or ideas were influential in the bhikkhuni Sangha, but not the bhikkhu Sangha, offers a plausible explanation for why these aspects of the bhikkhuni Vinaya are poorly integrated with the bhikkhu Vinaya.

9 The most important and linguistically interesting of these terms is *vuṭṭhāpana*, which is used in the sense of 'ordination'.[8] In non-technical

[6] VON HINÜBER, p. 20.

[7] It has been criticized by ANĀLAYO, 'Theories on the Foundation of the Nuns' Order'. Notice that when Anulā and the '1000' royal women (twice the number of Mahāpajāpatī's followers) wait for the arrival of Saṅghamittā, they, like Mahāpajāpatī and her royal women, don the ocher robes without a formal ordination (chapter 7.71–74).

[8] *Vuṭṭhāpana* usually appears in its verbal form, *vuṭṭhāpeti*. From an initial impression from the Pali, it would seem that the term is based on *vy-ud-√sthā*. However it is, rather, a dialectical variant stemming from *upa-√sthā*. It appears in this form in both Hybrid Sanskrit Lokuttaravāda and Sanskrit Mūlasarvāstivāda. The Pali form is the same as the term to 'rehabilitate' from an offence. But the Lokuttaravāda differentiates these two, having *vyutthāpayitum* in this meaning (ROTH p. 235 § 207; note also the double-causative form *vyutthāpāyayitum*). The Pali usually has the causative form (*vuṭṭhāpana* as a noun, or *vuṭṭhāpeti* as a verb). However in certain contexts the non-causative form *vuṭṭhāna* is found. This occurs specifically when the candidate for ordination requests the 'agreement for ordination' (*vuṭṭhāna-sammuti*, Pali *pācittiya* 64 at 4.320–321; *pācittiya*

contexts, *vuṭṭhāpana* is used of the 'setting up' or 'establishing' of a person in a particular post, such as the official town courtesan of Rājagaha.[9]

10 For our purposes, however, the important thing is not the derivation or grammar of *vuṭṭhāpana*, but its pattern of usage in conjunction with other special terms used by bhikkhunis. Here is a table with the relevant words and their meanings.

Table 6.1: Special terms in the bhikkhuni pāṭimokkha

Bhikkhu Vinaya		Bhikkhuni Vinaya	
upasampadā	Acceptance, entrance, full ordination.	*vuṭṭhāpana*	Establishment
upajjhāya	Lit. 'close reciter', i.e. mentor.	*pavattinī*	Lit. 'leader'.
saddhivihārika	Lit. 'one who dwells together', i.e. the student of an *upajjhāya.*	*sahajīvinī*	Lit. 'one who lives together, i.e. the student of a *pavattinī*

11 Each of these is an essential and well-established concept with a precisely defined meaning in Vinaya. To find three such terms so different in the bhikkhu and bhikkhuni Vinayas is extraordinary. The significance of this is not the meaning of the words as such, but the implications of their distribution in the Vinaya.

12 In the Mahāvihāravāsin texts, *vuṭṭhāpana* is found in the *pāṭimokkha* rules. Unlike the bhikkhus, the bhikkhunis have many rules dealing with

67 at 323–324). In other cases the phrase is used in reference to the bhikkhuni who confers the ordination, where the causative is used (*vuṭṭhāpana-sammuti* e.g. *pācittiya* 75 at 4.330). The difference is meaningful, since the bhikkhuni is the one who performs the ordination, so it is appropriate that a causative form be used to express her agency. I.B. Horner has captured the nuance by rendering *vuṭṭhāna-sammuti* as 'agreement as to ordination' (*Book of the Discipline* 3.368) and *vuṭṭhāpana-sammuti* as 'the agreement to ordain'. (*Book of the Discipline* 3.385, footnote 1 says: '*vuṭṭhāpana-sammuti*, to cause ordination (in another).') This nuance is not maintained in the Lokuttaravāda Hybrid Sanskrit tradition, which uses the causative form throughout (e.g. ROTH p. 29 § 29 *upasthāpanā-sammutin*). This is the same situation where the Pali uses the non-causative form, i.e. in reference to the candidate. When the bhikkhuni asks for agreement to give the ordination, the same form is used (ROTH p. 236 § 208). But the Mūlasarvāstivāda phrase *brahmacāryopasthāna* uses the non-causative form.

9 Various uses discussed in SHIH, chapter 5.5.1.1.

ordination actually in the *pāṭimokkha* itself.[10] In these rules, we always find *vuṭṭhāpana*, and never *upasampadā*. Similarly, *pavattinī* and *sahajīvinī* are always found in the bhikkhuni *pāṭimokkha*, and never their normal bhikkhu equivalents.

13 When we look in the *vibhaṅga* material that surrounds the *pāṭimokkha* rules in the canonical Vinayas, we find that the bhikkhus needed to insert their own explanations of these special terms. So in the word analyses, the distinctive bhikkhuni terms are explained by their corresponding bhikkhus' terms. Thus '*vuṭṭhāpana* means *upasampadā*';[11] '*pavattinī* means *upajjhā*';[12] and '*sahajīvinī* means *saddhivihārinī*'.[13] Here we can clearly discern the hands of the bhikkhu redactors at work. They had an oral text of the bhikkhuni *pāṭimokkha* which used unfamiliar terms for basic Vinaya concepts. So in composing their word-glosses, they substituted their own well-understood terminology for the obscure terms current among the bhikkhunis. There is nothing unusual in this, for the purpose of the word analyses is precisely to clear up the meaning of obscure terms.

14 In the background stories to these rules, the situation is more complex. In the majority of rules concerning ordination, the origin story is a mere back-formation from the rule. In such cases, the wording found in the background story derives directly from the rule, and merely adjusts the

---

[10] There is only one reference to ordination in the bhikkhu *pāṭimokkha*, which is in Pali *pācittiya* 65. Also, *anupasampanna* is used in the sense of 'one not fully ordained' in *pācittiyas* 4, 5, 8, and 9. The various Sanskrit *prātimokṣas* use the word the same way. The *kammavācās* also use *upasampadā*. A Sanskrit example is available at http://www.uwest.edu/sanskritcanon/Sastra/Roman/sastra68.html.

[11] Pali Vinaya 4.317: *Vuṭṭhāpeyyā'ti upasampādeyya*. SHIH (chapter 5.5.1.2) overlooks this when she argues that *vuṭṭhāpana* refers to the preliminary procedure by the bhikkhunis, while *upasampadā* is the second procedure performed by the bhikkhus, following which the candidate is 'really' ordained. The text clearly takes them as equivalent. Moreover, one ordained in front of bhikkhunis alone is always said to be *ekato-upasampannā*. SHIH goes on to argue, with admitted caution, that *vuṭṭhāpana* in *saṅghādisesa* 2, which prohibts giving *vuṭṭhāpana* to a woman thief without permission, originally implied 'raising someone out of an offence', and this was then developed into the meaning of 'ordination' in the *pācittiya* rules. However, her analysis of *vuṭṭhāpana* in *saṅghādisesa* 2 depends on the assumption that this usage is earlier, because it remains closer to a non-technical meaning of *vuṭṭhāpana*. However, the basic meaning of the term 'to raise up' would seem to apply perfectly well in the context of ordination.

[12] Pali Vinaya 4.326: *Pavattinī nāma upajjhā vuccati*. Note the feminine form *upajjhā*.

[13] Pali Vinaya 4.325: *Sahajīvinī nāma saddhivihārinī vuccati.*

case, syntax, etc., as appropriate, while preserving the bhikkhunis' special vocabulary unchanged. However, when the background story adds extra material that is not derived directly from the wording of the rule, the standard bhikkhus' terminology replaces the special bhikkhunis' terms.

15 An example of this pattern is found in *pācittiyas* 77 and 78. The first sentence of the background story, which does not correspond to anything in the rule itself, uses *upasampadā*, while the following sentences, which are directly derived from the rule, use *vuṭṭhāpana*. To make this point clear, here is the text from *pācittiya* 77, omitting the standard repetitions.

> 16 On that occasion a certain *sikkhamānā* approached Thullanandā bhikkhuni and asked for ordination (***upasampadā***). Thullanandā bhikkhuni, having said to that *sikkhamānā:* 'If, lady, you give me a robe then I will ordain you (***vuṭṭhāpana***)', neither ordained (***vuṭṭhāpana***) nor made efforts to have ordination (***vuṭṭhāpana***) given [by others].
>
> 17 Then that *sikkhamānā* told that matter to the bhikkhunis...
>
> 18 'And thus, bhikkhus, this training rule should be recited by the bhikkhunis:
>
> 19 'Should a bhikkhuni, having said to a *sikkhamānā*, "If, lady, you give me a robe then I will give you the ordination (***vuṭṭhāpana***)", afterwards, if she has no obstacle, she neither ordains (***vuṭṭhāpana***) nor makes efforts to have ordination (***vuṭṭhāpana***) given [by others], she incurs a *pācittiya*.'[14]

20 The first sentence sets the bare minimum of background for the story, with Thullanandā unimaginatively cast as the 'bad nun'. This is entirely artificial and the incongruities are, as usual, ignored: there is no way that the Sangha would have agreed to appoint Thullanandā as a mentor for a *sikkhamānā*. But even in this elementary elaboration, the text reverts to the bhikkhus' terminology: *vuṭṭhāpana* disappears, and *upasampadā* takes over. From the next sentence, whose wording is taken straight from the rule, *vuṭṭhāpana* returns.

---

[14] Pali Vinaya 4.332: *Tena kho pana samayena aññatarā sikkhamānā thullanandaṁ bhikkhuniṁ upasaṅkamitvā* ***upasampadaṁ*** *yāci. Thullanandā bhikkhunī taṁ sikkhamānaṁ—'sace me tvaṁ, ayye, cīvaraṁ dassasi evāhaṁ taṁ* ***vuṭṭhāpessāmī'ti*** *vatvā, neva* ***vuṭṭhāpeti*** *na* ***vuṭṭhāpanāya*** *ussukkaṁ karoti. Atha kho sā sikkhamānā bhikkhunīnaṁ etamatthaṁ ārocesi... 'Evañca pana, bhikkhave, bhikkhuniyo imaṁ sikkhāpadaṁ uddisantu—'Yā pana bhikkhunī sikkhamānaṁ—'sace me tvaṁ, ayye, cīvaraṁ dassasi, evāhaṁ taṁ* ***vuṭṭhāpessāmī"ti*** *vatvā, sā pacchā anantarāyikinī neva* ***vuṭṭhāpeyya*** *na* ***vuṭṭhāpanāya*** *ussukkaṁ kareyya, pācittiyan'ti.*

21 A similar pattern is found throughout the Mahāvihāravāsin Vinaya Suttavibhaṅga. In *saṅghādisesa* 2, *vuṭṭhāpana* is used in the rule, but the background story, which is highly developed, always uses *pabbajjā*, a term familiar from the bhikkhu Vinaya, and which here means full ordination (*upasampadā*).[15] Similarly, *pācittiyas* 68[16] and 70[17] use *sahajīvinī* in the rule, and the same is found in the background story derived from the rule. But *pācittiya* 74 does not use *sahajīvinī* in the rule, and the student in the background story is called *saddhivihārinī*.[18] Likewise, *pācittiya* 69[19] uses *pavattinī* in both rule and the background story derived from the rule, while *saṅghādisesa* 2, which does not mention the *pavattinī* in the rule, refers to the mentor in the word analysis as *upajjhā*.[20]

22 In all of these cases, then, the earlier portion of the text, that which is plausibly attributed to the oral tradition of the bhikkhunis themselves, uses their own distinctive terminology, while the later material uses the bhikkhus' vocabulary. The vocabulary was preserved unchanged, even when it meant using two words for the same thing in adjacent sentences.

23 So much for the *pāṭimokkha* and its *vibhaṅga*. What of the Bhikkhunikkhandhaka, where the ordination procedure is given in detail? The Bhikkhunikkhandhaka starts with the story of Mahāpajāpatī approaching the Buddha to ask for ordination. The word she uses is *pabbajjā*, which here just means 'ordination', not specifically novice ordination.[21] This is maintained through the discussion between Mahāpajāpatī and the Buddha, and the subsequent discussion with Ānanda. But when the Buddha is said to declare to Ānanda that acceptance of the eight *garudhammas* will constitute Mahāpajāpatī's ordination, he abruptly shifts to *upasampadā*.[22] *Upasampadā* is then used in the *garudhammas* themselves, specifically *garudhammas* 1, requiring

---

[15] Pali Vinaya 4.226. In later usage *pabbajjā* means novice ordination, but in the early texts this distinction is not consistent, and *pabbajjā* usually means the same as *upasampadā*.

[16] Pali Vinaya 4.324.

[17] Pali Vinaya 4.326.

[18] Pali Vinaya 4.329.

[19] Pali Vinaya 4.325.

[20] The gloss for *saṅghādisesa* 2 (4.227) does not comment on *vuṭṭhāpana*, but mentions the *upajjhā*; neither *upajjhā* or *pavattinī* appear in the rule.

[21] Pali Vinaya 2.253.

[22] Pali Vinaya 2.255: *Sace, Ānanda, mahāpajāpati gotamī aṭṭha garudhamme paṭigganhāti, sāvassā hotu upasampadā.*

that all bhikkhunis bow to all bhikkhus, 'even one ordained (*upasampadā*) that very day', and 6, which institutes the *sikkhamānā* training and the dual ordination. We have already discussed the *garudhammas* in detail, and have noted that their main purpose is to co-ordinate the bhikkhuni with the bhikkhu Sangha. Hence, the *garudhammas* are full of technical terms taken from the developed form of the bhikkhu Vinaya.[23]

24 The most important case here is *garudhamma* 6.

> 25 A *sikkhamānā* who has trained for two years in six rules should seek full ordination (***upasampadā***) in the dual Sangha... [24]

26 We shall discuss the exact interpretation of this rule in the next chapter. For now, it is sufficient to notice the use of *upasampadā*, which is said to be ordination 'in the dual Sangha', which of course refers to the ordination procedure for bhikkhunis found in all existing Vinayas, where the candidate receives ordination first from the bhikkhunis and then from the bhikkhus. This *garudhamma* is, however, closely related to *pācittiya* 63:

> 27 If any bhikkhunī should ordain (***vuṭṭhāpana***) a *sikkhamānā* who has not trained for two years in the six rules, there is an offense entailing expiation.[25]

28 Notice the important differences between these two rules. *Pācittiya* 63 refers to ordination with the term *vuṭṭhāpana*, while *garudhamma* 6 speaks of '*upasampadā* in the dual Sangha'. Thus, following the pattern we have described, the earlier term for ordination, found within the bhikkhunis' own oral literature, uses *vuṭṭhāpana*; this has been lifted out of that context, and placed in a context heavily dominated by the bhikkhus' technical vocabulary, and so the bhikkhus' term for ordination has been inserted.

29 But something else has appeared: the ordination 'in the dual Sangha'. This is yet another area where we are so heavily conditioned by the expectations of the traditional understanding that it is all but impossible to shake clear of it and read the texts on their own terms. For nowhere in the bhikkhuni *pāṭimokkha* do we find any mention of the dual Sangha

---

[23] E.g. *vassa, uposatha, pavāraṇā, mānattā.*

[24] Pali Vinaya 2.255: *Dve vassāni chasu dhammesu sikkhitasikkhāya sikkhamānāya ubhato saṅghe* ***upasampadā*** *pariyesitabbā...*

[25] Pali Vinaya 4.319: *Yā pana bhikkhunī dve vassāni chasu dhammesu asikkhitasikkhaṁ sikkhamānaṁ* ***vuṭṭhāpeyya*** *pācittiyan'ti.*

ordination, or any suggestion of the involvement of the bhikkhus at all. On the contrary, it is constantly said to be the bhikkhunis who give the ordination. This situation is maintained throughout most of the *vibhaṅgas*, too. With certain exceptions, such as the formal definition of a bhikkhuni, the notion that bhikkhus are involved in the ordination for bhikkhunis does not occur in the Suttavibhaṅga.[26]

30 If we consider the historical relationship between these two formulations of the rule regarding the *sikkhamānā*, it is apparent that the *pācittiya* 63 version must be the older and more authentic. This is generally true, of course, of all the *pāṭimokkha* rules: they underlie the entire Vinaya and must have pre-existed the Vinayas as they stand. In this case we also have a more specific reason for taking *pācittiya* 63 as older than *garudhamma* 6. For this rule, like many of the *garudhammas*, implies the existence of a developed bhikkhuni Sangha and an evolved form of the bhikkhuni Vinaya at a time when these simply did not exist. In fact, our text goes on to contradict itself: having established the dual Sangha ordination for bhikkhunis, it then raises the question of what to do with Mahāpajāpatī's companions, who also seek ordination. The Buddha is said to allow them to receive ordination from the bhikkhus. Much later, for different reasons, the allowance for the dual ordination is given. Thus the dual ordination is laid down twice, for different reasons, in one chapter. This internal incoherence shows beyond reasonable doubt that *garudhamma* 6 could not have been laid down at the start of the bhikkhuni Sangha, as depicted in the text, and must be a later addition. Hence it has almost certainly been adapted from the bhikkhuni *pāṭimokkha*, along with several other *garudhammas* which are also found in the *pāṭimokkha*, and the terminology and procedure 'updated' to conform with the practice of a later time.

31 Returning to our discussion of the use of terms for ordination within the Bhikkhunikkhandhaka, following the laying down of the *garudhammas* the text reverts to *pabbajjā* in Mahāpajāpatī's response to the Buddha's allowance and the Buddha's subsequent declaration of the dire consequences of bhikkhuni ordination.

32 Next, Mahāpajāpatī asks the Buddha what to do about the Sakyan ladies who have followed her. The Buddha allows them to be ordained by bhikkhus,

[26] For a possible exception to this, see the discussion of 'delayed consent' in chapter 8.66–85.

using the term *upasampadā*.[27] The statement here is purely formal; there is no discussion of how the bhikkhus were to perform the ordination. The Sakyan ladies then claim that Mahāpajāpatī is not properly ordained, and the Buddha declares that undertaking the eight *garudhammas* was her ordination (*upasampadā*).

33 The next section of the Bhikkhunikkhandhaka deals with other matters, and we return to the question of ordination in the third 'recitation section', where problems were said to arise due to women ordaining with various diseases. This is the start of the formation of the bhikkhuni ordination procedure as it is understood today. Throughout this section, ordination is referred to as *upasampadā*. Occasionally we find *pabbajjā*,[28] but never *vuṭṭhāpana*.

34 The ordination procedure also gives a few more clues as to the usage of the specific bhikkhuni Vinaya terminology. We cannot learn anything about the term *sahajīvinī*, for, like the corresponding masculine term *saddhivihārika*, it does not appear in the ordination procedure. However, the term for the ordination mentor, *pavattinī*, occurs no less than thirty times. In the list of questions which the candidate must answer before the ordination, the bhikkhuni candidate is asked for the name of her *pavattinī*,[29] just as the bhikkhus are asked for the name of their *upajjhāya*.[30] Similarly, in the formal statement of the ordination procedure, the candidate is said to have a *pavattinī* of such and such a name.[31] Both of these passages are fundamental parts of the oral text of the ordination procedure, and would have been regularly used within the bhikkhunis' own communities.

35 However, when we depart from the actual oral text of the bhikkhunis and look into the background material that describes the ordination procedure, we find the word *upajjhā*. Before the candidate is instructed regarding

---

[27] Pali Vinaya 2.257.

[28] In two cases: that of Aḍḍhakāsī, who had 'gone forth' (*pabbajitā*) and was seeking full ordination (*upasampadā*). An allowance is made for ordination 'by messenger' if the road is too dangerous to travel from the bhikkhunis to the bhikkus. (Pali Vinaya 227–8). Here *pabbajjā* evidently means the *sāmaṇerī* ordination, or perhaps the *sikkhamānā*, although there is no mention of her being a *sikkhamānā*. A little later (Pali Vinaya 2.278) *pabbajjā* is used to refer to a bhikkhuni.

[29] Pali Vinaya 2.271*ff*: *Kānāmā te* ***pavattinī****?*

[30] Pali Vinaya 1.94.

[31] *Itthannāmā saṁghaṁ upasampadaṁ yācati itthannāmāya ayyāya* ***pavattiniyā****...*

the obstacles, she is led into the Sangha, where the *upajjhā* first takes up the bowl and robes, then describes each of them for the candidate and asks her to go to one side for instruction.[32] This section has been simply copy-&-pasted from the bhikkhus' ordination procedure, adding the extra two robes for bhikkhunis.[33]

36 A similar situation recurs elsewhere in the Khandhakas, where texts dealing with the female Sangha have been copied from the bhikkhus' texts. For example, the Vassūpanāyikakkhandhaka deals with various cases when a bhikkhu may have an excuse for leaving the monastery during the rains retreat. One of these cases is if there is a *sikkhamānā* who wishes to take *upasampadā*.[34] Since the bhikkhus must go for this, it is obviously a dual ordination. Curiously, a similar procedure is laid down in the case of a *sāmaṇerī* who wishes to take *sikkhamānā* precepts during the rains retreat. She may send a messenger to the bhikkhus, who should strive to assist 'even if not sent for, still more if sent for'.[35] Similar statements are found in the Sarvāstivāda,[36] Mūlasarvāstivāda,[37] and Dharmaguptaka.[38] Yet the procedures for *sikkhamānā* ordination as described in the Vinayas do not mention the involvement of bhikkhus at all. Clearly, then, we are seeing different takes on the *sikkhamānā* ordination preserved within the same Vinaya. This could have a number of explanations. Perhaps it is just a textual oversight. Perhaps the description of *sikkhamānā* ordination in the Pali has suffered loss, and really should involve the bhikkhus. Or perhaps

[32] Pali Vinaya 2.272: *Paṭhamaṁ* ***upajjhaṁ*** *gāhāpetabbā.* ***Upajjhaṁ*** *gāhāpetvā pattacīvaraṁ ācikkhitabbaṁ: 'Ayaṁ te patto, ayaṁ saṅghāṭi, ayaṁ uttarāsaṅgo, ayaṁ antaravāsako, idaṁ saṅkaccikaṁ, ayaṁ udakasāṭikā; gaccha amumhi okāse tiṭṭhāhī'ti.*

[33] Pali Vinaya 1.94.

[34] Pali Vinaya 1.146: *Idha pana, bhikkhave, sikkhamānā upasampajjitukāmā hoti. Sā ce bhikkhūnaṁ santike dūtaṁ pahiṇeyya...*

[35] Pali Vinaya 1.147: *Idha pana, bhikkhave, sāmaṇerī sikkhaṁ samādiyitukāmā hoti. Sā ce bhikkhūnaṁ santike dūtaṁ pahiṇeyya.* The passage does not explicitly refer to the *sikkhamānā*, but merely to a *sāmaṇerī* who wishes to 'undertake the training'. But the exact idiom 'undertake the training' is used a little previously to refer to a *sikkhamānā*. (*Sā ce bhikkhūnaṁ santike dūtaṁ pahiṇeyya: 'Sikkhā me kupitā, āgacchantu ayyā, icchāmi ayyānaṁ āgatan'ti, gantabbaṁ, bhikkhave, sattāhakaraṇīyena, appahitepi, pageva pahite—'sikkhāsamādānaṁ ussukkaṁ karissāmī'ti..*) There is little doubt this is how the text should be read here.

[36] T23, № 1435, p. 175, a13–16.

[37] T23, № 1445, p. 1043, b10–12.

[38] T22, № 1428, p. 833, a17–21. For translations, see 'In the Vassa Chapter'. https://sites.google.com/site/sikkhamana/inthevassachapter

we are witnessing a parallel to the same process I have described for the bhikkhunis: the ordination was originally to be done by the bhikkhunis alone, and this situation is preserved in the earlier oral texts of the bhikkhunis themselves. The later texts compiled by the bhikkhus require that the bhikkhus play a part in the ordination.

37 The usage for *pavattinī* and *upajjhā* in the Bhikkhunikkhandhaka, then, follows the pattern we have seen in the *Suttavibhaṅga*. In the oral parts of the text, those used regularly by the bhikkhunis in their internal procedures, *pavattinī* occurs, while in those sections that are not part of the regular recitation, and which appear to have been influenced by the bhikkhus, we find *upajjhā*. In each case, it is clearly the bhikkhunis' own oral text that has the claim to historical priority.

38 But the situation with *vuṭṭhāpana* and *upasampadā* is different. The Bhikkhunikkhandhaka has entirely abandoned *vuṭṭhāpana*, and only uses *upasampadā*. Why is this so? It seems to me that we should look to the overriding agenda of the Bhikkhunikkhandhaka, which begins with the story of Mahāpajāpatī's ordination. That story, and the eight *garudhammas* that were the legal issue of the event, are clearly intended to subsume the bhikkhunis within the legal structure of the bhikkhus' Vinaya. I have argued earlier that this agenda has been overstated in most modern studies, and falls far short of a charter for dominance and control of nuns by monks.[39] Nevertheless, there is no doubt that the pattern of the *garudhammas* sets the bhikkhunis, in their relation to Vinaya, at an inferior level to the monks, and in some cases subject to their decisions. Nowhere is this more potent than the dual ordination. While the bhikkhus may ordain among themselves, and the bhikkhunis need not be involved at all, the bhikkhunis can only complete an ordination with the goodwill and assistance of the bhikkhus. The institution of the dual ordination constitutes a major point of control by the bhikkhus over the bhikkhunis.[40] Perhaps the Mahāvihāravāsin Vinaya preserves, in its intriguingly precise pattern of

[39] Chapter 2.114–122.

[40] A similar strategy is used in Thailand, where the legally constituted Sangha Act centralizes ordination under Bangkok control, so that no monk may act as an *upajjhāya* without permission of the central authorities. This centralizing movement caused considerable controversy and rebellion when it was first introduced, but by now is considered normal, although it has no precedent in Vinaya.

distinct ordination vocabularies for bhikkhus and bhikkhunis, a trace of a time when the bhikkhunis performed ordination by themselves, without the involvement of the bhikkhus.

39 This thesis should be tested against the other bhikkhuni Vinaya that we have in complete Indic form, the Lokuttaravāda. In the Lokuttaravāda *saṅghādisesa* 7, parallel to Mahāvihāravāsin *saṅghādisesa* 2, where the Pali uses *vuṭṭhāpana* the Lokuttaravāda uses its Hybrid Sanskrit form *upasthāpana*. As the Pali *vibhaṅga* says that '*vuṭṭhāpana* means *upasampadā*', the Lokuttaravāda says that '*upasthāpana* means *upasampadā*'.[41] And as the Pali background story uses the better known terms *pabbajjā* and *upasampadā* in the background stories, except in phrases that are directly derived from the rule, so too the Lokuttaravāda background story uses *pravrajitā* and *upasampaditā* except where it directly derives from the rule, when it reverts to *upasthāpana*.[42]

40 Similarly in *pācittiyas* 92,[43] 93,[44] and 94[45] the text uses *upasthāpana* in both rules and background stories derived from the rule. In *pācittiya* 95, the background story is developed independently, and where the phrasing does not mirror the rule, ordination is *pravrajitā* and *upasampaditā*, whereas when the phrasing copies from the rule, *upasthāpana* returns.[46] *Pācittiya* 96 departs from this pattern a little, as the first line of the background story, which is similar to the phrasing of the rule, uses *upasampadā*, and later when it recurs *upasthāpana* is used.[47] The standard pattern returns in *pācittiya* 97,[48] 98,[49] and 99.[50]

41 The only substantive difference as compared with the Pali is that *vuṭṭhāpana* does appear in the text where the ordination procedure is given in full. This is comparable to the Bhikkhunikkhandhaka of the Pali; but in the

---

[41] *Upasthāpayed iti upasampādayet*. This is stock, and occurs at Lokuttaravāda *saṅghādisesa* 7 (ROTH p. 137 § 159); *pācittiya* 94 (ROTH p. 26 § 208), *pācittiya* 96 (ROTH p. 239 § 210), etc.

[42] ROTH pp. 135–6 § 158.

[43] ROTH pp. 232–3 § 206.

[44] ROTH pp. 234–5 § 207.

[45] ROTH pp. 235–6 § 94.

[46] ROTH p. 237 § 209.

[47] ROTH p. 238 § 210.

[48] ROTH pp. 240–2 § 211.

[49] ROTH pp. 242–3 § 212.

[50] ROTH pp. 243–4 § 213.

Lokuttaravāda it is given at the start of the Bhikkhuni Vinaya, as part of the explanation of *garudhamma* 2. This text, like the Pali, does indeed use *upasampadā* mostly during this section. However there is a preliminary passage where the 'agreement to ordain' (*vuṭṭhāpana-sammuti*) is asked from the Sangha. This precedes the *upasampadā*. The key to distinguishing this extra 'motion & three announcements' from the ordination as such is that it occurs before the preceptor is appointed and the candidate is taken outside the Sangha for the instruction in private.

42 The same procedure occurs in the very closely related Mahāsaṅghika Vinaya. There, after completion of the *sikkhamānā* training, the preceptor requests the 'karma of taking on a disciple'.[51] Here the term for 'disciple' (弟子) appears to stand for *upasthāpita*. However, there is nothing in the Chinese word itself that would allow us to make this connection, since 弟子 is neither phonetically nor etymologically linked with *vuṭṭhāpana*; only the context permits the connection.

43 I have attempted to discern whether the patterns of usage evident in the Indic texts are evident in the Chinese Vinayas. However, the variability and vagueness of translation do not permit a clear picture. Several terms are used for ordination, and it is difficult if not impossible to tell which Indic terms are being represented.

6.2 Basic Dharma Bhikkhuni

44 The term 本法 (basic dharma) is sometimes used to describe a bhikkhuni who has received the ordination from the bhikkhunis before she receives it from the bhikkhus. This term is best known in the context of the procedure of 'establishing the holy life' (*brahmacāryopasthāna*; in Chinese 梵行本法 or 淨行本法). This term is found only in the Mūlasarvāstivāda Vinaya, not in any other Chinese Vinaya. Here 淨行 or 梵行 render *brahmacārya*, while 本法, 'root dhamma', renders *upasthāna*. The reason for this choice of rendering is a little obscure, but √*sthā*, among its dozens of other meanings, can imply 'basis, foundation', so it was probably interpreted here as being a foundational or preliminary procedure, and is clearly related

[51] T22, № 1428, p. 756, c28–29: 時諸比丘尼。便度盲瞎癃躄跛聾瘖瘂及餘種種病者

to the ordination term *vuṭṭhāpana/upasthāpana*. It is not clear why the Mūlasarvāstivāda prefaces the term with *brahmacārya.*

45 The usage of the term in the Mūlasarvāstivāda Vinaya is as follows.

46 The ordination procedure in the Mūlasarvāstivāda Vinaya differs from that in all other Vinayas. After training in 6 *dhammas* and 6 *anudhammas* for 2 years, she should request the *upasampadā*, find robes and bowl, and get a preceptor. Having gathered the minimum of 12 bhikkhunis, they should all agree to give the *brahmacāryopasthāna.*[52] This is the procedure that is equivalent to the *vuṭṭhāpana-sammuti* as told in full in the Lokuttaravāda/Mahāsaṅghika, although here it is just mentioned in passing. When all these things are complete, she should be taken for the instruction in private,[53] following which the teacher returns to the midst of the Sangha and calls the candidate in.[54] She then returns to the Sangha, pays respects, and requests to be given the *brahmacāryopasthāna* (淨行本法).[55] In the *saṅghakamma*, she asks to be given the *upasampadā*. But then she specifically requests that the bhikkhuni Sangha give her the *brahmacāryopasthāna.* This usage is maintained consistently: the ordination in front of bhikkhunis alone is called *brahmacāryopasthāna*, and is not the *upasampadā.*[56] Following this is the repeat of the questioning regarding the obstructions, then the bhikkhuni Sangha gives the *brahmacāryopasthāna* by motion & single announcement (*ñattidutiyakamma*). Then she is led to the place where the bhikkhus are (苾芻入壇場 *bhikkhumaṇḍala*). (At this stage the candidate is referred to as 'ordinand',[57] not 'basic dharma bhikkhuni'.) Here she asks for *upasampadā* from the dual Sangha.[58] Then she is questioned in the dual Sangha. Finally there is the motion and three announcements,[59] during which it is said: 'The bhikkhuni Sangha has already given the *brahmacāry-*

---

[52] T24, № 1453, p. 461, a21–22: 諸苾芻尼先可授其淨行本法

[53] T24, № 1453, p. 461, c3–p. 462, a17.

[54] T24, № 1453, p. 462, a17–22.

[55] T24, № 1453, p. 462, a22–23.

[56] E.g. T24, № 1453, p. 462, b27–28: 苾芻尼僧伽已與某甲受淨行本法

[57] T24, № 1453, p. 462, c3: 教受近圓者

[58] T24, № 1453, p. 462, c10–11: 願二部僧伽授我近圓. Compare previous parallel at T24, № 1453, p. 462, a27–28: 願苾芻尼僧伽授我淨行本法.

[59] T24, № 1453, p. 462, c20–p. 463, a15.

opasthāna',[60] and at the end of which it is said that 'the dual Sangha has now given *upasampadā*.'[61]

47 *Brahmacāryopasthāna* appears to be used only once elsewhere (unless a different rendering is used that escapes my searching). This is in a different part of the Vinaya, the Khuddhakavatthu, and a different rendering is used (梵行本法). Here it is allowed to give ordination by messenger. First she takes *brahmacāryopasthāna*,[62] then 'when that *upasthāna* is done'[63] she should quickly take *upasampadā*, which must be given by the dual Sangha.[64]

48 *Upasthāna*, without *brahmacārya*, as the 'basic dhamma' is mentioned in just one other place in the Mūlasarvāstivāda Vinaya, a summary verse.[65] Throughout the bhikkhuni *pāṭimokkha*, ordination is referred to as '*pabbajjā*, *upasampadā*',[66] with no mention of *brahmacāryopasthāna*.

49 The *brahmacāryopasthāna* is not the same as an *upasampadā*, although it follows a similar procedure, except for using the briefer motion & single announcement. This is confirmed throughout the Mūlasarvāstivāda Vinaya. A bhikkhuni is defined as *upasampannā*, and *upasampannā* is defined as having received ordination by motion & three announcements; therefore *brahmacāryopasthāna* is not *upasampadā*.[67] Again, it is said that *anupasampannā* means one not ordained by bhikkhus and bhikkhunis.[68]

50 This usage of *brahmacāryopasthāna* is unique to the Mūlasarvāstivāda. However, the Mahīśāsaka Vinaya uses the term *upasthāna* (本法), without *brahmacārya*, once in the same sense.[69]

51 The related phrase 'basic dharma bhikkhuni' (本法尼) is found in several later texts, including Dharmaguptaka *kammavācās*, of which T № 1804 and T № 1808 were by Dao Xuan, who lived between 596–667, and T № 1809

[60] T24, № 1453, p. 462, c24–25: 苾芻尼僧伽已與作淨行本法

[61] T24, № 1453, p. 463, a12–13: 二部僧伽已與某甲受近圓. Again compare with the bhikkhunis at T24, № 1453, p. 462, b27–28: 苾芻尼僧伽已與某甲受淨行本法

[62] In a family [?] at T24, № 1451, p. 368, b10–11: 往彼家中作梵行本法

[63] T24, № 1451, p. 368, b12: 至其家內與作本法已

[64] T24, № 1451, p. 368, b16: 僧尼二眾應授法與近圓

[65] T24, № 1453, p. 500, a22 與式叉本法

[66] 出家，近圓

[67] T23, № 1443, p. 913, c22–23: 云何苾芻尼性。謂受近圓。云何近圓。謂白四羯磨

[68] T23, № 1443, p. 972, a28–29: 未近圓人者。有兩種圓具。謂苾芻苾芻尼。餘並名爲未圓具者

[69] T22, № 1424, p. 219, a5: 先明本法

and T № 1810 were by Huai Su, 624–697.[70] Here it is used to signify the bhikkhuni who has received the first half of the *upasampadā*, in front of the bhikkhunis. But when describing the 'one who has been ordained' and is taken over to the bhikkhus for the second half of the *upasampadā*, the actual Dharmaguptaka Vinaya itself uses the phrase 'ordinand' (受戒者), both in the Suttavibhaṅga[71] and the Bhikkhunikkhandhaka.[72] This agrees with the Mahāsaṅghika,[73] Lokuttaravāda,[74] and Pali[75] traditions.

52 Thus it seems that the term 'basic dharma bhikkhuni' was unknown to the original Dharmaguptaka Vinaya as translated in Chinese, and was adopted as a later usage, perhaps influenced by the Mahīśāsaka, or perhaps all these were influenced by the oral developments in Vinaya terminology among the Chinese Sangha. It may be significant that the Mahīśāsaka Vinaya was brought from Sri Lanka, around the same time as the Sri Lankan bhikkhunis came to perform the *upasampadā*. The Mūlasarvāstivāda Vinaya was not translated until 710, by which time the term was already current.

6.3 Conclusion

53 The texts speak of bhikkhuni ordination as *vuṭṭhāpana*, and there is no suggestion that the bhikkhus were involved.[76] This is represented by the bhikkhuni *pāṭimokkha* and the Therīgāthā. If this textual strata represents a genuine historical stage, then I conclude that the bhikkhus did not, during the Buddha's lifetime, take part in the bhikkhuni ordination. Later the bhikkhus introduced the dual ordination. This found its textual form in the narrative of Mahāpajāpatī as the founder of the bhikkhuni order, and the subsequent developments in the Bhikkhuni Khandhaka and the *vibhaṅga* to

[70] T40, № 1804, p. 152, b1: 本法尼; T40, № 1808, p. 500, a29: 本法尼; T40, № 1809, p. 515, c28: 本法尼， 本法尼; T40, № 1810, p. 543, a8: 本法尼

[71] T22, № 1428, p. 757, c12.

[72] T22, № 1428, p. 925, a26.

[73] T22, № 1425, p. 473, b1: 我已與某甲受具足

[74] ROTH p. 44 § 58.

[75] Pali Vinaya 2.273–274.

[76] Here I omit consideration of whether, prior to such formal procedures, there were earlier generations of bhikkhunis who were ordained by the 'Come, bhikkhuni' formula spoken by the Buddha, or by the three refuges.

the bhikkhuni *pāṭimokkha*. The dual ordination was introduced before the first schism, probably as part of the general reforms and Vinaya tightening that followed the Second Council.

54 This evolution of the forms of the ordination procedure is mainly inferred from the pattern of distribution of the special terminology for bhikkhunis in the Mahāvihāravāsin and Lokuttaravāda Vinayas. In addition, it explains the unique nature of the Mūlasarvāstivāda bhikkhuni ordination procedure, where the *brahmacāryopasthāna* ordination in front of bhikkhunis alone is by motion and two announcements, and is not regarded as *upasampadā*; the *upasampadā* is accomplished in front of both Sanghas simultaneously. The Mūlasarvāstivāda *brahmacāryopasthāna* appears to be a relic of the *vuṭṭhāpana* ordination procedure, carried out by the bhikkhunis alone, without involvement of the bhikkhus.

55 The dual ordination is mandated in all existing Vinayas, so it would be controversial to suggest that single ordination be applied in practice. My feeling is that it is nice for the bhikkhunis to take ordination from both Sanghas, and to experience a genuine acceptance from both the male and female communities. In fact, I would like to look at ways of mirroring the procedure, so that bhikkhus also went before the bhikkhuni Sangha to have their ordination acknowledged.

56 Nevertheless, it remains the case that the dual ordination is potentially a powerful instrument of control by the bhikkhus. It seems undeniable that this was one of the purposes for introducing it in the first place. By having a power of veto over which women can receive ordination, the bhikkhu Sangha can in theory throttle any chance for the bhikkhuni Sangha to grow and thrive. In recent years in Korea one arm of the bhikkhuni Sangha, being disillusioned with their experience with the bhikkhu Sangha, has taken matters into their own hands and performs ordinations themselves. My research indicates that in doing so they are not making a radical new departure, but may be simply following the practice of the earliest bhikkhunis. Whether this is a wise move I cannot say; the mere contemplation of such an act is a sign that there are serious problems. In a situation where the bhikkhus were using their veto power in an unprincipled manner, the option of performing ordination by themselves remains one that the bhikkhunis can consider.

Chapter 7

WHO TRAINS FOR TWO YEARS?

A DISTINCTIVE ORDINATION PLATFORM FOR WOMEN, called the *sikkhamānā* (trainee), is found in all the Vinayas. The *sikkhamānā* training is described in the *pācittiyas* (and sometimes in the *garudhammas* and ordination procedure), where it is typically stated that a *sikkhamānā* must train for two years in the 'six rules' before taking higher ordination. There is no corresponding ordination platform for the bhikkhus.[1]

2 The *sikkhamānā* platform raises a whole host of difficulties that must be addressed if we are to further our understanding of women's ordination. A series of academic articles have addressed the issue, but one of the latest, by the philologist Oskar von Hinüber, ended with the dismal assessment: *non liquet*—it is not clear. In the present essay I wish to explain exactly why the situation is so unclear, and to raise a number of unresolved, and in some cases probably unresolvable, problems with the idea and practice of *sikkhamānā* training.

3 Underlying this entire issue is the question: why is there a special training for the women, extra to that of the men? It is often said that the purpose

[1] The term *sikkhamāna* is used once in the *pāṭimokkha* (*pācittiya* 71) to describe a bhikkhu who is still 'in training'. This non-technical usage, however, does not correspond to any formal ordination platform. This is a typical case where a non-technical term is found in the earlier text (the bhikkhu *pāṭimokkha*) and in the later text (bhikkhuni *pāṭimokkha*) it comes to have a defined technical sense.

was to prevent pregnant women from ordaining.[2] However, this reason is only found in a background story for one rule in the Sarvāstivāda Vinaya,[3] and the issue of pregnant nuns is dealt with elsewhere in the Vinayas by other means. The reason given in most of the background stories for instituting the *sikkhamānā* is that the bhikkhunis were uneducated and needed training. This is a sensible explanation, but it is far from certain. The origin stories for the *sikkhamānā* have, in all likelihood, been formed much later, and simply inferred back from the rule itself. Thus they provide little in the way of independent evidence for the original purpose of the rule. The real clue is simply the word *sikkhamānā*, which means 'trainee'.

4 It is tempting to infer that the *sikkhamānā* training was introduced for the women because of the inferior standards of education for women in ancient India. This would parallel the institution of the fortnightly exhortation, which we also interpreted as an educational requirement. While this explanation is plausible, we should be wary of accepting it as the final word on the matter, for it rests on slim evidence.

5 Von Hinüber has suggested an alternative, or perhaps complementary, explanation: the *sikkhamānā* period was adopted from the Jain Vinaya.[4] This must remain speculative, especially since the evidence he presents for the training period in Jainism is slim, and it is not at all clear how much it actually has in common with the Buddhist *sikkhamānā*. However, in the light of the other similarities between the Jain and bhikkhuni Vinaya, it is plausible. And it explains, with a single conservative thesis, just why the *sikkhamānā* period appears to be so variously understood or misunderstood in the Buddhist tradition, and why it seems so poorly integrated with the rest of the Vinaya.

6 If the *sikkhamānā* period was really adopted from the Jain Vinaya, along with a series of other influences, then there is no need to assume it had

---

2 E.g. VAJIRAÑĀṆAVARORASA Vol 3, p. 254. A false objection to this idea is sometimes raised: why, if the object was to prevent pregnant women from ordaining, is it necessary to wait for 'two years'? But the Indic word for 'year' is *vassa* ('rainy season'), so that 'two years' might be as little as the period encompassing two *vassas*, that is, a little over one year. And one *vassa* might be as little as three or four months. So if the rule merely required one *vassa* training, this would not be enough to be sure the candidate was not pregnant.

3 Sarvāstivāda *pācittiya* 111 at T23, n. 1435, p. 326, b5–b15.

4 VON HINÜBER, p. 20. Also discussed above chapter 6.7–8.

anything to do with differences in educational levels at the time of the Buddha, for the Jains use it for both their male and female Sanghas. It becomes merely an evolutionary artifact, evidence of the sometimes arbitrary and random course that Buddhism has charted over the millennia. Biologists are familiar with the fact that organisms inherit many useless or dysfunctional aspects which are mere remnants of their evolutionary heritage, and cannot be explained as functional in the present context. This is one of the most cogent arguments against Creationism in its various forms: design is frequently unintelligent. Nevertheless, organisms will frequently make innovate use of apparently superfluous items, turning a useless leftover into a beneficial new structure. Similarly, as Buddhists we inherit much that has outgrown its original context, and which would never have been instituted in the current context by an Intelligent Designer, who created the entire Vinaya from his Omniscient Knowledge.

7 It is normally assumed that all women must spend two years training as a *sikkhamānā* before ordaining as a bhikkhuni. However, the main canonical passages regularly apply the *sikkhamānā* training in the case of teenage girls, and there is scarce canonical support in the Pali texts for the universal application of *sikkhamānā* training. Ann Heirmann has already proposed that the *sikkhamānā* period may not have been required for all women at the earliest stage, but, she says, it soon became a universal requirement.[5] I would agree with this assessment, but would want to qualify Heirmann's vague 'soon'. The Vinayas as we have them were compiled over hundreds of years. I hope to show that evidence of a period where *sikkhamānā* was intended only for teenage girls are still prominent in the existing Vinayas, and hence that there is no evidence that the *sikkhamānā* training was considered mandatory before the Aśokan period.

8 One thing should be clarified from the start: omission of the *sikkhamānā* period does not in any way invalidate the ordination. It is at most a procedural flaw that results in a *pācittiya* offense for the ordaining bhikkhuni. Hence many candidates for bhikkhuni ordination in the present—and, it seems, the past as well—do not see this training as essential. Nevertheless, this attitude is sometimes regarded as a failure to live up to the highest standards of the Vinaya. I would suggest that this is an area where the

---

5 HEIRMANN, *Rules for Nuns*, V^{OL} 1, pp. 9–5.

application of legal principles beyond their legitimate scope should not be mistaken for scrupulousness. In fact, the Buddha said that we should neither add to nor take away from the rules. Overinterpretation of rules is just as harmful as laxity, for it obscures the original purpose, and diverts attention from those aspects of monastic life that are of genuine spiritual relevance.

7.1 The 'Six Rules'

9 The general idea of the *sikkhamānā* is more or less consistently presented in the different Vinayas. A *sikkhamānā* should train for two years in six rules before taking full ordination. However, when we look more closely, the different Vinayas reveal tremendous variations.

10 Even the number of rules is not consistent, with the Mūlasarvāstivāda acknowledging twelve rules, and the Mahāsaṅghika group having eighteen. The fact that both of these are multiples of six suggests that the shorter list was the earlier one, expanded by the schools in accordance with their needs of the time. Indeed, the Mūlasarvāstivāda rules (but not the Mahāsaṅghika) are divided into six major and six minor, maintaining the pattern of six. So we are on fairly safe ground in assuming that the 'six rules' was the original number.

11 But in the realm of content, we have no such assurance of being able to trace an original at all. The Mahāvihāravāsin and Mahīśāsaka say the six rules are the five basic precepts, with the third strengthened to include chastity rather than simply not committing sexual misconduct, and the addition of the sixth of the eight or ten precepts, forbidding taking food at the wrong time (after noon).

12 The Dharmaguptaka has instead the four *pārājika* offenses for bhikkhus, as well as not drinking alcohol and not eating after noon. These are, however, not too dissimilar to the previous rules, for the four *pārājikas* are merely serious instances of breaking the first four precepts. For example, the first precept concerns killing any living being, while the third *pārājika* concerns killing a human being. As well as being strengthened, the *pārājikas* are distinguished from the five precepts due to their distinctive sequence.

13 The first four of the 'six rules' in the Sarvāstivāda are also equivalent to the four bhikkhu *pārājikas,* but the final two of the Sarvāstivāda rules are two of the bhikkhuni *pārājikas*: having lustful contact with a man, and doing the 'eight things' (kinds of sexual conduct short of intercourse).

14 The Mūlasarvāstivāda has a list of six main rules and six minor rules, which are almost completely different from the other versions. The Mahāsaṅghika/Lokuttaravāda tradition increases these to eighteen, with again no important commonalities.[6] In both of these cases, the lists of rules draws upon various precepts and practices, such as the *pārājikas, saṅghādisesas, pācittiyas,* and various minor rules.

15 It is true that these lists contain important areas of overlap, and this might be seen as a sign that they harked from an early pre-sectarian source. Here, however, the nature of the commonalities weighs against such a conclusion, for the rules overlap precisely where they are identical with other lists. We know that the five and eight precepts and the four *pārājikas* are held in common from an early time by all the schools. It is entirely plausible that, in formulating the list of 'six rules', the schools independently drew upon such widely known and accepted lists. So the fact that the lists of 'six rules' share features in common may just as well, or better, be explained by the schools independently drawing on their common sources, rather than because they possessed an accepted ancient list of 'six rules'. The Mahāvihāravāsin and Mahīśāsaka drew on the eight precepts, the Dharmaguptaka and Sarvāstivāda drew on the *pārājikas,* and the Mūlasarvāstivāda and Mahāsaṅghika developed entirely independent schemes for training by drawing freely on various Vinaya sources.

16 It is particularly important to note that the Sthavira group of schools differs entirely from the Mahāsaṅghika group in both content and number of rules. Since these groups parted ways at the 'first schism', agreement between these schools is usually taken as evidence of a pre-sectarian heritage. The complete disagreement means we have no objective criteria for positing the content of the 'six rules' in the pre-sectarian period. The disparity in the lists of 'six rules' is most naturally explained by the thesis that the schools inherited from the pre-sectarian period some *pāṭimokkha*

6 See 'Six Precepts' for full lists and references. https://sites.google.com/site/sikkhamana/6rules

rules that referred to the *sikkhamānā* and her 'six rules', but the tradition of what those six rules were became lost by the time the canonical Vinayas were redacted.

17 How could this happen? We know that bhikkhunis existed and played prominent roles in the Aśokan period, for they are referred to in the edicts. The bhikkhunis, together with the bhikkhus, are warned against causing schism in the Sangha—which means they must have had political power—and they are encouraged to study the Buddhist suttas—which means they must have been educated. So if they were prominent in the time of Aśoka, how could the knowledge of the *sikkhamānā* period disappear so quickly in the post-Aśokan era when the Vinayas were finalized? Again, we can only speculate, but I would point to three factors. One is the generally poor state of the bhikkhuni Vinaya, resulting from their marginalization in the process of unifying the textual redaction through the Councils. The second is the idea that the *sikkhamānā* training may have been adopted from the Jains, and was hence never well understood or adapted within the Buddhist framework. Finally, there is our suggestion that the *sikkhamānā* training was originally intended for young girls. Since not all women went through the process, the details became forgotten in various communities.

18 There is one further problem with the 'six rules'. Normally in Buddhism, a higher status is conferred through the undertaking of a higher number of precepts. Thus the ordinary lay follower is expected to keep five precepts; a lay follower in periods of special devotion should keep eight; the *sāmaṇeras* and *sāmaṇerīs* should keep ten; and the bhikkhus and bhikkhunis have their long lists of hundreds of *pāṭimokkha* rules. But the *sikkhamānā* interrupts this neat picture. She has only six precepts, yet is said to be at a higher status than the *sāmaṇeras* and *sāmaṇerīs*.

19 For this reason, in modern Sri Lankan practice, the *sikkhamānā* period is usually omitted, and candidates are expected instead to take *sāmaṇerī* ordination for two years, following the reasoning that the *sāmaṇerī* outranks the *sikkhamānā* anyway. This interpretation, however, flies in the face of

the status of the *sikkhamānā* as depicted in the canons, where she always occupies a higher rank than the *sāmaṇerī*.[7]

20 The higher status is signified by the fact that the *sikkhamānā* is ordained through a *saṅghakamma* procedure that is more formal and developed than the corresponding novice (*sāmaṇera/sāmaṇerī*) ordination. And while the *sāmaṇerī* ordination is available for young girls,[8] *sikkhamānā* ordination is meant for eighteen year old girls.[9]

21 Thus modern Sri Lankan practice in this regard does not enjoy the support of the canonical Vinayas. Nor can it claim authority from the Mahāvihāravāsin tradition, for Buddhaghosa states that even a woman who has gone forth (as a *sāmaṇerī*) for 60 years must still undergo the two years' training in the six rules. Nevertheless, this modern innovation is understandable, for there is a genuine problem with the relation between the *sikkhamānā* and the *sāmaṇerī*.

22 Another possible explanation for the relation between these two platforms is that the *sikkhamānā* training is higher, not because of the number of precepts, but because of the strictness which which she holds them: while a *sāmaṇerī* might be forgiven certain laxities in some of the rules, a *sikkhamānā* must keep her precepts unbroken, or else she must start her training again.[10]

---

[7] Some examples in the Pali: *pācittiya* 59 (Pali Vinaya 4.121): '*Yo pana bhikkhu* ***bhikkhussa*** *vā* ***bhikkhuniyā*** *vā* ***sikkhamānāya*** *vā* ***sāmaṇerassa*** *vā* ***sāmaṇeriyā*** *vā sāmaṁ cīvaraṁ vikappetvā appaccuddhāraṇaṁ paribhuñjeyya, pācittiyan'ti.* Vassūpanāyikakkhandhaka (Pali Vinaya 1.139 & *passim*): *Anujānāmi, bhikkhave, sattannaṁ sattāhakaraṇīyena pahite gantuṁ, na tveva appahite.* ***Bhikkhussa, bhikkhuniyā, sikkhamānāya, sāmaṇerassa, sāmaṇeriyā, upāsakassa, upāsikāya***; *pārājika* 1 (Pali Vinaya 3.40): *Tena kho pana samayena vesāliyaṁ licchavikumārakā bhikkhuṁ gahetvā* ***bhikkhuniyā*** *vippaṭipādesuṁ...* ***sikkhamānāya*** *vippaṭipādesuṁ...* ***sāmaṇeriyā*** *vippaṭipādesuṁ...*; *Pārājika* 4 (Pali Vinaya 3.107): *Idhāhaṁ, āvuso, gijjhakūṭā pabbatā orohanto addasaṁ* ***bhikkhuniṁ****... addasaṁ* ***sikkhamānaṁ****... addasaṁ* ***sāmaṇeraṁ****... addasaṁ* ***sāmaṇeriṁ*** *vehāsaṁ gacchantiṁ*. In the Mahāsaṅghika/Lokuttaravāda, the first of the 18 *sikkhamāna* rules states she sits below the bhikkhunis but above the *sāmaṇerīs* (T22, № 1425, p. 535, a17; Roth p. 26). In the Dharmaguptaka (as in the Pali) the relevant non-offence clauses always list the *sikkhamānā* before the *sāmaṇerī*.

[8] While the age for *sāmaṇerīs* is not mentioned in the Pali, presumably it would be the same as for the *sāmaṇeras*, which is either fifteen, or big enough to scare a crow (Pali Vinaya 1.78).

[9] Leaving aside the problematic case of the *gihigatā*, discussed below.

[10] The concept of having to go back to the beginning of one's training is reminiscent of the procedure of 'sending back to the beginning' (*mūlāyapaṭikassanā*, Pali Vinaya 2.43) a

23 This interpretation might claim some support from the passage in the Mahāvihāravāsin ordination procedure where the *sikkhamānā* candidate declares her intention to keep the six rules for two years 'without transgression'.[11] The exact term for 'without transgression' (*avītikkamma*) is not found in similar rule formulations for the *sāmaṇera*, or indeed anywhere in the Pali Vinaya. Nevertheless, the text does not state what the consequences are if she does in fact transgress one of the rules. A survey of the Pali commentarial literature also turns up nothing on this point. However, an almost identical term is found in the formula for each of the eight *garudhammas*: they are said to be taken up and 'not to be transgressed for one's whole life'.[12] In this case, we know that transgression of a *garudhamma* did not result in expulsion or having to restart one's training.

24 It would, therefore, be overinterpreting the Pali text to insist that it states that she must start again with her training, no matter how minor an infringement occurs. And we should be clear about this: it is perfectly possible to break some of the 'six rules' of the Pali tradition without doing anything unethical. One might, for example, eat something in the afternoon that was reckoned as 'food'. While tucking into an evening sandwich would be clearly against the Vinaya, the exact boundary between what constitutes 'food' and what is allowable 'medicines' is extremely hard to draw, and in practice almost every community decides this point in slightly different ways. It is hard to believe that a *sikkhamānā* would have to start her training again for such a trifle.

25 The Dharmaguptaka says that major transgressions (normally equivalent to a *pārājika*—but note that this also includes any transgression of the rules against eating after noon and taking alcohol, which are mere *pācittiyas* for bhikkhunis) result in expulsion, and presumably she may not be ordained at all. Minor transgressions result in her taking the precepts again, which Heirmann interprets to mean that her *sikkhamānā* period would be extended; she does not say if that means literally starting over.[13] In any case, the text does not explicitly state that she would have to start

---

bhikkhu who trangresses again while undergoing penance for *saṅghādisesa*. But there is no discussion of such a procedure in the context of the *sikkhamānā*.

[11] Pali Vinaya 4.319: *Pāṇātipātā veramaṇiṁ dve vassāni* ***avītikkamma*** *samādānaṁ samādiyāmi...*

[12] Pali Vinaya 2.255: *Yāvajjīvaṁ anatikkamanīyo.*

[13] HEIRMANN, *Rules for Nuns*, p. 801, note 182.

her two years again. The Mahāsaṅghika Vinaya *sikkhamānā* rule 12 states that if she breaks one of the last four of the eight *pārājikas*, she must start her two years' training over again; but the Lokuttaravāda, extraordinarily, differs completely from the Mahāsaṅghika in this and following rules. I cannot find statements elsewhere that show that a *sikkhamānā* must definitely start her precepts again if she breaks one of them.

26 There is, therefore, no consensus in the traditions that a violation of any rule by the *sikkhamānā* would necessarily result in her having to start her two years over. In certain cases, usually those corresponding to the *pārājika* offenses, she is expelled or has to restart. But this is similar for the *sāmaṇeras/sāmaṇerīs*, who may also be expelled for breaking *pārājika* or even lesser offenses.[14] In fact, the Pali text clearly allows expulsion of *sāmaṇeras/sāmaṇerīs* who break serious precepts, while this is not made explicit in the case of *sikkhamānās*. There seems no reason, then, to accept a difference in the strictness of keeping precepts as marking a clear upgrade from the *sāmaṇerī* to the *sikkhamānā*.[15]

27 Even if the foregoing reasoning is not acceptable, and one continues to think that the difference in strictness marked the difference between the two platforms, this would not eliminate the problem, but merely shift the ground. It remains the case that nowhere is the difference between two ordination platforms marked by a decrease in number of precepts and an increase in strictness. However we try to explain it, the *sikkhamānā* is simply an oddity, who does not fit easily within the normal pattern of Buddhist ordination.

7.2 The Sikkhamānā Training Framework

28 In general, the process of *sikkhamānā* training is this. The applicant requests *sikkhamānā* training from the Sangha. She is either a maiden of eighteen or a *gihigatā* of ten. This is the basic age requirement. If the Sangha

[14] E.g. Pali Vinaya 1.84: *Anujānāmi, bhikkhave, dasahaṅgehi samannāgataṁ sāmaṇeraṁ nāsetuṁ. Pāṇātipātī hoti, adinnādāyī hoti, abrahmacārī hoti, musāvādī hoti, majjapāyī hoti, buddhassa avaṇṇaṁ bhāsati, dhammassa avaṇṇaṁ bhāsati, saṁghassa avaṇṇaṁ bhāsati, micchādiṭṭhiko hoti, bhikkhunidūsako hoti*; for the Dharmaguptaka, see HEIRMANN, *Discipline*, p. 102, note 54.

[15] See SHIH, chapter 6.3.

agrees, the applicant is given the *sikkhamānā* ordination.[16] She must be taught the training requirements, especially the 'six rules' (*deśitaśikṣam*).[17] Then she must train in those rules for two years. When she has completed the training she requests the Sangha to give the *vuṭṭhāpana*.[18] If the Sangha agrees a skilled bhikkhuni of minimum twelve years standing is appointed as the mentor, and she makes the formal motion to the Sangha, which consents in silence.[19]

29 To understand the *sikkhamānā* better, we will start with Pali *pācittiya* 63, which provides the overall framework for *sikkhamānā* training.[20] The rule itself reads as follows:

> 30 If any bhikkhunī should ordain (*vuṭṭhāpana*) a *sikkhamānā* who has not trained for two years in the six rules, there is an offense entailing expiation.[21]

31 *Pācittiya* 63 does not tell us who must undergo *sikkhamānā* training, but rather that whoever has undertaken the *sikkhamānā* ordination should fulfill the required precepts for the required period of time before taking higher ordination. The rule is specifically concerned with the prerequisites for conferring higher ordination on someone who has undertaken the

---

[16] Pali *pācittiya* 63.

[17] ROTH, p. 242 § 211.

[18] Mahāvihāravāsin (4.321): *Ahaṁ ayye itthannāmā itthannāmāya ayyāya dve vassāni chasu dhammesu sikkhitasikkhā sikkhamānā saṅghaṁ vuṭṭhānasammutiṁ yācāmīti... Dutiyampi... Tatiyampi...*; Lokuttaravāda (ROTH p. 29 § 29): *Vandāmi ārya-saṁghaṁ ahaṁ itthannāmā aṣṭādaśa-varśa kumāribhūtā dve varṣāṇi deśita-śikṣā paripūri-śikṣā. Sā ahaṁ saṁghaṁ upasthāpanāsaṁmutiṁ yācāmi. Sādhu me āryā saṁgho upasthāpana-saṁmutiṁ detu. Dvitīyampi... Tṛtīyampi...*

[19] In the Pali (4.321) this is a motion and single announcement, while in the Lokuttaravāda (ROTH p. 29 § 29) it is a motion and three announcements. This is a sign of greater development in the Lokuttaravāda text. It is also more developed in that the initial request by the candidate who has completed the training is preceded by an announcement by a bhikkhuni to the Sangha that the candidate will ask for the agreement to ordain (ROTH p. 28 § 28). This rule and explanation is also found in the Lokuttaravāda, but they have taken the next step of copying the extra procedure into the full ordination text.

[20] *Pācittiya* 64 is marginal for our study, for it merely requires that the bhikkhuni who gives the *sikkhamānā* ordination be formally agreed upon by the Sangha. A similar stipulation is made in *pācittiyas* 67 and 73 and their parallels.

[21] Pali Vinaya 4.319: *Yā pana bhikkhunī dve vassāni chasu dhammesu asikkhitasikkhaṁ sikkhamānaṁ vuṭṭhāpeyya pācittiyan'ti.*

sikkhamānā training, not with the ordination of women in general. Hence the focus of the rule is on maintaining the integrity of *sikkhamānā* training.

32 This rule is paralleled in *garudhamma* 6:

33 > A *sikkhamānā* who has trained for two years in six rules should seek full ordination (*upasampadā*) from the dual Sangha...[22]

34 Here too the rule stipulates that one who is a *sikkhamānā* should have fulfilled the training in six rules for two years before taking higher ordination, but does not say that all bhikkhunī candidates need to do *sikkhamānā* training.

35 Notice the important difference between these two rules. *Pācittiya* 63 refers to ordination with the term *vuṭṭhāpana*, while *garudhamma* 6 speaks of '*upasampadā* in the dual Sangha'. In chapter 6.12–30 we discussed the significance of this: *vuṭṭhāpana* is the earlier term, found only within the bhikkhuni *pāṭimokkha*, and evidently deriving from an ancient oral tradition among the bhikkhunis. The dual-Sangha *upasampadā* is evidence of the importing of bhikkhus' Vinaya terminology into the bhikkhuni Vinaya. In chapter 6.53, I suggested that the introduction of the dual–Sangha *upasampadā* for bhikkhunis occurred in the wake of the Second Council.

36 As far as the other Vinayas are concerned, Mahīśāsaka *pācittiya* 113 is similar to the Pali, except that it simply says 'two years' training, omitting mention of the six rules.[23] The background story and *vibhaṅga* for this rule are negligible.

37 Sarvāstivāda *pācittiya* 111 refers to a 'disciple' (弟子) rather than specifically a *sikkhamānā*. The background story is substantial, and concerns a woman who ordained when she was already pregnant. This situation is dealt with in other contexts in other Vinayas, and the Sarvāstivāda is unique in associating the *sikkhamānā* period with pregnancy. The *vibhaṅga* for this rule includes the entire *sikkhamānā* ordination procedure.

38 Mūlasarvāstivāda *pācittiya* 119 (in Chinese; or 80 in Tibetan) similarly lacks specific mention of the *sikkhamānā*, and prohibits giving ordination to a 'woman' who has not trained for two years in the six rules and six

---

[22] Pali Vinaya 2.255: *Dve vassāni chasu dhammesu sikkhitasikkhāya sikkhamānāya ubhato saṅghe upasampadā pariyesitabbā...*

[23] T22, № 1421, p. 92, a6–11.

lesser rules.[24] It has a brief, formulaic origin story and *vibhaṅga*. Notice that there is, as usual, no reason to think that the origin stories in any of these versions share any common heritage.

39 In summary, then, the Mahāvihāravāsin and Mahīśāsaka traditions prohibit full ordination for a *sikkhamānā* who has not completed her full two years' training. This wording implies nothing as to whether all women, in fact, must ordain as *sikkhamānā*. The Vinayas of the Sarvāstivāda group, on the other hand, prohibit full ordination for any woman who has not completed the two years' training. The Dharmaguptaka and the Mahāsaṅghika/Lokuttaravāda do not have a close parallel with this rule.

7.3 Gihigatā & Kumārībhūtā

40 After *pācittiya* 63 has provided the framework for *sikkhamānā* training, the Pali text defines in two sets of parallel clauses (*pācittiyas* 65–67, 71–73) who is eligible for ordination. These passages treat in parallel terms two categories of candidates who seek bhikkhunī ordination at a young age, the *gihigatā* and the *kumārībhūtā*.

41 Before discussing this rule in particular, we must acknowledge the difficulty with the term *gihigatā*.[25] There are three distinct and probably unresolvable areas of controversy. First is the meaning of the word. Etymologically, it has two elements, *gihi* ('layperson') and *gata* (literally 'gone', but having a more abstract sense of 'become'). It is interpreted in the traditions as a 'married woman', an interpretation reinforced by the fact that *gihigatā* appears in sets of rules parallel with *kumārībhūtā*, which, mercifully enough, clearly means 'maiden, girl'. However, as von Hinüber points out, 'married' is clearly too narrow a term, for there are many women who are neither married nor virgins. As well as the obvious case of women who have had sex before marriage, there are widows, divorcees, prostitutes, and so on. Both Pali[26] and Sanskrit[27] sources, according to von Hinüber,

[24] T23, № 1443, p. 1007, b8–9: 若復苾芻尼知女人二歲學六法及六隨法了。不與受近圓者波逸底迦

[25] BHS (Lokuttaravāda) *gṛhicaritā*; Skt. (Mūlasarvāstivāda) *gṛhoṣitā*. Von Hinüber interprets these as corrupted forms created when the original Pali was no longer understood.

[26] Pali Vinaya 4.322: *Gihigatā nāma purisantaragatā vuccati.*

[27] ROTH p. 245 § 214: *Gṛhicaritā'ti vikopitabrāhmacāryā.*

accordingly understand *gihigatā* in this context to mean 'non-virgin', a sexually experienced woman.

42 However, as von Hinüber also points out, *gihigatā* has a different meaning in the only early Pali passage where the word appears outside this context. This is in the narrative of the First Council, where Mahākassapa argues that the 'lesser and minor rules' should not be rescinded because they are 'current among the householders'.[28] If this meaning were to be adopted, it would suggest that the original purpose of the rule was to ensure that the female candidate for ordination had good references and reputation among the layfolk. However, this interpretation does not explain why the rules for the *gihigatā* should parallel those for the *kumārībhūtā*. And there is no reason why *gihigatā* should not have different meanings in different contexts, especially if it is a euphemistic idiom for sexual experience. We will, accordingly, assume that *gihigatā* probably means 'non-virgin' for the purpose of this essay.

43 The second major point of uncertainty is simply the nature of marriage and sexual relations in ancient India, and how they are to be applied in our present day society. We know little about the marital relations in the time of the Buddha, as most of our ancient texts stem from communities of celibate ascetics. Much of our information on marriage stems from the much later Dharmaśāstras, which are not a reliable source for the Buddha's period. How are we to compare the marital status of women in the Buddha's day with unmarried women today? What about those in same-sex relationships? The topic is too complex to go into here, but suffice to say that any rule which is predicated upon specific cultural relations must be reinterpreted if it is to be applied to a different cultural context.

44 The final problem is that the *gihigatā* is said to be 'ten years' when undertaking the *sikkhamānā* training, and 'twelve years' when she completes it.[29]

---

[28] Pali Vinaya 2.288: '*Santamhākaṁ sikkhāpadāni gihigatāni. Gihinopi jānanti—"idaṁ vo samaṇānaṁ sakyaputtiyānaṁ kappati, idaṁ vo na kappatī"ti.*' 'Our training rules are current among the householders. The householders know: "This is allowable for the Sakyan sons, this is not allowable for them."' This passage, incidentally, refutes the commonly accepted idea that Vinaya rules should not be taught to those who are not ordained.

[29] There are a couple of instances where the texts differ as to the age, but these are likely to be mere textual corruption. See discussion in 'Evolution of Rules Concerning the

But it is uncertain whether this means she is ten/twelve years old,[30] or ten/twelve years as a *gihigatā*.[31] The weight of the traditions, both canonical and commentarial, favors the former reading. Heirmann points out that in all the canonical contexts she has found, the texts either imply that she is 10/12 years old, or they are ambiguous. No canonical texts assume that she is 10/12 years married. In addition, the most authoritative commentators within the Pali (Buddhaghosa), Chinese (Dao Xuan) and Tibetan (Guṇaprabha) traditions all concur on this point.[32]

45 Nevertheless, von Hinüber points out that in Pali, phrases of the form 'number-years x' always mean 'the number of years in the state of being x', and never mean 'one who is this number of years old and is an x'.[33] This would mean that the *gihigatā* would have to have been in that state for 10 years, i.e. married for ten years, not ten years old and married.

46 In support of his argument, von Hinüber points out that this interpretation removes any conflict with the normal Vinaya requirement for ordination at a minimum age of twenty; and that the Vinaya typically makes things harder for women, so an allowance for women to ordain younger than men is implausible. He admits that it is difficult to explain why the numbers ten and twelve years are chosen, but refers to a number of similar cases in Buddhist and Jain Vinaya where the number of years appears to be similarly arbitrary. Von Hinüber regards the problem as solved, and bemoans the amount of ink that has been wastefully spilt on what he regards as an 'almost non-existent problem'.

47 But the matter is not as simple as he makes out. Indeed, von Hinüber appears to contradict himself a little later in the essay, when he argues that in one passage, the reference to the *kumārībhūtā* must refer to her age.[34] The compilers of the ancient texts and their commentators were well aware of the contexts where 'number-years x' means 'in a state of x for this number of years', and persisted in interpreting the phrase as

---

Two-Year Training'.
https://sites.google.com/site/sikkhamana/evolutionofrulesconcerningthetwo-yeartra

[30] As, for example, K.R. NORMAN's translation of *pācittiya* 65, NORMAN and PRUITT, p. 185.

[31] For example, I.B. HORNER, *Book of the Discipline*, 3.369.

[32] HEIRMANN, *Discipline in Four Parts*, VOL 1, pp. 82–88. See also discussion in SHIH, chapter 8.

[33] VON HINÜBER, pp. 7–9.

[34] VON HINÜBER, pp. 14–5.

'one who is this number of years old, and is in the state of x'. They were using their native language or a language close to their native language, and must have had access to a vast range of linguistic contexts beyond the few examples preserved in our texts. Language is a flexible, sometimes arbitrary and unpredictable beast, and the rules of the philologists don't always work. There is no reason why a particular phrase should not be used in one way in a dozen contexts, and a different way in the thirteenth.

48 The contradiction with the normal ordination age, which von Hinüber repeatedly cites as a major objection to the idea that the *gihigatā* ordains at twelve years of age, should not be seen by us as a bigger problem than it was for the Sangha of old. The Pali commentary passes quietly over this point and in all probability this was seen as merely an exception to a general rule.

49 And, in contradiction to von Hinüber, there are many instances where the Vinaya allows a milder treatment of women than men, and even where the men are positively discriminated against, a few of which I have mentioned above in chapter 2.118–122. None of this is to say that von Hinüber's conclusions here are wrong, it is just that the matter is not as settled as he presents it. I cannot decide for myself what the most plausible interpretation is here, and so will simply proceed with the traditional assumption that the *gihigatā* takes full ordination at twelve years of age, though bearing in mind the inconclusiveness of the matter.

50 With all these uncertainties taken together, the reality is that in the present day, the *gihigatā* is not of practical relevance in bhikkhuni ordination. No-one has, to my knowledge, advocated ordination for teenage girls who were married young, and no-one has advocated that women of sexual experience be required to wait ten years after losing their virginity before they can take *sikkhamānā* ordination. Like so many aspects of the bhikkhus' Vinaya, this has been quietly laid to one side. And we will follow suit. Rather than trying to solve the unsolvable, we will concentrate mainly on the more important case of the *kumārībhūtā*.

51 Returning to our study of the relevant rules, *pācittiyas* 65 and 71 tell us the age requirements: a *gihigatā* must be at least 12 years old, and a *kumārībhūtā* must be 20 years old before she can take full ordination. Then *pācittiyas* 66 and 72 tell us the training requirement: the *gihigatā* who has

just turned 12 and the *kumārībhūtā* who has just turned 20 must have completed *sikkhamānā* training before they are eligible for full ordination.

52 The crucial rule for our purposes is *pācittiya* 72, which reads as follows:

> 53 If any bhikkhuni should ordain (*vuṭṭhāpeyya*) a maiden who is fully twenty years of age [but] who has not trained for two years in the six rules, there is an offense entailing expiation.'[35]

54 The subject of this rule is not women in general (*itthī* or *mātugāma*) but a girl or maiden (*kumārībhūtā*).[36] The rule analysis refers to a *kumārībhūtā* of eighteen years of age. This age is also mentioned repeatedly and consistently in all other Vinaya recensions.

55 The statement that she must be fully twenty years of age is a standard idiom in Pali, which would normally mean 'at least twenty years'. But in this context such a reading is misleading: the rule is not about anyone who is twenty, but about a 'girl' of twenty. Since this rule is specifically about the ordination of girls, it cannot have been meant to apply to all women.

56 Thus this rule specifically refers to an allowance for giving *sikkhamānā* training to 18 year-old girls, who must train for two years in the six rules before taking full ordination. It cannot be construed as a general requirement for all female ordination candidates to undertake *sikkhamānā* training.

57 It is possible to interpret this rule as referring to a candidate of eighteen years of age, and the earlier discussed *pācittiya* 63 as referring to mature women. This is the suggestion of Vajirañāṇavarorasa, though he carefully notes that: 'According to the *sikkhāpada* in the Bhikkhunī *pāṭimokkha* which forbids giving *upasampadā* both to *sikkhamānā* and to *kumārībhūtā* who have not yet trained in the six rules for two years, or who have trained without (formal) agreement of the Sangha, it would seem that *sikkhamānā* means those already past the (minimum) age of *upasampadā*, and *kumārībhūtā* means those not yet old enough for *upasampadā*—but this is not explained.'[37] No matter what interpretative strategy we adopt, it remains

[35] Pali Vinaya 4.328: *Yā pana bhikkhunī paripuṇṇavīsativassaṁ kumārībhūtaṁ dve vassāni chasu dhammesu asikkhitasikkhaṁ vuṭṭhāpeyya pācittiyanti.*

[36] The PTS Dictionary for *kumārī*: 'a young girl Vin ii.10; v.129 (*thulla°*); A iii.76; J iii.395 (*daharī k°*); Pug 66 (*itthī vā k° vā*).' The last reference is especially pertinent, as it shows a 'woman' (*itthī*) is clearly distinct from a *kumārī*.

[37] VAJIRAÑĀṆAVARORASA 3.254.

the fact that these rules repeat material in different contexts, and do not contain any explanation of how these repetitions are to be understood.

7.4 The Pali Context

58 *Sikkhamānā* training does not play an integral role in passages about bhikkhuni ordination found elsewhere in the Pali. The absence of *sikkhamānā* training within these contexts, while not decisive, tends to support a reading which narrows the scope of *sikkhamānā* training to younger women.

59 The *sikkhamānā* is entirely absent from the description of bhikkhuni ordination in the Bhikkhunikkhandhaka. In addition, although the story which details the inception of the bhikkhuni order mentions the *sikkhamānā* training in the sixth *garudhamma*, there is no record that Mahāpajāpatī or the Sakyan women actually undertook this training. Further, there is no mention of the *sikkhamānā* in the standard definition of a bhikkhuni. Thus the Vinaya as a whole, while recognizing the *sikkhamānā* training, does not support the idea that it was intrinsic to all bhikkhuni ordinations.

60 *Sikkhamānā* training is mentioned occasionally in the Therīgāthā.[38] The word *sikkhamānā* appears in several verses.[39] In these cases, however, it seems to be used in a non-technical sense, not referring to a specific ordination platform. The commentary to Therīgāthā 104 explains *sikkhamānā* here as one who is pursuing the three trainings (ethics, samadhi, understanding). This is borne out by the contexts, which say, for example, 'For me undergoing training, the divine eye is purified';[40] or 'the six clear knowledges and the highest fruit were realized while training'.[41]

[38] See discussion in SHIH, chapter 6.2.1–2.

[39] Therīgāthā 99, 104, 330, and 516.

[40] Therīgāthā 104; 330 is similar.

[41] Therīgāthā 516. In addition, *sikkhamānā* appears twice in the rubrics (short descriptions of the verse context), saying that the verse in question was frequently taught by the Buddha to Muttā the *sikkhamānā* (Therīgāthā 2), or to Nandā the *sikkhamānā* (Therīgāthā 19–20). The verses themselves do not suggest that she was a *sikkhamānā*, nor do they give any information as to her age. The commentary adds nothing on this point. Hence we cannot draw any conclusions from these mentions, which are just notes added by the redactors.

61 The verses of Sakulā are more of a challenge for our hypothesis.[42] Therīgāthā 98 says that she abandoned son, daughter, money, and grain before going forth; while not definitive, this suggests Sakulā was of a mature age. Therīgāthā 99 says that while she was *sikkhamānā* she abandoned greed and hatred, together with the associated defilements; the commentary confirms the obvious interpretation that this refers to the 'third path', i.e. the state of a non-returner (*anāgāmī*). Therīgāthā 100 and 101 say she took bhikkhuni ordination and subsequently became an arahant. So it seems that here the text implies that a woman of mature age took *sikkhamānā* ordination, became an *anāgāmī*, then took bhikkhuni ordination at a later time.

62 This contradicts our thesis, but a number of factors must be considered. Firstly, this is a verse text, and should not be relied upon for definitive judgments in Vinaya. It gives an example of what one woman did, not a rule governing what all women must do. Secondly, there clearly seems to have been change and variation in the *sikkhamānā* training, so this may be just an example of this. Finally, we remember that we have no clear evidence that Sakulā was in fact of mature age. Perhaps she was a *gihigatā*, who married in her early teens, and had a son and daughter before going forth. Such cases would not have been unusual in India, where marriage has often been consummated at much younger ages than wẹ find acceptable today. This is, of course, assuming that the *gihigatā* is understood as twelve years of age.

63 Apart from this singular case, the Therīgāthā verses do not imply that the term *sikkhamānā* refers to the formally instituted period of preliminary training. Rather it seems to be a non-technical use simply meaning training in ethics, samadhi, and understanding.

64 This usage finds an echo in the bhikkhu Vinaya, which also refers to a monk who is 'training', with no technical meaning. The analysis to this rule simply says ' "trainee" means one who desires the training'.[43] Furthermore, other accounts in the Therīgāthā depict the Buddha giving bhikkhuni ordination to women without the period of *sikkhamānā* training, such as Bhaddā Kuṇḍalakesā. Hence, while Therīgāthā verses 97–101 suggest that

[42] Therīgāthā 97–101.

[43] Pali Vinaya 4.142.

sikkhamānā training may have undertaken by some mature women, other contexts suggests that it was not required.

65 There are in fact several Vinaya rules that depict women ordaining without first going through the *sikkhamānā* training. *Pācittiya* 61 concerns the case of a woman who took ordination while pregnant, which obviously could not have happened if she had followed the two years *sikkhamānā* training. Similarly, *pācittiya* 62 concerns a woman who took ordination while breast-feeding a child. The Bhikkhunikkhandhaka also contains procedures for how to deal with the child if a bhikkhuni gives birth, including the appointment of a companion for her.[44] If *sikkhamānā* training was required from the start of the bhikkhunī order, as stated in the story of the ordination of Mahāpajāpatī, supposedly the first bhikkhunī, then these cases could never have arisen.

66 One might try to resolve this inconsistency by pointing out the evident fact that the story of Mahāpajāpatī's ordination has little or no historical credibility, and that the *sikkhamānā* ordination must have been introduced later. The existence of rules concerning a pregnant nun are simply left over from an earlier period. While this argument makes sense, it is *ad hoc* and requires internal support before it can be accepted. We need an independent reason for thinking that these rules pertain to an especially early period of the bhikkhuni Sangha—but no such internal reason is evident. And a perfectly reasonable alternative hypothesis is available: if the *sikkhamānā* training applies only to women under twenty, it would indeed be possible to ordain a woman who is pregnant or breast-feeding, hence the need for rules to prevent this. The presence of several rules, and a developed procedure for dealing with the situation, does suggest that we are looking at something more significant for the bhikkhuni Sangha than a one-off event that was quickly ruled out by the institution of a two-year *sikkhamānā* training.

67 And there are other cases where the *sikkhamānā* period is omitted, yet which cannot be explained away as stemming from a time before the *sikkhamānā* was instituted. These include Mahāvihāravāsin *saṅghādisesa* 2, which concerns giving the ordination to a wanted criminal. An adulteress, so the story goes, is on the run from her husband—with a considerable

---

[44] Pali Vinaya 2.278–9.

quantity of his wealth in hand. Thullanandā gives her ordination, and the Buddha lays down a rule to prevent this.[45] *Pācittiya* 70 stipulates that a woman who has received ordination (*vuṭṭhāpana*) should be 'taken away' for a distance of five of six *yojanas*[46] after the ordination, a precaution which, according to the background story, was necessary because the husband came to bring his wife back.[47] In both of these cases, the origin story clearly shows that the woman was given full ordination immediately, and that there could have been no *sikkhamānā* period. Yet the origin stories, as we have consistently seen, stem from a much later period than the rules themselves. Thus, as usual, the origin stories for these rules in, for example, the Mahāsaṅghika[48] and Dharmaguptaka[49] are quite different. Hence the rules governing *sikkhamānā* training must have already existed when these origin stories were formed.

68 I would also draw attention to *pācittiyas* 68 and 69, which say that a student (*sahajīvinī*) should be supported by her mentor (*pavattinī*) for a minimum of two years following ordination. In a phrasing that exactly duplicates the reasons for insisting on the necessity of two years' training for the *sikkhamānā*, the background story says that students who ordained

---

[45] In the story, ordination is *pabbajjā*, while in the rule it is *vuṭṭhāpanā*. As usual, the rule preserves the earlier terminology. That *pabbajjā* here, as so often, is simply a synonym for full ordination, not a term for novice ordination, is confirmed in the rule analysis, which speaks of seeking for a 'group' to perform the ordination, establishing a *sīmā*, and performing the *kammavācā*, all of which pertain to bhikkhuni ordination, not to novices.

[46] A *yojana* is perhaps 12 kilometres.

[47] This rule also raises a question as to whether all the nuns actually had the permission of their husbands to ordain. Interestingly, the word analysis for these rules defines 'without permission' (*ananuññātā*) as 'without asking' (*anāpucchā*). This perhaps suggests that the 'permission' was purely a formal matter, where the candidate was expected to request, but not necessarily receive, 'permission'. This phrase does not occur in the *pāṭimokkha* for the bhikkhus, so this is, I believe, the only place in the Pali where it is commented on in this context. I would also raise a problem with the next series of *pācittiyas* 77–81, all of which deal with problems that arise with the improper ways of giving *vuṭṭhāpana* to *sikkhamānās*: in each case, the Pali background says the teacher was Thullanandā, who did not act properly and necessitated the laying down of the rule. But surely Thullanandā, the most notorious bad nun in the Vinaya, would never have been agreed upon by the Sangha to take students. This demonstrates, yet again, the artificial character of the background stories.

[48] Mahāsaṅghika *saṅghādisesa* 8 (HIRAKAWA, p. 153*ff.*), *pācittiya* 108 (HIRAKAWA, p. 319*ff.*)

[49] Dharmaguptaka *saṅghādisesa* 4 (HEIRMANN, *Discipline*, p. 335*ff.*) Pali *Pācittiya* 70 has no parallel.

but did not follow and receive support from their mentor for two years were foolish, uneducated, and did not know what was suitable or what was not suitable. One wonders, if they had indeed all undergone the two years *sikkhamānā* training, what exactly they had learnt in that time, if they were still so ignorant when the time came for full ordination. The same reason is given in the background story for *pācittiya* 74, which stipulates that a *pavattinī* must have been ordained for at least twelve years before ordaining disciples, and *pācittiya* 75, which requires that the *pavattinī* be appointed by the Sangha; and again, we would question why the students are still foolish, in exactly the same way as those who did not receive *sikkhamānā* ordination. Similar reasons are given for these rules in other Vinayas.

69 Reading the texts in a way that restricts the application of *sikkhamānā* ordination to younger women provides a simple explanation for all of these cases. We do not have to invent reasons to explain these several curious artifacts, nor to assume that they all happened before the formation of the *sikkhamānā* training. Instead, we have a single simple thesis that provides a clear explanation for a range of cases. Of course, we have to accept that the origin story of the bhikkhuni Sangha as presented in the texts is wrong; but this is obvious in any case.

70 Turning from the canonical literature to a brief survey of some of the later Pali texts, a similarly ambiguous image of the *sikkhamānā* emerges. The story of how the bhikkhuni order was introduced to Sri Lanka gives us some hints.[50] It is not clear how literally these details should be taken, as the accounts are full of the most exuberant fancies. Nevertheless, used with caution, they do contain some genuine history, and perhaps more important, they tell us how the Sangha of Sri Lanka wanted this process to be seen. The texts are concerned to establish the legitimacy of the lineage, and so are unlikely to include anything that would raise doubts.

71 The story begins with a great gathering of bhikkhus and bhikkhunis at the Aśokārāma in Pāṭaliputta, presided over by King Aśoka himself. At that gathering, the king's son Mahinda, being twenty years of age, was given

---

[50] This account is recorded in the Sinhalese Vinaya Commentaries the Samantapāsādikā in Pali, and the Sudassanavinayavibhāsā in Chinese translation (T № 1462). It is also found in the chronicles the Dīpavaṁsa and the Mahāvaṁsa, although it seems likely that these texts relied mainly on the Vinaya commentary for their source.

the full ordination, with Moggaliputtatissa as the *upajjhāya*, Mahādeva as the teacher for the going forth, and Majjhantika as the teacher for the full ordination. The king's daughter Saṅghamittā, being only eighteen, was only given the going forth and 'established in the training'. The ceremony was performed in the 'very same *sīmā*' within the Aśokārāma. Her *upajjhāya* was Dhammapālī, and her teacher was Āyupālī. The various accounts agree in most details,[51] with the Sudassanavinayavibhāsā adding that in being established in the training, Saṅghamittā was in fact undertaking the 'six precepts', thus confirming that *sikkhamānā* ordination is meant here.[52] The event of Saṅghamittā's full ordination is not recorded.

72 It is fascinating that Mahinda's *upasampadā* teacher (*kammavācācariya*) is Majjhantika. He is famous in both Southern and Northern traditions as the founder of Buddhism in Kaśmīr. The (Mūla) Sarvāstivādin texts constantly list him as one of the five founding Dhamma Masters who passed down the unbroken lineage from the time of the Buddha to Aśoka.[53] So one of the basic lineage masters of the Mūlasarvāstivāda is the ordination teacher of the founder of Sri Lankan Buddhism. Saṅghamittā's ordination was held in the same monastery at the same time, so she must also have been ordained in the same lineage. There are, accordingly, no grounds for asserting that the Mūlasarvāstivāda and the Mahāvihāravāsins have separate ordination lineages. On the contrary, they both stem from exactly the same circle of monastics, who became separated only because they fulfilled their Dhamma duty of propagating Buddhism in different countries.

73 Some time later, Mahinda established Buddhism in Sri Lanka, and a group of 1000 women headed by Princess Anulā wished to take ordination. Mahinda sent for his sister Saṅghamittā, and meanwhile the women stayed in the Upāsikā-vihāra in expectation, having taken on themselves the ten precepts and wearing the ocher robes, but without having received formal ordination.[54] Saṅghamittā came to Sri Lanka (with eleven other

---

[51] Samantapasādikā 1.51–52; Sudassanavinayavibhāsā T24, № 1462, p. 682, a4–12; Mahāvaṁsa 5.204–208; Dīpavaṁsa 7.21–3.

[52] T24, № 1462, p. 682, a11–12: 於戒壇中即與六法

[53] Kassapa, Ānanda, Majjhantika, Śāṇavāsin, Upagupta.

[54] Samantapāsādikā 1.80–81; Sudassanavinayavibhāsā T24, № 1462, p. 691, b26–28; Mahāvaṁsa 18.9–12; Dīpavaṁsa 15.83–4.

bhikkhunis[55]), where she gave ordination to the 1000 women headed by Princess Anulā.[56] The Sudassanavinayavibhāsā adds the detail that Anulā 'immediately gave them bhikkhuni ordination'.[57] This is not stated explicitly in the Pali accounts, but seems to be implied by the context. The Pali accounts refer to ordination as 'going forth' (*pabbajjā*), which in these texts refers to any kind of ordination, usually *upasampadā*, for both men and women. There is, however, no doubt that bhikkhuni ordination is meant, as the following verses routinely refer to the bhikkhunis.[58] Hence the information in these texts supports our interpretation: *sikkhamānā* ordination was used only for teenagers.

74 That the *sikkhamānā* may not have been a normal stage in a woman's monastic career in Mahāvihāravāsin circles is possibly hinted at in the Sammohavinodinī, the commentary to the Abhidhamma Vibhaṅga, which gives a detailed list of the stages of a woman's career in the Buddhasāsana. It goes from a laywoman to a *sāmaṇerī* to a bhikkhuni, and makes no mention of the *sikkhamānā*.[59]

75 However, a different picture emerges in the Samantapāsādikā's comment on *pācittiya* 63. Here is a translation of the relevant portions:[60]

> 76 'To give the agreement to training': why did he give it? Thinking: 'Women are wanton (*mātugāmo nāma lolo hoti...*). Not fulfilling the training in the six rules for two years they are stressed, but having trained, afterwards they are not stressed, they will cross over', he gave it.
>
> 77 ... These six trainings should be given to one who has gone forth even for 60 years; one should not give full ordination to anyone who has not trained therein.

---

55 Mahāvaṁsa 19.5. The eleven companions seems calculated to bring the total up to twelve bhikkhunis, including Saṅghamittā herself. It is often said that twelve is the minimum number for a bhikkhuni ordination, although this requirement is not found in the Pali Vinaya to my knowledge.

56 Samantapāsādikā 1.101; Sudassanavinayavibhāsā T24, № 1462, p. 693, b24–27; Mahāvaṁsa 19.64–5; Dīpavaṁsa 16.41–2.

57 T24, № 1462, p. 693, b25: 僧伽蜜多即度爲比丘尼

58 Mahāvaṁsa 19.67, 70, 77, 79, 81–3.

59 Vibh-a 383, 12–15: *Tato saraṇagatāya, pañcasikkhāpadikāya, sāmaṇeriyā, puthujjanabhikkhuniyā, sotāpannāya, sakadāgāminiyā, tato anāgāminiyā vītikkame mahāsāvajjo, khīṇāsavāya pana bhikkhuniyā ekantamahāsāvajjova.*

60 Samantapāsādikā 4.940.

78 Here we find the reassuring clarity and assertiveness so lacking in the canonical contexts. Perhaps this decisiveness results from the commentator's belief that the extra training is essential due to the 'wanton' nature of women. This attitude of the middle period of Buddhism is blatantly misogynist and must be rejected. It has no support in the canonical texts on the *sikkhamānā*, and is refuted, as we all know, by the vast weight of evidence on the capacities and strengths of women. There are countless bhikkhunis today who live active, strong, and beneficial lives in service of the Dhamma, who have never been through the *sikkhamānā* period.

79 This statement, or anything like it, is absent from the Sudassanavinayavibhāsā, a Chinese translation of a Sinhalese Vinaya commentary in many ways similar to the Samantapāsādikā (T № 1462). We have seen that the Therīgāthā commentary (by Dhammapāla rather than Buddhaghosa) appears to vacillate between seeing *sikkhamānā* as simply meaning the threefold training, and seeing it as the specific stage of ordination status; and the Sammohavinodinī omits the *sikkhamānā* entirely. It is therefore unclear to what extent Buddhaghosa's comments in the Samantapāsādikā represent the Sinhalese tradition in general.[61]

7.5 Sikkhamānā in the Ordination Questions

80 The ordination candidate in the Mahāsaṅghika group of schools is questioned as to whether she has completed her *sikkhamānā* training.[62] This may be taken as implying that the *sikkhamānā* stage must have been essential for all bhikkhuni candidates.

81 When we look closer at the ordination questions, moreover, it becomes less clear exactly what they imply. It is normally assumed that the candidate has to give the 'correct' answer to these questions, and if they cannot they may not ordain. But, although the questions are said to be regarding 'obstacles' (*antarāyikā dhammā*) it is not, to my knowledge, ex-

[61] A cursory survey of later sub-commentaries has turned up nothing on this point.

[62] Mahāsaṅghika T22, № 1425, p. 471b; Lokuttaravāda (Roth, p. 32 § 35). In addition, the candidate is questioned in the Dharmaguptaka and Sarvāstivāda Vinayas, but only in the second part of the ordination, when in front of the bhikkhu Sangha. This case is discussed below.

plicitly stated that failure to make the 'correct' answer necessarily bars ordination. The basic purpose of a question is not to prohibit, but to elicit information. When we fill out a form, we do not expect that in each case there is a right and a wrong answer, but merely that the relevant information is required. Similarly, in the case of ordination, there are clearly some cases where it is simply impossible to give the 'right' answer. For example, the candidate is asked whether they have the permission of their parents, and in the case of women, the permission of their husbands. Obviously, this may frequently be impossible: the parents may be dead, or unknown, or mad, or incapacitated, and similarly with the husband, and of course a woman may not even be married. Some Vinayas—such as the Mahāsaṅghika and Mūlasarvāstivāda—acknowledge this problem, by allowing that if the parents are dead this question may be skipped; but this is only a partial solution.

82 Many of the other questions concern various matters which, based on guidelines found elsewhere in the Vinaya, may not completely bar ordination. This requires some explanation. The first chapter of the Khandhakas describes the evolution of the ordination procedure in great detail. It contains very many prescriptions and requirements for ordination, and conditions that should be met for ordination to take place. It is often assumed that all these requirements are necessary. But it is not difficult to find examples of cases where less than complete adherence to all these rules is found, and yet the ordination is regarded as still carried out.

83 Thus the Mahāvihāravāsin Vinaya contains two distinct types of imperfections in the ordination procedure. In some cases, it is said that a certain thing should not be done, and if it is done, the candidate is 'to be expelled' (*nāsetabbo*). In other cases, a thing should not be done, but if it is done, there is an offense of wrong-doing (*āpatti dukkaṭassa*), which evidently falls to the *upajjhāya*. The cases involving an 'offense of wrong-doing' typically involve minor matters, while those meriting expulsion are more serious. Thus, for example, someone who ordains someone who has no bowl or

robe incurs an offense of wrong-doing;[63] but if one ordains a matricide or patricide, they are 'to be expelled'.[64]

84 Once this distinction is recognized, it cannot escape notice that many of the items found in the ordination questions incur an offense of wrong-doing, not expulsion. These include ordaining someone with the 'five diseases',[65] one who is under government service,[66] one who is in debt,[67] and one who does not have bowl and robes. On the other hand, if one ordains someone who is under twenty years from conception, or who is not a human, they can definitely not remain. The case of giving ordination to one who is not a male is ambiguous: it seems that a woman who snuck into a bhikkhu ordination might well be accepted as a bhikkhuni.

85 Another point to notice is that the Vinayas vary considerably in their questions. For example, the Mūlasarvāstivāda bhikkhuni ordination has around 36 questions, and lists about 33 diseases, while the Mahīśāsaka has about 15 questions and mentions 7 diseases.[68] Even within the Pali tradition there seems to be some disagreement: the main passage on bhikkhuni ordination lists 24 questions,[69] but the Parivāra mentions 11.[70] We are not dealing with a closed and definitive list of criteria, but a somewhat flexible standard, which may well have admitted of some variation from the earliest times. At the very least we must admit that the Vinaya falls short of definitively stating that anyone who fails to give the 'correct' answer can never ordain under any circumstances. Thus the fact that the candidate is asked, in the Mahāsaṅghika group, whether she has completed the two years *sikkhamānā* training cannot be accepted as definitive evidence that this was essential, even within that group of schools.

---

[63] Pali Vinaya 1.90. Other examples include ordaining someone if there is a fault with the preceptor, or with various diseases and disabilities.

[64] Pali Vinaya 1.88. Other examples include ordaining a eunuch or hermaphrodite, one who has fraudulently donned the robes, one who has gone over to another sect while still a bhikkhu, an animal(!), one who has raped a bhikkhuni, killed an arahant, caused a schism in the Sangha, or injured a Buddha.

[65] *Na, bhikkhave, pañcahi ābādhehi phuṭṭho pabbājetabbo. Yo pabbājeyya, āpatti dukkaṭassāti..*

[66] *Na, bhikkhave, rājabhaṭo pabbājetabbo. Yo pabbājeyya, āpatti dukkaṭassāti..*

[67] *Na, bhikkhave, iṇāyiko pabbājetabbo. Yo pabbājeyya, āpatti dukkaṭassāti.*

[68] It is not always possible to determine exactly how to count the questions in the Chinese translations.

[69] Pali Vinaya 2.271.

[70] Pali Vinaya 5.140.

7.6 Sikkhamānā in the Ordination Procedure

86 In addition to the mention of the *sikkhamānā* in the ordination questions, she is mentioned in the ordination procedure in all extant Vinayas, with the sole exception of the Mahāvihāravāsin.[71] I have left this until last for I believe it is the most powerful evidence that the bhikkhuni ordination candidate was generally expected to have completed the *sikkhamānā* training. Nevertheless, I believe that even here, a careful evaluation reveals a more nuanced historical picture. The development of the *sikkhamānā* as depicted in the Dharmaguptaka Vinaya is highly suggestive as to the probable historical situation.

87 The sequence of events starts with the ordination of young girls, which caused various problems due to their immaturity. The Buddha therefore allowed the *sāmaṇerī* training for such girls. There follows the allowance for giving the *sikkhamānā* training to girls of 18 years of age, followed by the requirement that she must train for two years in the six rules. Next the text goes on to describe the bhikkhuni ordination. When the first part of the ordination, in front of bhikkhunis, is completed, the candidate is led to the bhikkhu Sangha. There she is questioned again before the bhikkhus give the final statement of the ordination. In this final questioning, the candidate is asked an extra question, not found in the earlier part of the ordination procedure: 'Have you completed the [*sikkhamānā*] training in the precepts?'

88 Only here, right at the end of the whole procedure, is the requirement of *sikkhamānā* presented as if it applies to all women. Even here it is, given the context, ambiguous, since we started out talking about young girls. But the striking thing is that the requirement is made specifically by the bhikkhus. It is as if the text is trying to tell us: 'The *sikkhamānā* training was originally laid down for young girls, but the bhikkhus applied it to all women'.

89 A similar pattern is found in the Sarvāstivāda. There, too, the questions in front of the bhikkhuni Sangha do not mention the *sikkhamānā*,[72] but

[71] Sarvāstivāda (T23, № 1435, p. 332, b26), Mūlasarvāstivāda (T24, № 1453, p. 462, b12–13), Mahīśāsaka (T22, № 1421, p. 188, a17), Mahāsaṅghika (T22, № 1425, p. 472, c14), Lokuttaravāda (Roth p. 38 § 47), and Dharmaguptaka (T22, № 1428, p. 757, c18–21).

[72] T23, № 1435, p. 332, b12–23.

when she is led in front of the bhikkhus they ask if she has completed the two years' training.[73]

90 While not sharing this inconsistency in the questions, the Mūlasarvāstivāda, Mahāsaṅghika, and Lokuttaravāda Vinayas, like the Dharmaguptaka and Sarvāstivāda, depict a situation where the candidate is said to be a *sikkhamānā*, usually specified as a *kumārībhūtā* who started the training at eighteen and has now completed it at twenty.[74] So all these procedures appear to arise out of the specific context of giving ordination to young girls.

91 The ordination procedures as they appear in our existing Vinayas depict the most complete situation, one that covers the entire spectrum of ordination possibilities. This is characteristic of the literary style of these texts, which tend to accumulate passages and move towards comprehensiveness. Having designed the text to encompass the most complete possible procedure, it would be only natural that, with time, each step of the procedure should come to be regarded as essential. Such developments are the norm in Buddhism, and may be constantly observed in the realm of doctrinal development through the Abhidhamma and commentaries.

92 As so often, then, one will reach different conclusions if one brings different assumptions. If, as is common in the Buddhist traditions, one believes that every requirement of the ordination is absolutely necessary, and that the mention of the *sikkhamānā* in most Vinayas is evidence that it is intrinsic to the Vinaya, then one will conclude that *sikkhamānā* training is necessary. On the other hand, if one accepts that the ordination procedure as described is an ideal case, which in practice must have admitted of much variation; and one sees the absence of questions about the *sikkhamānā* in some Vinayas as evidence for the diversity of ancient practice, and the probable evolution of the *sikkhamānā* platform, one will conclude that the *sikkhamānā* training is optional for mature women.

---

[73] T23, № 1435, p. 333, a14–15.

[74] The Mahīśāsaka text appears to be incomplete in this section, so cannot be evaluated.

7.7 Conclusion

93 The *sikkhamānā* training was intended as an extra allowance so that young women could undertake a training similar to that of the bhikkhunis at an earlier age. The idea that *sikkhamānā* training is integral for the ordination of all women is not supported in the earliest texts. The universal requirement for *sikkhamānā* training appears in later passages of the Vinaya and commentaries, where it has evidently been introduced by the bhikkhus. It is not clear whether the opinions were shared by the bhikkhunis, or to what extent women have actually practiced this training.

94 The historical situation I would suggest here is simple. The *sikkhamānā* stage was introduced, possibly by former Jain nuns, as a means of helping young women train for full ordination. When the time came for compiling the detailed instructions on ordination procedure, the texts followed on from the introduction of the *sikkhamānā* in such cases, tracing the career of the young woman through to full ordination. Such a presentation naturally suggests that *sikkhamānā* is a normal part of all ordinations. This agrees with the general tendency of the Vinaya to make the ordination more stringent and more complex, and to make things that were earlier regarded as desirable into things that are essential. It also agrees with the movement to making the *sāmaṇera* ordination, which was originally intended for boys, into a stage required for all men before full ordination. This development, carried out in parallel fashion across the Buddhist world, resulted in most Vinayas stating or implying that all female candidates must complete the *sikkhamānā* training. The Mahāvihāravāsin Vinaya is alone in not mentioning the *sikkhamānā* in the bhikkhuni ordination procedure. In this respect, as in the ordination procedures generally, it shows its archaic nature. The situation found in the canonical Vinayas of other schools is found in the Pali school only in its commentaries.

95 Such an unclear textual situation has definite ramifications in the context of modern bhikkhuni ordination. It is difficult to justify the perpetuation of this difference between the male and female ordination procedures, which inevitably will be seen as embodying chauvinist attitudes. Such a perspective can hardly be dismissed when the central passage in the Pali commentary that stipulates the universal requirement for the *sikkhamānā*

training is, in fact, blatantly chauvinist. Since there are serious textual objections to the belief that such a universal requirement was ever intended by the Buddha, an insistence on the *sikkhamānā* training will be interpreted, rightly or wrongly, as nothing more than the perpetuation of such attitudes.

96 All this, of course, has precisely nothing to do with the question of whether it is a good thing to do two years' training before ordination. In Thailand today monks will typically take full ordination with little or no preliminary training; and the truly dismal state of the Sangha that has resulted is a good argument for requiring a training period. In some of the Mahāyāna lands, for example Korea and Taiwan, the monastics must undergo a rigorous and extensive training before taking ordination. In the Thai forest tradition of Ajahn Chah, candidates will typically spend up to a year as an *anāgārika* (eight-precept postulant in white) and a further year as a novice (*sāmaṇera* or *sāmaṇerī*) before taking full ordination. The end result is a two year training period, which in effect reflects the *sikkhamānā* training, although this is pure coincidence. This system works well in this context. No doubt other systems work well in different places, and the preferred procedure will be influenced by local conditions, such as the age and educational level of the candidates, the number of candidates relative to teachers, the emphasis on meditation, study, or service, the personal style of the local Sangha, and many other variables. The great variations in the list of 'six rules' for the *sikkhamānā* is irrefutable evidence that this training was treated differently in different communities of ancient Indian Buddhists. The same remains the case today, and so it will be always. In such a case the wise course will be to encourage and support any community that is working to apply Vinaya with sincerity and integrity, even if their interpretation may not agree with our own.

Chapter 8

A BHIKKHUNI MISCELLANY

In this chapter I gather several shorter notes on aspects of Vinaya that have come up from time to time in the context of bhikkhuni Vinaya.

8.1 Communion

2 Following is a sketch of the notion of *saṁvāsa* ('communion') as found in the Pali Vinaya. Communion is relevant in the context of bhikkhuni ordination, as it is sometimes questioned whether groups of monastics from different traditions may perform *saṅghakamma* such as ordination together. One reason why this may not be possible would be if the two groups of Sangha were in a schismatic relation, which would be the case if the ancient schools of Buddhism had arisen through a formal *saṅghabheda*. However, I argued in *Sects & Sectarianism* that there is no serious evidence that this was the case. On the contrary, the ancient schools grew apart because of geography or doctrinal developments, and not due to schism over Vinaya. Indeed, the three existing Vinaya lineages—Mahāvihāravāsin, Dharmaguptaka, and Mūlasarvāstivāda—share very close roots in ancient times, and all stem from the same tightly knit group of Elders around the time of Aśoka.[1]

3 A further possibility that might prohibit the performance of bhikkhuni ordination with bhikkhus from the Theravāda and Central Asian lineages

[1] Chapter 7.71–74.

with bhikkhunis stemming from East Asian traditions is the concept of 'separate communion' (*nānāsaṁvāsa*). This is a state of division within the Sangha that falls short of a true schism, and yet still disallows the performance of mutual *saṅghakamma*. In modern times, this concept is applied very liberally and casually, and in the Thai forest tradition where I trained, any bhikkhu who comes from a different background is assumed to be of a different communion. However, the Vinaya itself applies the concept much more narrowly.

4 The notion of *saṁvāsa* is originally laid down in the context of *uposatha*, and there it functions primarily as an indicator of who is to be included in the unified Sangha. A unified Sangha is regularly defined as one that is of the same communion, remaining in the same *sīmā*. (*Samaggo nāma saṅgho samānasaṁvāsako samānasīmāyaṁ ṭhito.*) The same definition is used in the context of *pavāraṇā*. One should not perform either *uposatha* or *pavāraṇā* with bhikkhus who are *nānāsaṁvāsa*. If one does not know that the other party is *nānāsaṁvāsa*, there is no offense in performing *uposatha* with them.[2]

5 The other rules regarding *nānāsaṁvāsa* include prohibitions against traveling on *uposatha* or *pavāraṇā* day to a group of *nānāsaṁvāsa* bhikkhus. These restrictions are similar to those that apply to one undergoing disciplinary measures such as *parivāsa*, *mānattā*, etc.

6 One who is *nānāsaṁvāsa* cannot be the completing member for a quorum in *saṅghakamma*.[3] Nor can they object to an act that is being carried out.[4] The protest in the midst of the Sangha of one who is *nānāsaṁvāsa* is not valid. But acts carried out in different communions are valid for those communions.[5] Generally, one should not bow to one of a different

---

2 Pali Vinaya 1.133.

3 Pali Vinaya 1.319: *Catuvaggakaraṇañce, bhikkhave, kammaṁ... nānāsaṁvāsakacatuttho kammaṁ kareyya... akammaṁ na ca karaṇīyaṁ.* A *kamma* that is carried out with a group of four... should they do this *kamma* with one of a different communion as fourth... this is not *kamma*, and should not be done.

4 Pali Vinaya 1.320: *Nānāsaṁvāsakassa, bhikkhave... saṅghamajjhe paṭikkosanā na ruhati.*

5 Pali Vinaya 1.339: '*Te ce, bhikkhu, ukkhittānuvattakā bhikkhū tattheva antosīmāya uposathaṁ karissanti, saṅghakammaṁ karissanti, yathā mayā ñatti ca anussāvanā ca paññattā, tesaṁ tāni kammāni dhammikāni kammāni bhavissanti akuppāni ṭhānārahāni. Tumhe ce, bhikkhu, ukkhepakā bhikkhū tattheva antosīmāya uposathaṁ karissatha, saṅghakammaṁ karissatha, yathā mayā ñatti ca anussāvanā ca paññattā, tumhākampi tāni kammāni dhammikāni kammāni*

communion, but exception is made for one who is senior and a speaker of Dhamma.[6] One must be of the same communion to cause a *saṅghabheda* (schism), which seems strange; but it makes sense, because in order to accomplish a formal *saṅghabheda* two groups of bhikkhus must perform separate *uposathas*.[7]

7 There are two (and apparently *only* two) grounds for regarding someone as *nānāsaṁvāsa*:

> 8 There are, monks, these two grounds for belonging to a different communion: by oneself one makes oneself of a different communion; or a Sangha in unity suspends one for not seeing [an offense] or not making amends, or for not relinquishing. These are the two grounds for belonging to a different communion.
>
> 9 There are, monks, these two grounds for belonging to the same communion: by oneself one makes oneself of the same communion; or a Sangha in unity rehabilitates one who was suspended for not seeing [an offense] or not making amends, or for not relinquishing. These are the two grounds for belonging to the same communion.[8]

10 The way in which communion is described in the Vinaya requires a definite act of decision. It is never simply assumed that other bhikkhus or bhikkhunis are of different communion. Even if in fact they are of different communion, it is no offense to perform *saṅghakamma* together with them if one does not know (if one does know it is a *dukkaṭa*). However they may not complete the quorum.

11 In any case, it is obvious that the Sanghas as they are constituted today cannot be considered as of 'different communion' according to the standards of the Pali Vinaya. There is, accordingly, no justification in using this argument to oppose bhikkhuni ordination within the Theravāda Sangha.

---

bhavissanti akuppāni ṭhānārahāni. Taṁ kissa hetu? Nānāsaṁvāsakā ete bhikkhū tumhehi, tumhe ca tehi nānāsaṁvāsakā.

[6] Pali Vinaya 161: *Nānāsaṁvāsako vuḍḍhataro dhammavādī vandiyo.*

[7] Pali Vinaya 2.203: *Bhikkhu kho, upāli, pakatatto, samānasaṁvāsako, samānasīmāyaṁ ṭhito, saṅghaṁ bhindatī.*

[8] Pali Vinaya 1.339: *Dvemā, bhikkhu, nānāsaṁvāsakabhūmiyo—attanā vā attānaṁ nānāsaṁvāsakaṁ karoti, samaggo vā naṁ saṅgho ukkhipati adassane vā appaṭikamme vā appaṭinissagge vā. Imā kho, bhikkhu, dve nānāsaṁvāsakabhūmiyo. Dvemā, bhikkhu, samānasaṁvāsakabhūmiyo—attanā vā attānaṁ samānasaṁvāsaṁ karoti, samaggo vā naṁ saṅgho ukkhittaṁ osāreti adassane vā appaṭikamme vā appaṭinissagge vā. Imā kho, bhikkhu, dve samānasaṁvāsakabhūmiyoti.*

8.2 Living in the Forest

12 It is commonly believed that bhikkhunis are forbidden from living in the forest. This may not be such a problem for bhikkhunis in traditional Buddhist countries, where only a small percentage of the Sangha preserves the forest lifestyle, but it is a major issue for bhikkhunis from non-traditional backgrounds. Experience has shown that almost all the bhikkhus who have taken ordination from Western countries prefer to live in forest monasteries, and almost all the successful monasteries for local people in non-traditional countries are situated in the forest. If bhikkhunis are to be required to live in the town, it is almost certain that there will be few candidates in countries such as Australia who would be interested.

13 One red herring should be disposed of first. It is sometimes said that the rule against living in a forest was based on the episode when Uppalavaṇṇā, one of the great arahant bhikkhunis, was raped.[9] But there is no mention in this sad episode that she was living in a forest, nor is any mention made of forbidding forest dwelling. Rather, the point of this story is to make it clear that a bhikkhuni who is raped does not fall into any offense.

14 The rule against living in a forest, or wilderness (*arañña*), is found in the Bhikkhunikkhandhaka.

15
> Now on that occasion bhikkhunis lived in the forest. Bandits attacked them. The Blessed One declared regarding that matter: 'Monks, bhikkhunis should not dwell in a wilderness. For one who should so dwell, there is an offense of wrong-doing.'[10]

16 We have already remarked that rape and other physical violence against bhikkhunis is a serious issue that needs to be addressed directly. Certainly no-one would wish to place women at risk. The question here, however, is simply: what is a wilderness?

17 'Wilderness' is not defined in this context, so we shall have to look elsewhere, and consider whether other contexts give us a reasonable basis for inference. Typically the texts contrast the *arañña* with the *gāma*, or village. One important context is *pārājika* 2, where the bhikkhus (and bhikkhunis)

---

[9] Pali Vinaya 3.35.

[10] Pali Vinaya 2.278.

are forbidden from stealing anything from the 'village or wilderness'. Here these terms are defined thus:

> 18 **'Village'** means: **one hut (*kuṭi*) is a village**, also two huts... three huts... four huts... with people... without people... enclosed... unenclosed... a cattle-ranch... and even a caravan that is camped for more than four months is a village.
>
> 19 **'Village vicinity'** means: for an enclosed village, the distance an average man could throw a clod of earth while standing at the village gate; for an unenclosed village, the distance an average man could throw a clod of earth while standing in the vicinity of a house.
>
> 20 **'Wilderness'** means: apart from the village and the village vicinity, all else is called wilderness.[11]

21 This is straightforward: just one hut is sufficient to constitute a 'village'. However, elsewhere dwelling in a 'building' might also be in a 'wilderness'.

> 22 Now on that occasion venerable Udāyin dwelt in a wilderness. His dwelling (*vihāra*) was beautiful, attractive, delightful...

23 Yet again, when dwelling in a monastery had not yet been allowed by the Buddha, the monks were living in wilderness, at the roots of trees, mountains, or caves. When requested, the Buddha allowed five kinds of shelter, which include a dwelling (*vihāra*).[12] In this context, a 'dwelling' seems to be contrasted with a 'wilderness'.

24 For the purposes of establishing a 'boundary' (*sīmā*) for Sangha acts, if no boundary has been formally appointed, then if the Sangha is in a village, the 'village or town boundary' will suffice, and if in the wilderness, a distance all around of about 100 metres.[13]

---

[11] Pali Vinaya 3.46: ***Gāmo*** *nāma* ***ekakuṭikopi gāmo***, *dvikuṭikopi gāmo, tikuṭikopi gāmo, catukuṭikopi gāmo, samanussopi gāmo, amanussopi gāmo, parikkhittopi gāmo, aparikkhittopi gāmo, gonisādiniviṭṭhopi gāmo, yopi sattho atirekacatumāsaniviṭṭho sopi vuccati gāmo.* ***Gāmūpacāro*** *nāma parikkhittassa gāmassa indakhīle ṭhitassa majjhimassa purisassa leḍḍupāto, aparikkhittassa gāmassa gharūpacāre ṭhitassa majjhimassa purisassa leḍḍupāto.* ***Araññaṁ*** *nāma ṭhapetvā gāmañca gāmūpacārañca avasesaṁ araññaṁ nāma.* The further definition of wilderness in this rule is not relevant here. (Pali Vinaya 3.51: *Araññaṁ nāma yaṁ manussānaṁ pariggahitaṁ hoti, taṁ araññaṁ.*) This applies only in the context of stealing: one can only steal from a wilderness that which belongs to someone.

[12] Pali Vinaya 2.146: *Anujānāmi, bhikkhave, pañca leṇāni—vihāraṁ, aḍḍhayogaṁ, pāsādaṁ, hammiyaṁ, guhanti.*

[13] Pali Vinaya 1.110–111: *Asammatāya, bhikkhave, sīmāya aṭṭhapitāya, yaṁ gāmaṁ vā nigamaṁ vā upanissāya viharati, yā tassa vā gāmassa gāmasīmā, nigamassa vā nigamasīmā, ayaṁ tattha*

25 It would seem, then, as if we have a number of indications, which are not totally consistent. This is not a problem, as the different ideas of the wilderness are applied in different contexts, and it would be unreasonable to expect total agreement. Our question is simply, which is the most applicable in the case of bhikkhunis living in the 'wilderness'?

26 It seems clear enough that the purpose of the rule was for the safety of the bhikkhunis, so the definition we choose should be based on the grounds of safety. It seems to me that the idea of being included in the village boundary as determined by the civil authorities has little or no effect on safety. Indeed, in many places today city environments are less safe than the country.

27 The only thing that seems to me to be relevant from a point of view of safety is having a hut, preferably a lockable one. This allows the bhikkhuni a degree of protection. This would suggest that the first definition, 'even one *kuṭi* is a village' should be applied here.

28 This suggests that this rule is connected with the fact that, for the bhikkhunis, there are only three 'supports' mentioned in their ordination: alms-food, robes, and medicine. The fourth support is typically 'dwelling at the root of a tree'. This is not mentioned for the bhikkhunis.[14] It would seem that the idea is that bhikkhunis should not dwell literally 'in the forest', staying at the roots of trees, but that they should have a decent dwelling place to ensure their safety.[15]

8.3 Going to court

29 Bhikkhuni *saṅghādisesa* 1 is understood to be a prohibition against bringing lawsuits. This has a significant practical effect on modern bhikkhunis, as there has been a substantial resistance to the notion that bhikkhunis are entitled to seek legal protection. On the one hand, this is seen as a radical renunciation, throwing oneself onto the winds of uncertainty, and trust-

---

samānasaṁvāsā ekuposathā. Agāmake ce, bhikkhave, araññe samantā sattabbhantarā, ayaṁ tattha samānasaṁvāsā ekuposathā.

[14] In most Vinayas. The Dharmaguptaka has four supports. This would seem to be yet another instance of late influence from the bhikkhu Vinaya on the Dharmaguptaka.

[15] See VAJIRAÑĀṆAVARORASA, 3.259.

ing in the Dhamma of forgiveness; certainly, no-one wants to see litigious monastics. Yet it also breeds disempowerment and disenfranchisement; bhikkhunis become easily victimized, whether it be through physical attacks, defamation, or theft of monastery property. In recent years, several cases have been brought to court by bhikkhunis, in the face of criticism by the Sangha generally. The problem is that in many cases their position is obviously just. All should be entitled to protection under the law. And so, when bhikkhunis seek to exercise this basic right, it becomes either an occasion to criticize the bhikkhunis, or an occasion to criticize the Vinaya. Once again, so it is argued, we can see how the Vinaya is irrelevant and cannot be applied in our modern world.

30 Following our usual method, we will start with the assumption that Vinaya is reasonable and ethical. Nothing should follow from Vinaya that entails harm. If Vinaya is interpreted in a way that leads to harm, we would return to a close examination of the actual texts to see how the harmful principles may have come about, and whether they are actually justified by the texts themselves.

8.3.1 What does 'ussaya' mean?

31 This rule pivots on the term *ussaya*. The bhikkhuni is forbidden from being a 'speaker of *ussaya*'. Unfortunately, *ussaya* appears nowhere else in the Vinaya, and indeed, so far as I am aware, nowhere else in the Pali canon. The Lokuttaravāda Vinaya uses the Hybrid Sanskrit form *utsada(ya)*.[16] The fact that such an unusual term is found in both of these Indic texts suggests that it is intrinsic to the rule from its origin.[17]

32 The Pali Text Society Dictionary takes *ussaya* as a variant of *usuyya*, itself related to the Sanskrit *asūya*. These words mean envy, jealousy; and *asūya*, according the Monier-Williams Sanskrit Dictionary, can mean 'calumnious'. Accordingly, both I.B. Horner and K.R. Norman translate *ussaya* as 'envy'.

---

[16] V.l. *utsada(va)*. The title to the rule uses *ussaya*.

[17] As usual, the Chinese Vinayas are not much help in determining the exact meaning of an Indic term. The Dharmaguptaka, Sarvāstivāda, and Mahāśāsaka just have 言 'say', which the Sarvāstivāda qualifies with 恃勢 'relying on power'. The Mahāsaṅghika has more explicitly 諍訟相言 'bring a law suit'.

33 However, there are a number of serious objections to this translation. Firstly, the Sanskritized form in the Lokuttaravāda Vinaya is not *asūya* but *utsada(ya)*. Perhaps this is simply a case of incorrect Sanskritization from an earlier form; but perhaps it is the modern etymology that has gone astray. A second problem is that the derivation of *ussaya* from *asūya* via *usuyya* does not seem at all straightforward. The third, and critical, problem is that nothing in the rule, the background stories, or the analyses has anything to do with 'envy'.

34 There is another possible derivation. Pali[18] and Sanskrit[19] dictionaries both acknowledge a √*si*, meaning 'to bind'. The Sanskrit sources recognize a form of the word in this sense that uses the prefix *ut-*. The derivation is straightforward if we take it as a causative form, 'having bound'. The Lokuttaravāda form would, under this interpretation, be related to the Sanskrit causative verb *sāyayati*.

35 The PTS Dictionary supplies a reference to the Pali commentaries where √*si* is equivalent to √*bandh*, cognate to the English 'bind'. This very word appears in the background story of the Pali version of our rule, when the lay people accuse the bhikkhunis of 'having a person imprisoned' (*bandhāpesu*). It seems that this is the actual act that causes the laying down of the rule; and here, √*bandh* in causative form plays the same function that *ussaya* does in the rule itself.

36 I would therefore propose that *ussaya* be understood as a noun related to a causative form of √*si* in the sense of 'causing [someone] to be imprisoned'.

8.3.2 Mahāvihāravāsin

37 The Mahāvihāravāsin Vinaya tells of a lay supporter who gave a store-house to the bhikkhunis. He died, leaving two sons, one with faith, the other faithless. The sons argued about whether they or bhikkhunis were the rightful owners. They dealt it out—apparently deciding by chance who should inherit it—and the faithless son received it, went to the store-house, and asked the bhikkhunis to leave. Thullanandā objected, and they took

[18] PTS Dict., p. 710: *Sinoti* [*sā* or *si*; Vedic *syati* & *sināti*; the Dhtp 505 gives *si* in meaning '*bandhana*'] to bind; DhsA 219 (*sinoti bandhatī ti setu*).

[19] MONIER-WILLIAMS, p. 182: *ud*-√*si*, p. *-sināti*, to fetter, chain, RV. 1, 125, 2; *utsita*, mfn. fettered, entangled, AV. Vi, 112, 2; 3; p. 1212: *si*, to bind, tie, fetter.

the matter to the Ministers, who agreed that the offering had been made properly to the bhikkhunis, and this had been witnessed by the Ministers themselves. They dismissed the case and the bhikkhunis retained control. The defeated son abused the bhikkhunis, and Thullanandā reported this to the Ministers. They then had the faithless son punished (probably flogged). After his punishment, the faithless son then instigated some naked ascetics to abuse the bhikkhunis. Thullanandā complained to the authorities again, and they had the man fettered. People criticized it, saying: 'First the bhikkhunis had a store-room taken away from the man, then had him punished, then had him fettered. Next they'll have him killed.'[20] Accordingly, the rule was laid down:

> 38 Should a bhikkhuni be one who speaks in order to have someone imprisoned, whether concerning a householder or householder's son or a slave or a tradesperson, or even an ascetic or wanderer, this bhikkhuni too has transgressed a rule that is an 'immediate-offense' *saṅghādisesa* involving being sent away.[21]

39 The Pali word analysis explains *ussaya* as meaning 'she is a maker of lawsuits'.[22] As often in the word analyses, it is not clear that they intend the definition to be a simple equivalence, or whether the definition is intended to clarify the meaning of the term in context. It is unclear, in other words, whether the word analysis means us to understand that '*ussaya*' means 'law-suit'; or that 'she is one who speaks *ussaya* and makes a law-suit.'

40 The non-offense clauses say there is an exemption if she goes being dragged along by people(!), if she asks for protection, or if she explains without being specific.[23] The last clause seems to mean that, for example, if she tells the police that the monastery has been robbed, or that she has been attacked, without accusing anyone specifically, there is no offense. The second clause also makes it clear that seeking legal protection cannot

---

[20] Pali Vinaya 4.224: *Paṭhamaṁ bhikkhuniyo udositaṁ acchindāpesuṁ, dutiyaṁ daṇḍāpesuṁ, tatiyaṁ bandhāpesuṁ. Idāni ghātāpessantīti.* The PTS reading omits *paṭhamaṁ*

[21] Pali Vinaya 2.224: *Yā pana bhikkhunī ussayavādikā vihareyya gahapatinā vā gahapatiputtena vā dāsena vā kammakārena vā antamaso samaṇaparibbājakenāpi, ayaṁ bhikkhunī paṭhamāpattikaṁ dhammaṁ āpannā nissāraṇīyaṁ saṁghādisesan'ti.*

[22] Pali Vinaya 2.224: *Ussayavādikā nāma aṭṭakārikā vuccati.*

[23] Pali Vinaya 2.225: *Anāpatti manussehi ākaḍḍhīyamānā gacchati, ārakkhaṁ yācati, anodissa ācikkhati...*

be an offense under any circumstances. But it is curious that this would seem to be what Thullanandā did in the origin story. She was seeking protection for the bhikkhunis from the aggressive and unscrupulous acts of a certain individual.

41 There are some serious problems with this rule, both ethical and formal. The ethical problem is clear enough. Originally, Thullanandā was defending the property rights of the bhikkhunis. Like anyone else, they have to live. If anyone could simply help themselves to the bhikkhunis' land and property, the Sangha could not survive. In the follow-up, she was protecting the bhikkhunis from deliberate and aggressive abuse. Again, it seems hard to find fault with this; on the contrary, she acted as protector of the Sangha. The right to protection under the law is, of course, a fundamental principle of human society.

42 The formal problems are no less acute. In the background story, there is no suggestion that she is instigating a legal proceedings or seeking punishment. Remembering that government in those days was much simpler than today, it would seem that the acts she carries out would not be matters for the court in the present day. In the first case, they together ask (*pucchiṁsu*) the Ministers regarding the property titles. As Thullanandā acted together with the son, this can clearly not be considered bringing a legal action. These days such an matter would be handled by a mere inquiry to the relevant government department. Following this, when the man is abusing or instigating others to abuse the bhikkhunis, Thullanandā is merely said to 'inform the Ministers of this matter' (*mahāmattānaṁ etamatthaṁ ārocesi*). It is the Ministers who impose a punishment on the man (*mahāmattā taṁ purisaṁ daṇḍāpesuṁ*). The people who complained that the bhikkhunis imposed these punishments, therefore, were wrong. In the present day, such matters would typically not be taken to court, but the complainant would first take the matter to the police. If the police were not effective to make the person stop his abuse, the appropriate State prosecution body might take it to court.

43 Next we have the rule, which introduces the term *ussaya*, which is found nowhere in the background story. Finally the analysis, which for the first time explicitly introduces the notion of a legal case (*aṭṭa*). This throws one fact into stark relief: in each of the three main sections (background story,

rule, word analysis), the term used to describe the forbidden act is quite different. In the background story the bhikkhuni is simply said to 'state a matter' (*etamatthaṁ ārocesi*); the rule itself forbids speech that is *ussaya*; and the analysis says that *ussaya* means a court case (*aṭṭa*).

44 As usual, we are thrown back on our interpretive suppositions. If we see the text as a coherent whole, then we would accept the *vibhaṅga's* equation of *ussaya* and *aṭṭa*, and take the background story, rule, and analysis as referring to the same type of event. Given that Thullanandā's acts in the background story do not seem to be unethical, we would have to suppose that even justifiable litigation is prohibited under this rule.

45 If we wish to take an analytical approach, we would see the background story, the rule, and the analysis as using quite different terminology, with only the analysis explicitly referring to legal cases.

46 However, given that the background story does not agree with the accusations of the laypeople (they say that the bhikkhunis had the man imprisoned, whereas the story says that the Ministers had him imprisoned), and given that Thullanandā seems to be simply seeking justifiable protection, which is said to be not an offense, it would seem reasonable to leave aside the background story and focus on what the bhikkhunis are accused of doing; that is, having someone imprisoned. Taking the equivalence of *ussaya* and *bandhāpesu* as our starting point, and combining this with the explanation of *ussaya* as meaning 'she is a maker of lawsuits', we would arrive at the interpretation: she instigates a lawsuit in order to have someone imprisoned.

47 In the passage where the lay people accuse the nuns, they mention a number of items: first, having the store-house taken away; second, having the man punished; third, having him imprisoned. These form a scale of severity; the next on the list is having the man killed. And the rule is only imposed after they 'have the man imprisoned'. This again suggests that the purpose of the rule is specifically to stop bhikkhunis from having people imprisoned.

48 The texts themselves are silent on the question of intention: what if she had no wish to see the man imprisoned, but the authorities did so anyway? It seems to me that in the spirit of the rule, the bhikkhunis could only be held responsible for an outcome they were actually seeking, not

an incidental result. This is supported by the background story to the Dharmaguptaka version, where the Buddha himself makes a statement that results in the Ministers being punished, even though he had no such intention.

8.3.3 Mahāsaṅghika/Lokuttaravāda

49 The Mahāsaṅghika and Lokuttaravāda Vinayas, as usual, have background stories that closely agree. The language is colorful and idiomatic—to say the least—and what follows is only a rough approximation.

50 The wall between the bhikkhuni monastery and the monastery of the nuns of another sect fell down. Thullanandā, who was the Sangha official in charge of maintenance, tells the other nuns that they are shameless, as they wander in and out naked; seeing them causes the defilements of the bhikkhunis to grow, so they must rebuild the wall immediately. One of the other nuns asks if they can wait until the end of the rainy season. Thullanandā insisted, and when the other nuns refused to start work immediately, Thullanandā abused them, saying: 'Short-lived ones! Drunkards! Donkey-riders! Naked, shameless ones of wrong views, destined for hell! Build the wall!' The other nun replied: 'You witch's daughter, fat as a pumpkin! I wouldn't build the wall even if you killed me.' Thullanandā then went to the court[24] and complained to the judge, asking him to make the other nun rebuild the wall. The judge had faith in Buddhism, so he summoned the other nun, roundly abused her, and told her to fix the wall straight away. They put the wall up, but it fell down because of the rain. Again and again they tried, and could not complete it during the three months of the rainy season. They said to the lay followers: 'Look at these worthy nuns! They made us labor for three months in the mud to put up this wall!' Word of this got to the Buddha. He called up Thullanandā, chastised her, and laid down the rule.

51 > Should a bhikkhuni be one who speaks in order to have someone imprisoned, whether concerning one dwelling at home or a wan-

[24] *Āsana.*

derer, for a day or a short period—even with monastery attendants or novices—this too is 'immediate-offense'.[25]

52 The rule analysis defines *utsada(ya)-vāda* as 'making arguments' (*kalaham kareya*). It says to merely announce it in a court or in government circles (*rājākula*) is a *thullaccaya*, but to have a person dragged into the courts is a *saṅghādisesa*. A bhikkhu, according to this Vinaya, also falls into a minor offense for similar acts. No non-offense clauses are mentioned.

53 Here Thullanandā is in fine form. I particularly like the way she describes the other nuns as 'shameless'. The fact that she claims to have been aroused by the sight of the naked nuns perhaps sheds an unexpected light on her sexual orientation—normally she's out for the guys. There's no doubt a *saṅghādisesa* is appropriate for this behavior, which is a classic example of what not to do, both when dealing with neighbors and with followers of other religions. And yet it has little in common with the Pali version; even the rule itself has quite different wording.

54 This version shares the critical term *ussaya*, although it is explained quite differently, as *kalaha* (argument) rather than *aṭṭa* (law suit). The *vibhaṅga* clearly assumes that it is not just an ordinary argument, but one that involves a legal judgment, so perhaps we should combine these interpretations. Building on from our understanding of the Mahāvihāravāsin rule, we could interpret *ussaya* as: making an aggressive or argumentative law suit in order to have someone imprisoned.

8.3.4 Dharmaguptaka

55 This version depicts the dispute as arising over the offering of a wilderness monastery.[26] Some time later, the bhikkhunis left the place, and the donor passed away. The son of the donor decided to plough the land, and bhikkhunis objected, saying it belonged to them. He argued that the land

---

[25] ROTH pp. 140–1 § 140: *Ya puna bhikṣuṇī utsada(ya)-vādā vihareyā āgārika-parivrājakehi divasmvā muhūrtam vā antamasato ārāmika-śramaṇ-uddeśehi sārdham ayampi dharmo prathamāpattiko.* Notice the unusual form *śramaṇ-uddeśa*, which occurs in the Pali bhikkhu pāṭimokkha as a term for novices (=*sāmaṇera*). The Mahāsaṅghika version is similar. T22, № 1427, p. 557, b3–5: 若比丘尼諍訟相言。若俗人若出家人晝日須臾。乃至與園民沙彌共鬪相言。是法初罪僧伽婆尸沙

[26] In apparent contradiction with the idea that bhikkhunis should not live in a wilderness, if this is interpreted as including a forest monastery.

was just being left vacant, and would not stop. The bhikkhunis went to see the judges and charged him. The judges fined the man and confiscated his possessions. The Buddha laid down the first version of the rule.

56 Later, a concubine of King Pasenadi offered a monastery to the bhikkhunis. They left it, and she offered it to a group of female brahman ascetics. The bhikkhunis returned and claimed the monastery back. The *brahmīs* took the matter to court, and the bhikkhunis were summoned. They did not know whether they were allowed to attend or not, and the Buddha said they should go when summoned. The bhikkhunis explained to the judges that the original donor still owned the monastery, although she allowed the bhikkhunis to stay there. The judges accordingly allowed the *brahmīs* to stay there. When this got back to the Buddha, he said that both the bhikkhunis and the judges were wrong: the original gift still stood, and the monastery belonged to the Sangha. When Pasenadi heard about this, he punished the judges. The Buddha then modified the rule, with the apparent intent to specify that a bhikkhuni only falls into an offense if she instigates the case.

57 If a bhikkhuni goes to see the judges and if she charges a householder or a householder's son, a slave or a servant, by day or by night, during the time of one thought, of one snap of the fingers or of one moment, then this bhikkhuni violates an immediate rule, a *saṅghādisesa* that involves being sent away.[27]

58 Again, this wording differs from the other versions. The *vibhaṅga* defines 'to charge' as 'to go see the judges and to debate together about right and wrong'. This gives another interpretation of what presumably was an original Indic term corresponding to *ussaya*. It is not dissimilar to the Mahāvihāravāsin definition.

59 If she does not mention the offender's name, it is a *thullaccaya* (in the Mahāvihāravāsin version this is no offense). It is no offense if she is summoned; if someone wants her to report something; if she has been taken

---

[27] T22, № 1431, p. 1032, a21–23: 若比丘尼詣官言。居士若居士兒。若奴若客作人。若晝若夜。若一念頃。若彈指頃。若須臾頃。是比丘尼犯初法應捨僧伽婆尸沙. The Mahīśāsaka offers a truncated version of this, identical except leaving out the detailed qualifications, from 'householder' to 'one moment'. T22, № 1423, p. 207, b25–26: 若比丘尼詣官言人。是比丘尼初犯僧伽婆尸沙可悔過

there by force or tied up; if her life or chastity are in danger; or if she says it to someone other than the judges.

60 While the background story, as usual, has nothing in common with the other Vinayas, the problem is similar to that found in the Pali. Unlike the Pali, however, the actions of the son, however unjustified, did not immediately threaten the bhikkhunis, so it appears as if their acts were less imperative. In the second case it is surprising to see the Buddha depicted as disagreeing with both the bhikkhunis and the judges; and ironic that it is the Buddha's statements that get the judges punished. It is important to note that there can be no offense if a bhikkhuni is responding to a threat to her physical safety, corresponding to the Pali allowance to ask for protection.

8.3.5 Conclusion

61 I do not have the time here to go into a detailed consideration of the other versions of this rule, which all involve similar complicated backgrounds. I will just mention the extraordinary phrasing of the Mūlasarvāstivāda version: 'Should any bhikkhuni, relying on a contract obtain for herself the possessions of a dead person…'.[28]

62 There is a genuine degree of discrepancy between the existing texts, and this compounds the ethical problem of whether it is justifiable or beneficial to require that bhikkhunis be unable to seek redress from the law. Adding to the complexity is the massive change in legal structures between the Buddha's day and our own. There is a range of possible perspectives that could be taken in considering these cases, and a corresponding range of policies in how the rule should be applied.

63 My own feeling is that this rule should only be applied where we are certain that the case is covered by the rule. This would be when the bhikkhuni, out of malice or argumentativeness, instigated a legal case with the intention to send someone to prison. We have noted that the element of malice is found in some of the canonical accounts; similarly, the Pali commentary

[28] T24, № 1455, p. 509, b28–c1: 若復苾芻尼依他舊契自爲己索亡人物者僧伽伐尸沙

specifies that the offense falls for one who acts with the malicious intent to harm.[29]

64 There is no offense if she is seeking protection. So if a bhikkhuni has been physically attacked, or if a monastery has been robbed, or similar cases, there can be no question of an offense. Similarly, if she reports a crime or misbehavior without specifying the person involved, there can be no offense. If she reports a crime, but does not instigate legal proceedings (*aṭṭakārikā*), again there can be no offense. Or if she does instigate legal proceeding but with no expectation or desire to have the opponent imprisoned, again there would be no offence. As we mentioned earlier, when lesser punishments were levied on the man in the Mahāvihāravāsin story, there was no question of a rule arising. In that case, the lesser punishment was probably a flogging. These days, it would more likely be a fine.

65 As a general principle, it is of course desirable for monastics to avoid getting entangled in court proceedings. It's messy and ugly and only the lawyers get anything out of it. In modern times, it would often be the committee who owns the monastery property and acts as steward for the Sangha who would take responsibility for legal action. This would especially be the case if there was a property dispute, as most of the background stories suggest. If it were a case of malicious intent on the part of the monastic, the committee should exercise discretion and leave the monastic to pursue their own course.

8.4 Delayed consent

66 Bhikkhuni *pācittiya* 81 presents a difficult interpretive problem, although the practical implications are less serious than some of the other cases we have considered. The main point of interest for us is that, under some interpretations, it could seem to imply that bhikkhus were involved in bhikkhuni ordination, and would thus be the only *pāṭimokkha* rule that suggested that bhikkhunis were ordained by a dual Sangha. The rule makes it an offense for a bhikkhuni to give the *vuṭṭhāpana* ordination to a *sikkhamānā*

---

[29] Samantapāsādikā 4.906: *Ussayavādikāti mānussayavasena kodhussayavasena vivadamānā. Yasmā pana sā atthato aṭṭakārikā hoti, tasmā 'ussayavādikā nāma aḍḍakārikā vuccatī'ti padabhājane vuttaṁ.*

by means of *pārivāsikachandadāna*. Unfortunately, the operative term *pārivāsikachandadāna* is obscure. It is comprised of three parts, *pārivāsika*, *chanda*, and *dāna*. Of these, only the last term *dāna* 'giving' is clear in meaning.

67 *Pārivāsika* is a personal term based on *parivāsa*, which is used in two senses in the Vinaya. The first, and by far the most common, is for the penance for bhikkhus who have committed a *saṅghādisesa*. The second is for the four months 'probation' period for one who was formerly an ascetic of another sect who wishes to ordain.[30]

68 The personal term *pārivāsika* only occurs in the former sense, meaning 'a bhikkhu who is undergoing *parivāsa*', but there is no grammatical reason why it should not also denote one who is on probation awaiting ordination. However, *pārivāsika* can also be interpreted a third way, 'one who is staying on', especially 'staying overnight'.

69 *Chanda* is similarly ambiguous, and is used in the Vinaya primarily to mean two things: either 'favoritism, preference' based on personal bias;[31] or 'consent' to a decision of the Sangha in one's absence.[32]

70 If *parivāsa* refers to the penance for a *saṅghādisesa*, which is practiced only by bhikkhus, not bhikkhunis, this would imply that bhikkhus were taking part in the *vuṭṭhāpana* ordination for bhikkhunis. If *parivāsa* is taken to mean 'staying overnight', then the rule prohibits the bhikkhunis from ordaining the candidate themselves 'on one side', and then having her ordain with the bhikkhus the following day. This, too, would require that the bhikkhus be involved in the ordination procedure. Hence, either of these interpretations challenge our suggestion that the *vuṭṭhāpana* ordination was originally given by bhikkhunis alone.

71 The Pali background story tells us that Thullanandā wished to give ordination for a *sikkhamānā*; rejecting the Elder bhikkhus, she assembled Devadatta and his cronies and did the ordination with them. The story does not use the term *pārivāsikachandadāna*, and it is not at all clear how the rule and story are meant to be related. One might assume that the problem was that she gave the ordination by 'favoritism' (*chanda*) for bhikkhus who

[30] Pali Vinaya 1.69.
[31] E.g. Pali Vinaya 4.38.
[32] E.g. Pali Vinaya 1.121.

are 'suspended' (*parivāsa*).[33] On the other hand, this interpretation has the glaring weakness that, while Devadatta and his mates were doubtless bad monks, there is no evidence that they were, at that time, actually undergoing *parivāsa*.

72 Other translators treat *pārivāsika* in the sense of 'delayed overnight'. Pruitt and Norman render the rule thus:

> 73 'If any bhikkhuni should sponsor a trainee by a giving of consent postponed overnight, there is an offence entailing expiation.'[34]

74 Ṭhānissaro adopts a similar rendering, but he suggests that the delay need not be overnight.[35]

75 Amid this confusion of interpretations, we can at least clear up some problems. The background story seems to suggest that 'favoritism' might be the issue: Thullanandā gets rid of the good monks so she can use some more to her taste. But the usage of parallel terms elsewhere in the Vinaya shows decisively that this is not correct.

76 In the chapters dealing with *uposatha* and *pavāraṇā*, there is a list of cases that invalidate the proceedings. One such case is if the Sangha performs *uposatha* by means of giving 'purity' that is *pārivāsika* (*pārivāsikapārisuddhidānena*).[36] Obviously this phrase is parallel to our bhikkhuni rule, and 'purity' (*pārisuddhi*) appears just where 'consent' (*chanda*) appears in the bhikkhuni rule. 'Purity' and 'consent' are closely related ideas. In the former, one who cannot come to the *uposatha* sends a bhikkhu in his stead to declare that he is pure in his precepts; in the second, one who cannot come to another

---

[33] This was I.B. HORNER's reading in *Book of the Discipline* 3.396–7: 'Whatever nun should ordain a probationer by showing favouritism to (monks) placed on probation, there is an offence of expiation.' The uncredited translation at http://www.metta.lk/tipitaka/1Vinaya-Pitaka/6Patimokkha/bhikkhuni-patimokkha-e.html treats it as if the candidate is the one under probation: 'If a bhikkhuni ordain a trainee under probation, showing favors, it's an offence for atonement.' WIJAYARATNA's translation (p. 199), on the other hand, omits the troublesome term altogether: 'Whatever bhikkhuni should ordain a postulant by showing favoritism, she is guilty of an offence of the *pācittya* category.'

[34] PRUITT and NORMAN, p. 189.

[35] http://www.accesstoinsight.org/tipitaka/vin/sv/bhikkhuni-pati.html#pc-part8

[36] Pali Vinaya 1.136. Incidentally, this is another case where a rule applies to the bhikkhus and bhikkhunis equally, but for the bhikkhus is buried away in the Khandhakas, while the bhikkhunis have it in the bhikkhuni *pāṭimokkha*, thus giving the erroneous impression that bhikkhunis have more rules.

kind of *saṅghakamma* sends a bhikkhu in his stead to declare his 'consent' to the decisions of the Sangha. The *pavāraṇā* is similar; here the phrase is *pārivāsikapavāraṇādānena*.[37]

77 The parallelism with *pārisuddhi* and *pavāraṇā* makes it clear that *chanda* here must mean 'consent', not 'favoritism'. We are left to wonder exactly why the background story seems to imply favoritism rather than consent; perhaps this was an early confusion.

78 We are still not entirely clear as to the meaning of *pārivāsika*, though. Elsewhere it always means 'a bhikkhu who is undergoing penance'. Here the phrase as a whole is glossed in the word analysis as 'when the assembly has arisen' (or 'by an arisen assembly', *vuṭṭhitāya parisāya*).[38] This suggests that the issue is whether the act of the Sangha is continuous, and hence supports the idea that *pārivāsika* means 'delayed'. The commentary interprets it in this way, giving four cases when a *saṅghakamma* might be delayed. The commentary is not explicit as to whether in each case it must be delayed overnight. Let us briefly survey the other Vinayas to see how they interpret the matter.

79 Dharmaguptaka *pācittiya* 139 tells us that the bhikkhunis performed the ordination on one day, then took her for the ordination in front of the bhikkhus the next day.[39] Apparently, they were full of diseases and destroyed the Sangha. Anyway, plausible or not, this version tells us that the Buddha then laid down a rule forbidding this procedure. The rule explicitly says that a bhikkhuni must not confer the ordination, then go to the bhikkhus to confer the ordination the next day.

80 As usual, the background stories are completely different. Mahīśāsaka *pācittiya* 119 similarly tells of bhikkhunis who gave ordination in the bhikkhuni Sangha, and then in the bhikkhu Sangha the next day.[40]

---

[37] Pali Vinaya 1.168. The PTS edition reads *pārivāsikassa*. However, it adopts this reading against all its manuscripts, which read *pārivāsikapavāraṇādānena* (Pali Vinaya 1.378: 14.4). The editor refers to the earlier passage on *uposatha*, where it also reads *pārivāsikassa* without, however, offering any variant readings in that case.

[38] This further cements the connection with the two cases described above, for they too refer to an 'arisen Sangha'.

[39] T22, № 1428, p. 764, b15.

[40] T22, № 1421, p. 92, b20–27.

81 Sarvāstivāda *pācittiya* 127 supplies an origin story featuring Ānanda and Bhadrā, and then goes into tremendous detail, but essentially concerns the same issue.[41]

82 The Chinese version of the Mūlasarvāstivāda *pācittiya* 139 reintroduces Thullanandā, with a similar problem, although this has the remarkable distinction that neither the rule nor the origin story mention ordination.[42] It is, rather, a general prohibition against giving 'consent' on an earlier day for a *saṅghakamma* the following day. The Tibetan text appears to omit this rule.

83 Mahāsaṅghika/Lokuttaravāda *pācittiya* 107 forbids bhikkhunis from giving *vuṭṭhāpana* to one who is pure on one side [i.e., has received bhikkhuni ordination from the bhikkhuni Sangha, but not the bhikkhu Sangha], and who is *parivāsikiniṁ*.[43] This time it is Jetā who wishes to give ordination, and she relies on Thullanandā to gather a group. Unfortunately, she gathers the disreputable group of six, and Jetā decides that she will not allow her student to be ordained by such a group. But it's too late to gather another group that day, so she waits overnight and performs the ordination the next day with well-behaved bhikkhus. The Buddha chastises her for two things: for looking down on the bhikkhus, and for waiting overnight to complete the ordination. Here, *parivāsikinī* clearly refers to staying overnight. The bad monks are brought in, but only as an excuse for delaying the ordination, and there is no suggestion that they are associated with the term *pārivāsika.*

84 So in all of these cases the issue is clearly about a giving of 'consent' on one day for an act of the Sangha that is carried out the next day. In all cases bar the Mūlasarvāstivāda the act concerned is ordination; but it would seem that any giving of consent—as with *pārisuddhi* and *pavāraṇā*—should only be effective on the day it is given. Most of the Vinayas attribute the problem to a delay between receiving the ordination in front of the bhikkhuni Sangha, then the bhikkhus. However, this is not intrinsic to the rule. In the Mūlasarvāstivāda the problem is the delay in consent among the bhikkhunis themselves. This much is implied by the analysis

---

41 T23, № 1435, p. 331, a17–b14.

42 T23, № 1437, p. 485, b17–18.

43 ROTH, p. 252 § 221: *Ya puna bhikṣuṇī ekato viśuddhaṁ parivāsikiniṁ upasthāpayet pācattikam.*

to the Pali version, which specifies that the bhikkhunis receive an offence as the *saṅghakamma* is completed, which surely must mean as their own *saṅghakamma* is completed. This makes sense of the 'unarisen assembly': if the Sangha continues in one session, the 'consent' given for that session remains valid; but once the Sangha has arisen the 'consent' is no longer effective. Given that, as usual, the background stories all differ, I would suggest that the motif of the involvement of the bhikkhus is secondary, and was introduced into the background stories, and from there into the rule in the Dharmaguptaka and Mahāsaṅghika/Lokuttaravāda Vinayas. There is no mention, from the rule itself in the remaining versions, of the involvement of the bhikkhus in the ordination.

85 I would suggest, then, that this rule concerns the giving of consent, primarily in the case of ordination. A bhikkhuni who is present within the *sīmā* but not able to attend the ordination itself may give consent to the bhikkhuni Sangha for performing ordination, but this consent only remains valid as long as the Sangha remains in session. If the session is disturbed or delayed for any reason, the bhikkhuni must give consent once more. The Pali is not explicit that the delay must be overnight; in any case, it would be prudent to ensure that the consent is refreshed if there is any interruption to proceedings. While this rule only applies directly to ordination, it seems reasonable that it should apply to all formal acts of the Sangha, as is implied by the similar rules for bhikkhus in the case of *uposatha* and *pavāraṇā*, which presumably would also apply to the bhikkhunis.

Chapter 9

CONCLUSION

9.1 Abhidhamma, Abhivinaya

EARLY BUDDHIST LITERATURE is normally thought of as 'Dhamma' and 'Vinaya', two complementary collections of early material. The Dhamma deals with doctrine, while the Vinaya focuses on monastic discipline. The third section of the Buddhist canons, the Abhidhamma, is seen as a later compendium, compiled largely after the early two were, in the main, fixed. But when we look a little more closely, this symmetry recedes and another emerges: the relation between the Vinaya and the Abhidhamma.

2 The term *dhammavinaya*, repeated countless times through the early texts, seems to presuppose some kind of basic duality between the doctrinal and disciplinary teachings. But it is not obvious that this corresponds in any simple way with the existing scriptural collections. For the Suttas—which normally seem to correspond more or less with the *dhamma*—contain large amounts of disciplinary material, in addition to their doctrinal matter. The teachings on monastic ethics and lifestyle from the earliest period of Buddhism are preserved here rather than in the Vinaya. So it is quite possible that, at least to some degree, the term *dhammavinaya* refers to the teachings found today within the Suttas.

3 The pair *sutta-vinaya* would seem to be a more promising reference to the early collections of Suttas and Vinaya. But here again there is uncertainty, for the *pāṭimokkha* (monastic code), which appears to be one of the earliest

forms of the *vinaya*, refers to itself as the *sutta*. It is really uncertain exactly what these two terms refer to in the earliest literature, or even whether they have a clear and consistent denotation.

4 In addition to these pairs, the early texts also refer to another pair, *abhidhamma* and *abhivinaya*.[1] The denotation of these is no less uncertain than that of the previous pairs. Obviously *abhidhamma* here cannot refer to the Abhidhamma-piṭakas as they exist today, or even anything similar. Nevertheless, it probably refers to an advanced or reflective inquiry into the subtleties of the Dhamma, which was the wellspring of the process that eventually led to the creation of the great Abhidhamma systems. It seems likely that a similar process was happening in the Vinaya as well, with a constant questioning and clarifying of the principles of Vinaya, partly driven by a wish for sheer theoretical clarity, and partly by the encounter with situations unforeseen in the texts existing to that date. This process would naturally have started during the Buddha's life, and continued for long afterwards.

5 Perhaps the earliest explanation of *abhivinaya* in the Pali texts is found in the late canonical Parivāra. It defines the *vinaya* as the rule which has been laid down, and the *abhivinaya* as the analysis of that.[2] Taking this definition literally, this means that the rules of the *pāṭimokkha* are the Vinaya, and the rest of the material in the Suttavibhaṅga is the *abhivinaya*. This is plausible and straightforward, and concurs with our historical understanding. Just as the Dhamma is the teaching of the Buddha, organized and preserved by his immediate disciples, and the *abhidhamma* is a later scholastic systemization of the Dhamma, so too the Vinaya (= *pāṭimokkha*) is the rules laid down by the Buddha, organized and preserved by his immediate disciples, and the *abhivinaya* (= Suttavibhaṅga) is the later scholastic systemization of the Vinaya.

6 Another interesting term is the *mātikā* (matrix). This usually refers to an abstracted scheme of items that form the backbone of an extended explanation or commentary. It is applied equally to *abhidhamma* or *abhidhamma*

---

1 I.B. HORNER discusses the Pali occurrences of these words at http://buddhanet.net/budsas/ebud/ebsut064.htm.

2 Pali Vinaya 5.2: *Ko tattha vinayo, ko tattha abhivinayoti? Paññatti vinayo, vibhatti abhivinayo. Kiṁ tattha pāṭimokkhaṁ, kiṁ tattha adhipāṭimokkhanti? Paññatti pāṭimokkhaṁ, vibhatti adhipāṭimokkhaṁ.*

style texts, and to Vinaya. The *pāṭimokkha* is one of the earliest *mātikās*, and several 'Vinaya-mātikās' exist in the Chinese and Tibetan canons.

7 The literary form of the Suttavibhaṅga bears much in common with the Abhidhamma. Each rule is divided into three sections: the origin story, the rule itself, and the analysis of the rule. The bare list of rules (*pāṭimokkha*) is the *mātikā*, the fundamental scheme on which the system is built. The analysis is strikingly similar in form to the Abhidhamma work called the Vibhaṅga, which similarly takes up *sutta* passages and subjects them to a *vibhaṅga* analysis.[3] To briefly illustrate this, I will compare two sections, each chosen as a shortish example which nevertheless exhibits the main stylistic features of the texts in question: the section on the 'bases for success' (*iddhipādas*) from the Vibhaṅga, and the rule on false speech from the Suttavibhaṅga.

Table 9.1: Abhidhamma, Abhivinaya

Vinaya Suttavibhaṅga: false speech	**Abidhamma Vibhaṅga: bases for success**
Origin story	
Statement of the rule taken from *pāṭimokkha.*	Statements on *iddhipādas* taken from Saṁyutta Nikāya.
Word definition	Word definition
Permutations (*cakka*) applying the rule in different cases: the seen, heard, sensed, cognized, etc.	Permutations applying each *iddhipāda* with each *jhāna*, plane, and mode of practice.
	Permutations applying *iddhipādas* to each of the categories of the *mātikās.*
Non offence clauses	

8 It is immediately obvious that the Abhidhamma Vibhaṅga and the Vinaya Suttavibhaṅga share much in common in terms of their literary style and means of analysis. This strongly suggests that they emerged in a similar period, and for similar reasons: to systematize and clarify for students of a

3 This fundamental Abhidhamma work of the Mahāvihāravāsins was shown by FRAUWALLNER (*Studies in Abhidharma Literature*) to share a common basis with the Dharmaskandha of the Sarvāstivādins and the Śāriputrābhidharmaśāstra of the Dharmaguptakas.

later time the original texts that had been handed down from the earliest period. In the case of the Abhidhamma Vibhaṅga, these early texts were central passages from the Suttas, especially the Saṁyutta Nikāya; while for the Suttavibhaṅga, the early text is the *pāṭimokkha*.

9 Some aspects of the these texts are not shared. The origin stories are, of course, not abhidhammic in style, for the abhidhamma eschews all temporalization. But they do bear a marked resemblance to other strands of Buddhist literature that are also part of the later canon, especially the Jātakas. The Jātakas are based on verses, which summarize the climax of an event in a past life of the Bodhisatta, and encase these in an extended commentarial prose story, giving both the events in this life that provoked the story, and the full past life story. It is obvious that these are not, in the main, stories that could be with any plausibility attributed to the Buddha's own teachings on his past lives; rather they are mainly fables and tales that have become incorporated into the Buddhist world through this literary assimilation.

10 In a similar way, most of the so-called origin stories for the Vinaya rules have a minimal claim to plausibility. Frequently they are mere formulas, simply instantiated by back-formation from the rule itself; or they involve events that are inherently implausible, such as repeated variations on the same simple acts; or they involve bizarre perversions; or the story and the rule do not fit; or the various versions of the stories in the Vinayas all contradict each other; and so on. It seems inevitable that the vast majority of these stories were invented in later times, no doubt with the wish to emphasize the authenticity of the rules. But the inherent implausibility of the stories, many of which seem calculated purely to give a laugh, suggests that the redactors didn't expect them to be taken literally. They were used by Vinaya teachers to give life to their otherwise dry material. The composers of the stories of Udāyin's laundry or the robe he sewed for a bhikkhuni, for example, would be amused, and perhaps a little disconcerted, to find that future generations took their bawdy tales to be solemn fact. So, even though the origin stories are not similar to the Abhidhamma, they are similar to other forms that emerged in the later part of the early period of Buddhist literature.

11 Another strikingly abhidhammic feature of the Vinayas is that they are a system. The Suttas deal with one topic at a time, showing a particular aspect of that, or emphasizing a particular perspective. There is no parallel whatsoever within the Suttas for an integrated, massively detailed exposition of a single topic, intended to provide a single, overall syllabus. Again, this aspect of the Vinaya texts can only be reasonably compared with the Abhidhamma, where each 'book' is a clearly integrated systematic whole, and the books as a collection are also, more or less, integrated into one overarching system.

12 All of this confirms what we have seen again and again throughout this essay. The Vinayas, in their existing canonical forms, do not constitute an original Buddhist text, passed down unchanged since the time of the Buddha. They are products of the schools, who inherited the rules (*pāṭimokkha*) and procedures (*kammavācā*) from the early period, together with a loosely defined mass of explanation and background material, and construed that, each in their own way, into a complete Vinaya system, an Abhivinaya that would serve the more complex demands of developed Buddhism.

13 In the textual evolution of the Vinayas, the Second Council is of preeminent importance. It is the only major event in Buddhist history that revolves exclusively around a Vinaya dispute. The victory of the Pāveyyakas, the 'rigorist' Vinaya group at the Second Council, is consistent with a scenario that attributes the systematic formation of the Vinaya texts to this period.[4] Although the canonical accounts do not divulge what textual work may have occurred on that occasion, it seems likely that the form of the Vinayas we have today was a product of the Second Council; probably essential structures and themes were agreed there, while details were worked out in different monastic communities over subsequent generations, resulting in the different Vinayas we possess today.

---

[4] Contrary to popular belief, the rigorist victors at the Second Council can in no way be identified with the Theravāda we know today, as substantially similar accounts of the events are preserved by all schools, including the Mahāsaṅghika. Ironically enough, this polemical rewrite of history is maintained by the school that asserts it has never changed anything; even more ironically, many Theravādin monks actually follow practices of the laxist Vajjiputtakas, such as accepting money, taking the authority of the teacher as superseding that of the canon, etc.

14 If we are to take this scenario seriously, it suggests that the bulk of the Vinaya texts as we have them today were added well after the Buddha's death. This again contrasts with the Suttas, which appear to stem more directly from the Buddha, with more moderate editorial involvement. I would suggest that the proportion of authentic Buddhavacana in the Vinaya roughly compares with the proportion found in the early Abhidhamma works, such as the Vibhaṅga and Puggalapaññatti, which were probably composed around the same time.

15 Even with the recognition that perhaps 90% of the text of the Vinaya does not come from the mouth of the Buddha, this affects relatively little of how Vinaya is actually practiced. Yes, significant differences emerge when we treat the Vinaya according to historical principles—as we have seen in this work—yet in the main the *vibhaṅga* merely serves to clarify and define the existing rules, not to establish radically new principles.

9.2 The Peculiarity of the Pali

16 Shayne Clarke has recently pointed out that in certain respects the Pali Vinaya differs from all the others.[5] He cites the cases of the *śikṣādattaka*, a bhikkhu who has committed a *pārājika* offence, but due to extenuating circumstances, he is allowed to retain a limited role in the monastic community, without remaining as a fully-fledged bhikkhu. This allowance is found in all the Vinayas except for the Pali. He further cites the problem of stupa worship in early Buddhism. All the mainland Vinayas contain various precepts dealing with stupas, while the Pali Vinaya is alone in omitting all mention of them. He suggests that, rather than seeing the Pali as representative of the Indic tradition as a whole, it is perhaps an exception.

17 This raises the question: how did this situation come about? Clarke suggests a number of possibilities in the case of the *śikṣādattaka*. The similarities between the mainland Vinayas may be a case of lateral borrowing between the traditions; or the *śikṣādattaka* may been been included in an earlier redaction of the Pali and then removed; or the different traditions may have come up with the idea independently. By taking the cases that

[5] CLARKE, 'Monks Who Have Sex', p. 31.

Clarke mentions, and comparing them with various examples we have discovered in the bhikkhuni Vinaya, however, I think it is possible to come up with a firmer explanation.

18 We have found a similar case in the bhikkhuni Vinaya. Our discussion of the *sikkhamānā* showed that all the Vinayas apart from the Pali mention in the bhikkhuni ordination procedure that the candidate has completed the two years' training before taking full ordination.[6] The curious thing is that we find a similar proposition, not in the canonical Pali Vinaya, but in the commentaries. While the mainland Vinayas require that all women complete the two years' *sikkhamānā* training before taking bhikkhuni ordination, the Pali commentary, not the canon, has a statement to this effect.

19 If we re-examine the cases mentioned by Clarke, we notice a strange similarity. The worship of stupas is absent from the Pali canon, but found in the commentaries. Similarly, the *śikṣādattaka* is absent from the canon, but something similar is implied in the commentaries and later Theravāda.

20 In each of these cases a statement on the matter is found explicitly in all or most of the mainland Vinayas, while the Pali canon is silent, and the judgment is found in the commentary. There is an obvious explanation for this pattern: the Pali is earlier.

21 This primitive character of the Pali is confirmed by a number of considerations. Firstly, on purely internal considerations each of these cases feels like a late development. The worship of stupas is clearly not part of original Buddhism. The *śikṣādattaka* is a late legal attempt to deal with marginal cases, introduced by a ridiculous origin story involving a dead horse which turns out to be a deva—and let's leave out the rest of the details. The extension of the *sikkhamānā* training to include all women follows a universal pattern for ordination procedures to become more

---

[6] There may be some other similar cases in our study, but none so clear. For example, there is the question as to whether a bhikkhuni can re-ordain. We found that most of the mainland Vinayas prohibit a bhikkhuni from re-ordaining, while the Pali alone only prohibits re-ordination in the case of a bhikkhuni who goes over to another religion without first disrobing. The Dharmaguptaka and Mahīśāsaka, however, also appear to not prohibit re-ordination, so it is not sure whether this should be considered, or whether it is a common feature of the Vibhajjavāda schools. Nevertheless, it remains the case that the prohibition against re-ordination was adopted from the other Vinayas into the Vibhajjavāda commentaries.

complex, exclusive, and demanding over time, for example by making the novice ordination a necessary preliminary to *upasampadā*.

22 So in each case an internal reflection suggests they are probably late. Furthermore, we have the fact that they are absent from the Pali Vinaya, which suggests that they were added after this textual lineage had become textually separated from the other communities. And finally, in each case the missing part came to be included in the Pali tradition at a later time. This confirms that the situation should be explained by historical evolution, rather than cultural differences or sectarian divisions.

23 In all of these cases, the Pali version seems to be the most primitive. Sri Lanka is separated from the mainland, and the chronicles indicate that the physical isolation was also felt in a spiritual sense. It is a common tendency of culture that things tend to evolve more quickly in the central regions, while the isolated or outlying regions tend to remain more conservative. The Sinhalese, who had received the Dhamma only in the time of Aśoka, were anxious to preserve their new-found texts, and developments on the mainland took time to filter through. So the canonical texts remained relatively primitive, while the mainland Vinayas showed more flexibility in adapting to changes in culture. The Vinayas of the Sarvāstivāda and Dharmaguptaka, it is true, were similarly fostered in distant regions of the Buddhist domain; but in their case it was also a central conduit for trade, and a highly diverse region: all the invaders came to India through Kaśmīr/Gandhāra, and indeed the Greeks were ruling much of the region during the period the Vinayas were being redacted.

24 But if the Mahāvihāravāsin tradition remained slow to respond to the changes of the mainland, they did not remain a bastion of primordial purity. The influences of the later schools is felt, but came to incorporated in the commentarial literature, rather than the canonical texts. The Mahāvihāravāsin Sangha thus found its way to keep up with developments without adjusting their texts. It is not the case that the Sri Lankan Sangha remained forever the most primitive and pristine; rather, they struck a slightly different balance in how they reconciled the competing claims of conservatism and modernity.

25 The Theravādin assertion that the Pali Vinaya is the one true and accurate record cannot be sustained. When read together with the wealth of

early texts from other traditions it is undeniable that the Pali constitutes merely one voice among many. Nevertheless, it must be admitted that in many cases the Pali Vinaya does indeed seem to preserve archaic tendencies. The Mahāsaṅghika/Lokuttaravāda, despite claims to the contrary, shows a number of features indicating it was redacted later than the Pali. The Sarvāstivāda contains a greatly expanded list of *sekhiya* rules, and in its language and wording appears later than the Pali, while the Mūlasarvāstivāda is obviously a late compilation. And also the Dharmaguptaka and Mahīśāsaka show repeated indications of late development. It does seem that, as a very general rule of thumb, the Pali is still a serious contender for the title of the earliest Vinaya. But, it should never be forgotten, this is a generalization regarding the text as a whole, and has little meaning in considering any particular passage.

9.3 And Finally...

26 Many of the conclusions I have reached in this book will be controversial. The *sikkhamānā* stage was originally for teenage girls; bhikkhuni ordination was originally carried out by the bhikkhunis alone; the *garudhammas* were intended for Mahāpajāpatī; bhikkhunis may re-ordain; bhikkhunis may prosecute legal cases; bhikkhunis may travel without a bhikkhuni companion; bhikkhunis may live in the forest. Others have considered the same topics from a different angle, and have come to different conclusions. And more will do so in the future, continuing the ancient Buddhist tradition of discussion and clarification of the Buddha's message and how it can be applied in an immediate lived context.

27 In discussion with Sangha members about these issues, I constantly hear about what traditional monastics will or will not accept, about what is useful, or expedient to say publicly. Personally, I find that such attitudes are often highly patronizing. In my experience, 'traditional' monastics vary greatly, and are themselves engaged in a similar process of engagement with and interpretation of their tradition. This book is not written to persuade anyone that bhikkhuni ordination is a good thing. It is here to help those who are interested in bhikkhuni ordination, and want to learn how it may be done in the best way.

28 I have avoided the more urgent political ramifications of the bhikkhuni movement, such as the social impact that full ordination could have on women in Buddhist countries. Obviously, however, I wouldn't have spent so much time and effort to get to the bottom of things if I did not believe that bhikkhuni ordination was of tremendous benefit. In fact, I think the successful adoption of bhikkhuni ordination will be a life-changing revolution for those Buddhist traditions. The key word here is 'successful': there is no question but that bhikkhunis exist, and play their part in all Buddhist cultures. The question facing the Sangha is not 'should bhikkhunis exist or not?' but 'how are we to best respond to their presence?' In its answer the male Sangha has the chance to show its quality.

KATAÑÑUTĀ

KATAÑÑUTĀ IS A PALI WORD MEANING 'GRATITUDE'. It literally means 'knowing what has been done'. As a bhikkhu, 'what has been done' for me is virtually everything. The computer I write on, the books I refer to, the table I lean on, the coffee that keeps me going: all these are offered freely for no other reason than human kindness. If I were to mention all the ways that this book has been made possible by the help of others, it would be longer than the book itself. So I will be content to mention the names of some of those who have contributed to the many discussions and consultations that have informed this book.

Bhikkhu Brahmavaṁso, Bhikkhu Brahmālī, Bhikkhu Santidhammo (Kester Ratcliff), Bhikkhuni Tathāālokā, Bhikkhuni Chue Men, Bhikkhuni Jampa Tsedroen, Bhikkhuni Thubten Chodren, Bhikkhuni Tenzin Palmo, Bhikkhuni Dhammanandā (Chatsumarn Kabalsingh), Bhikkhuni Dhammanandā (Nguyen Huong), Bhikkhuni Wu Yin, Bhikkhuni Sobhanā, Bhikkhuni Lekshe Tsomo, Bhikkhuni Santinī, Bhikkhuni Sudhammā, Bhikkhuni Sucintā, Bhikkhuni Vāyāmā, Bhikkhuni Serī, Bhikkhuni Hāsapaññā, Bhikkhuni Nirodhā, Bhikkhuni Samacittā, Sāmaṇerī Adhimuttā, Sāmaṇerī Mahācittā, Jackie Miller, Paul Fuller, Justine McGill, Annie Keating, Bhikkhu Bodhi, Shayne Clarke, Ann Heirmann, Marcus Bingenheimer, Bhikkhu Anālayo, Rod Bucknell, Mark Allon, Peter Harvey, Rupert Gethin, Sāmaṇerī Jagarīyā (Chong Peng), Bhikkhu Jaganātha, Jennifer Proctor, Bhikkhuni Chao Hwei, Bhikkhuni Chi Kwang, Bhikkhuni Wei Chun, Bhikkhuni Upekkhā, Bhikkhuni Sudhammā, Bhikkhuni Munissarā.

ABBREVIATIONS

DN	Dīgha Nikāya
DĀ	Dīrgha Āgama (Taishō № 1)
MN	Majjhima Nikāya
MĀ	Madhyama Āgama (Taishō № 26)
SN	Saṁyutta Nikāya
SĀ	Saṁyukta Āgama (Taishō № 99)
SĀ2	'Shorter' Saṁyukta Āgama (T № 100)
AN	Aṅguttara Nikāya
EĀ	Ekottara Āgama (Taishō № 125)
T	Taishō edition of the Chinese Tripiṭaka

BIBLIOGRAPHY

Primary texts

References to the Pali Vinaya and commentary texts are to volume and page of the Pali Text Society editions. For Suttas, references are to discourse and section of *The Long Discourses of the Buddha* (WALSHE) and *The Middle Length Discourses of the Buddha* (ÑĀṆAMOLI and BODHI); *Saṁyutta* and discourse of *The Connected Discourses of the Buddha* (BODHI; this varies from the reckoning in earlier texts and translations, especially in SN 35); *nipāta* and discourse for the Aṅguttara Nikāya; *vagga* and discourse for the Udāna. For the Dīpavaṁsa I use the GRETIL text.

The Pali text is usually taken from the World Tipiṭaka online version at http://studies.worldtipitaka.org.

References to Chinese texts are to the CBETA edition of the Taishō canon.

Secondary literature

ANĀLAYO. 'The Buddha and Omniscience.' Indian International Journal of Buddhist Studies, V^OL 7, 2006.

———. 'The Development of the Pali Udāna Collection'. Bukkyo Kenkyu, V^OL 37, 2009.

———. 'Theories on the Foundation of the Nuns' Order—A Critical Evaluation.' Journal of Buddhist Studies (JCBSSL V^OL VI), Centre for Buddhist Studies, Sri Lanka.

———. *A Comparative Study of the Majjhima Nikāya*. Unpublished draft.

BAPAT, P.V. and HIRAKAWA, A. *Shan-Chien-P'i-P'o-Sha: A Chinese version by Sanghabhadra of Samantapāsādikā*. Poona: Bhandarkar Oriental Research Institute, 1970. (Note: this is the English translation of the text that I refer to by the Indic reconstruction of the Chinese title, Sudassanavinayavibhāsā.)

BLACKSTONE, Kate. 'Damming the Dhamma: Problems with Bhikkhunīs in the Pali Vinaya.' Journal of Buddhist Ethics, V^OL 6, 1999.

BODHI, Bhikkhu. *The Revival of Bhikkhunī Ordination in the Theravāda Tradition.* Inward Path Publishers, 2009.

———. *The Connected Discourses of the Buddha.* Wisdom Publications, 2000.

CHAU, Bhikshu Thich Thien. *The Literature of the Personalists of Early Buddhism.* Delhi: Motilal Barnasidass, 1996.

CHUNG, In Young. 'A Buddhist View of Women: A Comparative Study of the Rules for Bhikṣuṇīs and Bhikṣus Based on the Chinese Prātimokṣa.' Journal of Buddhist Ethics, Vol 6, 1999, pp. 29–105.

CLARKE, Shayne. 'Vinaya Matṛkā—Mother of the Monastic Codes or Just Another Set of Lists?' Indo-Iranian Journal, 2004, pp. 77–120.

———. 'Miscellaneous Musings on Mūlasarvāstivāda Monks'. Japanese Journal of Religious Studies 33/1, 2006, pp. 1–49.

———. 'The case of the nun Mettiyā reexamined.' Indo-Iranian Journal, Vol 51, 2008, pp. 115–135.

———. 'Monks Who have Sex: *Pārājika* Penance in Indian Buddhist Monasticisms.' Journal of Indian Philosophy, Vol 37, 2009, pp. 1–43.

———. 'Locating Humour in Indian Buddhist Monastic Law Codes: A Comparative Approach'. Journal of Indian Philosophy, Vol 37, 2009, pp. 311–330.

EDGERTON, Franklin. *Buddhist Hybrid Sanskrit Grammar and Dictionary.* Delhi: Motilal Barnasidass, 2004.

FRAUWALLNER, E. *Studies in Abhidharma Literature.* Albany: State University of New York Press, 1995.

———. *The Earliest Vinaya and the Beginnings of Buddhist Literature.* Roma: Istituto Italiano per il Medio ed Estremo Oriente, 1956.

GOODWIN, Allison. 'Right Views, Red Rust, and White Bones: The Eight Garudhammas and Buddhist Teachings on Female Inferiority Reexamined in Light of Psychological and Social Research.' (Unpublished)

GURUGE, Ananda W.P. 'Shan-Jian-Lu-Piposha as an authentic source on the early history of Buddhism and Aśoka.' *Dhamma-Vinaya: Essays in Honor of Venerable Professor Dhammavihari (Jotiya Dhirasekera).* Ed. Asanga TILAKARATNE, Toschiichi ENDO, G.A. SOMARATNE, and Sanath NANAYAKKARA. Sri Lanka Association for Buddhist Studies (SLABS), 2005, pp. 92–110.

GUTTER, Peter. 'Law and Religion in Burma.' Legal Issues on Burma Journal, № 8, April 2001. Burma Lawyer's Council.

HEIRMANN, Ann. 'Can We Trace the Early Dharmaguptakas?' T'oung Pao LXXXVII, 2000, pp. 396–429.

———. *Rules for Nuns According to the Dharmaguptakavinaya.* Delhi: Motilal Barnasidass, 2002.

———. 'Where is the Probationer in Chinese Buddhist Nunneries?' *Zeitschrift der Deutschen Morgenländischen Gesellschaft* 158.1, 2008, pp. 105–137.

———. 'Becoming a Nun in the Dharmaguptaka Tradition, *Buddhist Studies Review* 25.2, 2008, pp. 147–173.

HIRAKAWA, Akira. *Monastic Discipline for Buddhist Nuns (An English translation of the Chinese text of the Mahāsāṁghika Bhikṣuṇi-Vinaya).* K.P. Jayaswal Research Institute, 1999.

JAINI, Padmanabh S. *Gender and Salvation.* The University of California, 1991.

JOHNSON, Paul Christopher. ' "Rationality" in the Biography of a Buddist King: Mongkut King of Siam (r. 1851–1868).' In SCHOBER (ed.)

KABILSINGH, Chatsumarn. *The Bhikkhunī Pātimokkha of the Six Schools.* Thammasat University Press, 1991.
http://www.buddhanet.net/pdf_file/bhikkhuni_patimokkha.pdf

KHUANKAEW, Ouyporn. 'Buddhism and Domestic Violence'. *World Fellowship of Buddhists Review*, July–Dec 2002.

KUSUMĀ, Bhikkhuni. 'Inaccuracies in Buddhist Women's History.' In Karma Lekshe TSOMO, *Innovative Buddhist Women: Swimming Against the Stream.* Routledge, 2000, pp. 5–13.

LAMOTTE, Étienne. *History of Indian Buddhism.* Paris: Peeters Press, 1976.

LOTTERMOSER, Friedgard. 'Buddhist Nuns in Burma.' Sakyadhita Newsletter, Summer 1991, VOL 2, № 2.

MOFFAT, Abbot Low. *Mongkut the King of Siam.* Ithaca, New York Cornell University Press, 1968.
http://archive.org/details/mongkutthekingof002419mbp

MONIER-WILLIAMS, M. *A Sanskrit-English Dictionary.* Delhi: Motilal Barnasidass, 2002.

NA-RANGSI, Sunthorn. 'Administration of the Thai Sangha: Past, Present and Future.' *Chulalongkorn Journal of Buddhist Studies*, VOL 1, № 2, 2002.

NATTIER, Jan and Charles S. PREBISH. 'Mahāsaṅghika Origins.' *Buddhism: Critical Concepts in Religious Studies.* Paul WILLIAMS (ed.). VOL II. London: Routledge, 2005, pp. 199–228.

ÑĀṆAMOLI, Bhikkhu and Bhikkhu BODHI. *The Middle Length Discourses of the Buddha.* Wisdom Publications, 2005.

NOLOT, Édith. *Règles de Discipline des Nonnes Bouddhistes: le 'Bhikṣuṇīvinaya' de l'école Mahāsāṃghika-Lokottaravādin / traduit annotée, commentaire, collation du manuscrit.* Paris: Collège de France: diff. de Boccard, 1991.

PACHOW, W. *A Comparative Study of the Pratimoksa.* Delhi: Motilal Barnasidass, 2000.

PAW, Maung. *The Revival of Bhikkhuni Sasana in Today's Theravāda Buddhism.* California, 2005.

PIPAT, Kulavir P. 'Gender and Sexual Discrimination in Popular Thai Buddhism.' Journal for Faith, Spirituality and Social Change, VOL 1:1.

PREBISH, Charles S. *Buddhist Monastic Discipline.* Delhi: Motilal Barnasidass, 2002.

PRUITT, William, and K.R. NORMAN. *The Pātimokkha.* Pali Text Society, 2003.
PUNTARIGVIVAT, Dr. Tavivat. '200 Years After King Mongkut's Birth: A Review of Reform Movements in Thai Buddhism.'
ROCKHILL, W. Woodville. *The Life of the Buddha.* New Delhi: Asian Educational Services, 1992.
ROTH, Gustav. *Bhikṣuṇī Vinaya.* Patna: K.P. Jayaswal Research Institute, 1970.
SASANASOBHON, Phra. *His Majesty King Rama the Fourth Monkut.* Mahamakut Foundation, BE 2511 (1968).
SALGADO, Nirmala S. 'Eight Revered Conditions: Ideological Complicity, Contemporary Reflections and Practical Realities.' Journal of Buddhist Ethics, Vol 15, 2008.
SCHMIDT, Michael. 'Bhiksuni-Karmavacana, Die Handschrift Sansk. c.25(R) der Bodleian Library Oxford', in *Studien zur Indologie und Buddhismuskunde, Festgabe des Seminars für Indologie und Buddhismuskunde für Professor Dr. Heinz Bechert zum 60.* Geburtstag am 26. Juni 1992, M. HAHN (ed.), Bonn: Indica et Tibetica, 1993, pp. 239–288.
SCHOBER, Juliane (ed.). *Sacred Biography in the Buddhist Traditions of South and Southeast Asia.* University of Hawai'i Press, 1997.
SCHOPEN, Gregory. *Bones, Stones, and Buddhist Monks.* Honolulu: University of Hawai'i Press, 1997.
———. *Buddhist Monks and Business Matters.* Honolulu: University of Hawai'i Press, 2004.
SHIH, Juo Hsüeh. *Controversies over Buddhist Nuns.* Pali Text Society, 2000.
SKILLING, Peter. 'Nuns, Laywomen, Donors, Goddesses: female roles in early Indian Buddhism.' In Paul WILLIAMS (ed.) *Buddhism: Critical Concepts in Religious Studies,* Routledge, 2005, 1.272–298.
SPONBERG, Alan. 'Attitudes toward Women and the Feminine in Early Buddhism.' In José Ignacio CABEZÓN, ed., *Buddhism, Sexuality, and Gender.* State University of New York Press, 1992.
STRONG, John S. *The Legend and Cult of Upagupta.* Delhi: Motilal Barnasidass, 1994.
SUJATO, Bhikkhu. *A History of Mindfulness.* Taipei: Corporate Body of the Buddha Educational Foundation, 2006.
———. *A Swift Pair of Messengers.* Penang: Inward Path Publishers, 2001.
———. *Sects & Sectarianism.* Santipada Publications, 2006.
———. *White Bones Red Rot Black Snakes.* Santipada Publications, 2010.
TATHĀĀLOKĀ, Bhikkhuni (Yeo Kwang Sunim). *A Brief History of Bhiksuni Ordination.* (Unpublished notes.)
ṬHĀNISSARO, Bhikkhu. *The Buddhist Monastic Code 1.* Metta Forest Monastery, 1994.
TOMALIN, Emma. 'The Thai Bhikkhuni Movement and Women's Empowerment.' *Gender & Development,* Vol 14, № 3, November 2006.

TSOMO, Karma Lekshe. *Sisters in Solitude.* State University of New York Press, 1996.

VAJIRAÑĀṆAVARORASA, Somdet. *The Entrance to the Vinaya (Vinayamukha).* Mahāmakut Rrājavidyālaya. V^OL 1, 1992 (Thai edition first published 1916); V^OL 2, 1973 (Thai edition first published 1916); V^OL 3, 1983 (Thai edition first published 1921).

VON HINÜBER, Oskar. 'The Foundation of the Bhikkhunīsaṃgha.' Annual Report of the International Research Institute of Advanced Buddhology at Soka University for the Academic Year 2007, published 2008, pp. 3–29.

WALSHE, Maurice. *The Long Discourses of the Buddha.* Wisdom Publications, 1995.

WIJAYARATNA, Mohan. *Buddhist Nuns.* Colombo: Wisdom, 2001.

WYNNE, Alexander. 'How Old is the Suttapitaka?' Oxford Center for Buddhist Studies, 2003.

YIFA. *The Origins of Buddhist Monastic Codes in China.* Kuroda Institute, 2002.

YIN, Wu. *Choosing Simplicity.* Snow Lion Publications, 2001.

www.ingramcontent.com/pod-product-compliance
Lightning Source LLC
LaVergne TN
LVHW011346080426
835511LV00005B/157
* 9 7 8 1 9 2 1 8 4 2 1 5 3 *